"TRIUMPH IN OUR TROUBLED WORLD"

...Unleashing Your Bargaining Power With Advanced Intelligence

Copyright © 2024 by Richmond Asare

DEDICATION

I dedicate this book to my two 'mothers' who raised me in the way of the LORD: Madam Joana Charity Nketsiah and Mrs. Patience Nketsiah.

I will eternally be grateful to you both.

PREFACE

1. OUR TROUBLED WORLD TODAY

In a world whirling on the edge of uncertainty and turmoil, our hearts are heavy with the weight of countless challenges. We witness the relentless clash of political ideologies, the seething undercurrents of social unrest, the gaping gaps of economic disparities, the haunting specter of environmental degradation, and the relentless march of technological disruption. It is amidst this tempestuous storm that we must find the strength to weather the trials and navigate our way to a brighter future.

Our world today is at a stage where socio-political battles rage, leaving scars of division and uncertainty in their wake. The echoes of heated debates and impassioned protests reverberate through our souls, as we grapple with the fragile nature of our global governance systems. In these trying times, diplomacy, compassion, and unwavering determination become beacons of hope that guide us towards collective solutions.

The rapid advancement of technology casts both a mesmerizing spell and a daunting shadow upon our world. Artificial intelligence (AI), genetic engineering, and pervasive surveillance systems have the power to shape the very essence of our existence.

We find ourselves at the precipice of ethical dilemmas and questions of personal privacy, grappling with the consequences of progress. It is in our collective wisdom, our ability to temper innovation with compassion and our commitment to responsible stewardship that we can harness the potential of technology for the betterment of all.

Within the fabric of our society, we confront the deep wounds of social injustice, financial challenges, prejudice, and inequality. The despondency of marginalized voices echoes through the corridors of power, leaving countless dreams unrealized and potentials untapped.

We are called to bear witness to the human struggle against discrimination and exclusion, to rise above the divisions that threaten to tear us apart. It is in embracing empathy, fostering inclusivity, and championing the rights of every individual that we can pave the path towards a more equitable and harmonious world.

The recent pandemic has served as a stark reminder of our vulnerability and the fragility of our health systems. From the fear and isolation of lockdowns to the heart-wrenching loss of loved ones, we have felt the depths of human suffering. Access to quality healthcare, mental health awareness, and the pursuit of holistic well-being emerge as crucial components of our collective journey towards a healthier and more resilient world.

In the midst of these trials and tribulations, the voices of the youth resound with unwavering determination. They inherit a troubled world, burdened with the consequences of decisions made before their time. Yet, many refuse to succumb to despair.

They march, they organize, and they demand change. Their resilience, idealism, and boundless energy illuminate the path forward. It is incumbent upon society and leadership across board to empower them, guide them, to amplify their voices, and to provide them with the requisite tools and skills they need to be the architects of a brighter tomorrow.

2. DESPAIRED DEMOGRAPHY

Let's face it, the human race is in trouble, and many of us especially young people are feeling a bit lost in the face of these daunting challenges - socioeconomic issues, technological invasions, mental and other health issues, relationship and marriage crisis, political turmoil, you name it. It's like we're stuck in a never-ending race against time, trying to keep up with the fast-paced twenty-first-century ecosystems.

But hey, we're not alone! Countless people walk among us, wearing masks of contentment while carrying the weight of shattered dreams and lost hope. It's high time we shed those masks and find the knowledge, skills, and tactics to win the negotiation nukes of personal and professional life as the world continues to evolve in uncertainty!

You know, life is like a buffet of opportunities. It's all about spotting the right dishes ahead and gorging on them to satisfy your hunger for success. But here's the catch - you need to quickly identify those opportunities and bargain your way to gain, instead of whining about your stains and compounding pains.

3. YOU CAN DO IT TOO

Let me introduce you to Evelyn Johnson, the queen of reinvention. At the ripe age of forty-five, she found herself bored silly, and despondent, having dedicated her life to rearing three kids and mastering the fine art of diaper changing. But one day, she stumbled upon a sign that said, 'Free Seminar on Making Money in Cosmetics.' Evelyn thought, "Why not? I've got nothing to lose!"

In just sixty minutes, that seminar convinced her that she could sell to her friends, friends of friends, and pretty much anyone with a pulse. She dove headfirst into the business, bringing other women on board, and before she knew it, she was climbing the ladder of success in the cosmetics world.

Her husband couldn't be happier that she stepped outside her confinement and did something more with her life. Now, she's a top star in her organization, and she even got some fancy recognition for her achievements.

But here's the real kicker - her success isn't just about money and career. It has transformed her spiritually. You see, being a homemaker is no small feat, but after twenty-five years of it, Evelyn thought that was all she could do. Boy, was she wrong? She proved to herself that she can do so much more, and her self-esteem is through the roof! She's thrilled about helping other women realize their potential too. Turns out, they're a whole lot better than they think.

Evelyn J. is just one example of countless determined individuals who have defied the odds and risen above their circumstances. They have tapped into the greatness within and around them, maximized these for gain and so can you!

4. NEGOTIATE WITH ADVANCED INTELLIGENCE

Negotiation in the modern world requires more than just basic skills and techniques. It demands a higher level of awareness, a deeper understanding of human dynamics, and an ability to navigate the intricate web of interconnected interests. It is within this context that advanced intelligence emerges as a guiding principle for negotiators seeking to thrive amidst the turmoil.

My concept of Advanced Intelligence in this book is the power to tap into one's inner potential and reach out to those in-built traits, skills, and capabilities that enable you to navigate successfully any opportunity or deal you face. This concept equips individuals skillfully irrespective of age, race, color, education, gender, and even social status to not only survive but to excel at any endeavour, even in the face of unprecedented challenges.

At its core, my idea of advanced intelligence empowers individuals to navigate the troubled waters of our modern reality with clarity, conviction, and finesse. You will discover very intelligent stratagems in our modern boardrooms and even the alleys to tackle the various issues you may face. It enables you to transcend conventional limitations, become a strategic negotiator and leverage your intellectual, emotional, and interpersonal capacities to drive successful outcomes.

5. ACTIVATE YOUR BARGAINING POWER!!

Now, let's get down to business - the art of bargaining to gain in our troubled world today. My goal in writing this book is to ignite a fresh fiery passion within you to overcome challenges, traverse life's uncertainties, and make your dreams a reality. Consider this your survival manual for all the negotiating tables of life - business, ministry, profession, marriage, academics, you name it.

Sure, we all want to gain the luxurious things in life, but what's even more important is leaving a lasting impression. As the wise Maya Angelou once said, "People will forget what you said, people will forget what you did, but people will never forget how you made them feel." So let's aim to create positive and memorable experiences.

For you, young souls on the quest for love, don't settle for anything less than God's best in a partner. And to all you politicians, parents, pastors, and business executives out there, remember to consider the welfare of generations unborn as you make strategic decisions and sign those contracts. It's not just about the present; it's about creating a legacy.

In this classic manual, get ready to dive deep into the ever-evolving realms of life. We're about to unravel the intricate tapestry of our dynamic world, exploring the multitude of challenges that come our way. But we are not stopping there, oh no!

We're about to peel back the layers and reveal stories of resilience, the flickering flames of hope, and the incredible power of collective action. Brace yourself for heartfelt narratives, powerful anecdotes, and the wisdom of those who've weathered the storm. Get ready for some serious solace, inspiration, and guidance.

This book is bursting with mind-blowing, game-changing nuggets that'll turn you from a mere "survivor" into a fulfilled blessing. Get ready for an epic journey to the Palace of Life, where you'll challenge and transform yourself by applying these cutting-edge principles that have stood the test of time.

Whether you're a seasoned negotiator or a rookie, you've got what it takes to rise to the top and conquer all your aspirations in the fast-paced boardroom of life. In today's troubled world, it's time to uncover, understand, and effectively utilize all YOUR BARGAINING POWERS! Get ready to level up!

INTRODUCTION

In the realm of human potential, some stories defy expectations and shatter preconceived notions. They remind us that greatness knows no bounds and that strength can emerge from the most unexpected places. Our tale begins in a less privileged home, where adversity was a constant companion and hope seemed like a distant dream.

Meet our protagonist, a young man whose journey will inspire and amaze you. Born into a world where the odds were stacked against him, he faced the challenge of a physical disability and the absence of a father figure. But in the face of adversity, he discovered an extraordinary power hidden within himself.

While the world saw his disability as a limitation, he refused to succumb to self-pity or despair. Instead, he embarked on a remarkable journey of self-discovery, determined to rise above his circumstances. He knew that within the depths of his being lay a unique talent waiting to be unleashed.

Through unwavering determination, he ventured into a quest to identify his true calling. It was in the pursuit of his passion that he unearthed a skill that would become the foundation of his success. With resilience as his fuel and passion as his guide, he transformed his skill into a profitable endeavor.

But this story isn't just about the triumph of a single individual. It's a testament to the indomitable spirit that resides within each of us. It reminds us that our circumstances need not define us and that the power to shape our destinies lies within our hands.

As you delve deeper into the pages that follow, prepare to be captivated by the unwavering spirit of this extraordinary young man.

Through his trials and triumphs, you'll witness the sheer audacity of the human spirit and the incredible heights one can reach when fueled by determination and a touch of humor.

So, fasten your seatbelts and get ready for a journey that will make you laugh, cry, and ultimately, believe in the boundless potential that resides within all of us. Prepare to witness the remarkable story of a young man who defied the odds, embraced his uniqueness, and soared to unimaginable heights.

Get ready to meet a hero who proves that true greatness knows no limits and that sometimes, the greatest treasures lie hidden within the most unexpected places. Welcome to the extraordinary tale of a young man who transformed adversity into opportunity, and in doing so, became an inspiration to us all.

Let the journey begin!

4. EMMANUEL'S GOAL HAS GONE GLOBAL

"Determination gives you the resolve to keep going despite the roadblocks that lay before you" - and Ghanaian-born Emmanuel Ofosu Yeboah attests to this. Born with a severely deformed leg, Emmanuel was determined to show the people of Ghana and the world at large that those who are physically challenged are capable of great things.

So, he hopped on a bicycle and embarked on an improbable, Forrest Gump-like journey across the nation to prove just that. "I see how people are treated in Ghana, and that's why I am giving it my all," said the then 28-year-old man, who was born without a shin bone. "I don't want to give up. I don't want to give up," he reiterated, probably pedaling away with his one good leg.

Emmanuel's goal has gone global!

According to the 2021 Population and Housing Census, People living with Disabilities (PwDs) or the physically challenged account for approximately 8 percent of Ghana's population, which represents 2,098,138 individuals. Most of them face numerous challenges, including social stigma and limited opportunities for education and employment. But Emmanuel's story is here to change that narrative.

Enrollment of children with disabilities in Ghanaian schools remains "very low," according to a report by the National Development Planning Commission (NDPC). Children with disabilities have lower enrollment rates compared to those without disabilities at all levels of pre-tertiary education, particularly at the SHS and Technical and Vocational Education and Training (TVET) levels.

The report further highlights substantial gaps in learning outcomes in reading, writing, and mathematics for pupils with and without disabilities. But Emmanuel's journey defies these statistics and brings a glimmer of hope for those facing similar challenges.

Emmanuel was born without the lower part of his right leg, with a normal-sized foot essentially dangling from his thigh instead of a knee. Because of his disability, his mother, Comfort, was advised to either kill him or leave him in the forest to fend for himself or die.

As a result of his physical challenge, his father, Dickson, abandoned the family. But Yeboah refused to accept such a cruel fate. He decided to use his limited resources, his unwavering determination, and a touch of humor to change the world's perception of what people with disabilities can achieve.

"His mission is to change perceptions. He's the epitome of doing what you can with limited resources," said Bob Babbit, a co-founder of the California-based Challenged Athletes Foundation, which provided Yeboah with the bicycle that jump-started his quest for greatness.

Yeboah, shining shoes for three Ghana cedis (GH¢ 3.00/UDS $0.40) per day, was trying to make ends meet for himself and his family when he learned about CAF's grant program through a Missionary in town. Praying to God while writing his first letter to America, Yeboah asked for a bike he could ride across the country - more than 370 miles - to disprove the stereotype about the disabled.

After getting the hang of this awkward activity - basically pedaling with his healthy leg while his right foot resting on the frame - Yeboah secured enough sponsors to begin his ride. Skepticism hounded him, but he pressed on, and as he gained momentum, so did the publicity surrounding his remarkable journey.

EMMANUEL NEVER GAVE UP…

Wearing a red, yellow, and blue striped shirt, Yeboah rolled through village after village as wide-eyed children chased behind him in awe and celebration. In April 2003, he was fitted with a prosthetic right leg. The next year, he shaved three hours off his time in the same event.

He even made it to California in 2003, where he attended ESPN's ESPY Awards, an honor given to courageous athletes named after the late tennis star Arthur Ashe. "I believe that if it's not coming from your heart, you give up," Yeboah said, probably flashing his infectious smile. "But if it is coming from your heart, you never give up," he added, inspiring everyone within earshot. "I believe that I'm not going to end it here," Yeboah reiterated. "I'm going to continue until the time that I will die."

And this is how I introduce this wonderful book to you, my precious reader. The fact that you have this book in your hand means you have taken a great step to bargain for something greater in life, no matter the pain. Get ready to receive an incredible dose of ministration and direct impartation from the divine that will catapult you to the next level.

As the title suggests, "TRIUMPH IN OUR TROUBLED WORLD"...*Unleashing Your Bargaining Power with Advanced Intelligence;* you may wonder why such an introduction. Well, great lessons can be learned from Emmanuel's remarkable journey, as he recognized his potential and used his limited resources to achieve greatness.

He is a shining example of someone who bargained with the little he had to gain a great game, overcoming his battles along the way. And this is exactly what this book is all about.

To bargain is to strike an agreement between two parties, where each promises to offer something in exchange for something else. So, the question arises: What did Emmanuel offer to live, and what did he get in return? What were his bargaining powers? Let's dive into his extraordinary story and uncover the secrets that can empower us all.

EMMANUEL'S SUCCESS STORY

Five things stand out in Emmanuel's journey that contributed to his remarkable success. With unwavering determination, he offered his head, his hands, his health, his heart, and his happiness. In return, he has reaped immeasurable rewards: a profound sense of satisfaction, a true sense of belonging, and a profound feeling of importance.

Emmanuel's actions have not only transformed his own life but have also made a positive impact on the lives of his family, as well as countless others who are less privileged and facing physical or mental challenges worldwide.

Emmanuel's story serves as a powerful reminder that when we wholeheartedly devote ourselves to a cause, utilize our unique abilities, and embrace challenges, we can overcome seemingly insurmountable obstacles and achieve greatness. This book, "TRIUMPH IN OUR TROUBLED WORLD"...*Unleashing Your Bargaining Power with Advanced Intelligence*,' takes inspiration from Emmanuel's journey and that of many others and explores the principles and practices that can empower individuals to harness their potential and navigate life's challenges with confidence.

As we delve into the pages that follow, we will uncover valuable insights and practical strategies that enable us to identify our strengths, negotiate effectively, and seize opportunities for personal growth and fulfillment. Just as Emmanuel bargained with determination and resilience, we too can discover our bargaining powers and unleash our full potential in the pursuit of our dreams.

So, let us embark on this transformative journey together, as we learn from Emmanuel's remarkable example and unlock the power of bargaining effectively with our potential to create a life of purpose, achievement, and profound impact.

1. His Head

"You can chain me, you can torture me,
you can even destroy this body,
but you will never imprison my mind."
Mahatma Gandhi

First and foremost, Yeboah had a sharp mind. He was wise enough to seize the opportunity he learned from the missionary in town and went all in. Just because he had a physical disability didn't mean his mind was disabled too. His mental prowess was as strong as ever, allowing him to use his thoughts to navigate life's challenges.

You see, your thoughts have tremendous power. The ideas you dwell on often have a way of manifesting in reality. When you invest your mental energy into the same thoughts day after day, you gain strength and start shaping your attitude, expectations, behavior, and actions. Remarkably, these thoughts can even be subconsciously perceived by others, who may offer you help or present opportunities, just like what happened to Yeboah.

Our thoughts have the incredible ability to attract corresponding events, situations, and opportunities into our lives. However, not every thought automatically becomes reality. It takes consistent repetition, fueled by desire and action, for a thought to come true. Doubts, fears, and worries are the enemies that can dismantle what you've built with the power of your mind. To succeed in life, it's crucial to clear your mind of negativity and doubt, paving the way for your path to success.

Emmanuel, this determined young man, refused to let his physical limitations hold him back from pursuing his dreams. He engaged in a negotiation with his mind, seeking solutions to his challenges, and eventually achieving his desired outcome. His mind acted as a magnet, attracting the right ideas and opportunities into his life.

PLAY TO WIN THE GAME

2. His hands

"Each player must accept the cards life deals him or her: but once
they are in hand, he or she alone must
decide how to play the cards to win the game."
Voltaire

Secondly, let's talk about Emmanuel's entrepreneurial spirit and his bargain with his hands. Despite not having the privilege of attending top universities or prestigious schools, Emmanuel took matters into his own hands, quite literally. He decided to write a letter to America, seeking a bike that would enable him to embark on his ambitious journey across the nation.

You see, Emmanuel didn't wait for perfect circumstances to unfold before taking action. He grabbed a pen and paper and penned that first letter with determination and grit. He turned his ideas into tangible actions, recognizing that great plans and dreams alone are not enough. As the saying goes, a dream without an actionable plan is nothing more than a wish. And let's face it, if wishes were horses, beggars would be riding in the Kentucky Derby!

But Emmanuel was no beggar. Prior to this incredible endeavor, he worked diligently as a shoe shine boy, using his hands to earn a living. Instead of relying on handouts or passively hoping for a change in his circumstances, he hustled and put his hands to work. He refused to be a wishful-thinking dreamer.

Emmanuel's story teaches us an invaluable lesson. He understood the power of utilizing what he possessed to achieve what he desired. He didn't shy away from his predicaments; instead, he embraced them and used them as stepping stones toward a better future.

By leveraging the work of his hands and penning that impactful letter, he caught the attention of others and opened doors of opportunity. So, let Emmanuel's story inspire you to work hard and let God bless the labor of your hands, for prayers alone won't magically bring success.

Remember, my friend, it's not just about praying for a horse, but rather putting in the effort to learn how to ride and steer that horse in the direction of your dreams.

EMMANUEL TRADED HEALTH FOR WEALTH

3. His health

"To keep the body in good health is a duty...otherwise we shall not be able to keep

Buddha

Emmanuel, the determined go-getter that he was, didn't let his physical limitations dampen his spirit. Despite being born without a shin bone, he knew that true wealth lay in his health. It was a trade he was willing to make.

Like a true sportsman, Emmanuel trained tirelessly, taking meticulous care of his body. He didn't let the temptation of indulgent pleasures or unhealthy foods distract him from his goal. He knew that a healthy life was the key to his success. And boy, did it pay off! Running across an entire nation wouldn't have been possible for him if he hadn't committed to a lifestyle of fitness and well-being. It was the ultimate investment that yielded incredible dividends.

You see, many people have big dreams and aspirations, but they neglect the basics of personal hygiene and healthy living. They devour anything at any time, expecting their bodies to magically stay strong and vibrant. But let me tell you, my friend, if you want to achieve greatness and go the distance, you need to offer life your very best.

So, trade in those unhealthy habits for a vibrant and energetic life. Embrace healthy practices, nourish your body with the right fuel, and watch as the wealth of well-being becomes your greatest prize in the end. After all, it's not just about having a fat bank account but having a healthy and fulfilling life that truly counts.

A DETERMINED HEART WINS!!

4. His heart

"Beginnings are usually scary and endings

are usually sad, but it's everything in between

that makes it all worth living."

Sandra Bullock

Determination and courage, the dynamic duo of success, were the driving forces behind Yeboah's remarkable journey. With an unwavering will and an insatiable hunger for achievement, he proved that nothing could hold him back. His heart beat with an unyielding strength.

He defied the odds stacked against him, rising above the limitations imposed by his family background and the challenging environment he grew up in. He fearlessly challenged the status quo, leaving an indelible mark on the world. With a heart brimming with determination, he embarked on a journey of negotiation, and in the end, he emerged victorious and renowned.

The beginning of any venture is often fraught with challenges, but Yeboah's steadfastness enabled him to endure those initial obstacles and ascend to the pinnacle of his potential. He possessed an unwavering faith in his abilities and exuded confidence, and that belief propelled him forward. He offered his heart to the pursuit of his dreams, and in return, he garnered the hearts of millions who admired and honored his remarkable efforts.

When the day of his appearance in villages arrived, throngs of people, both young and old, flocked to witness the resolute spirit of the athlete. Winning a medal was undoubtedly a great achievement, but capturing the hearts of those who faced similar challenges or even greater ones was the true measure of fulfillment. Yeboah touched the hearts of multitudes around the globe, leaving an indelible impact that transcended mere athletic triumph.

His story serves as a testament to the power of determination, courage, and the ability to win not just medals, but the hearts of people. Yeboah's resolute heartbeat is in harmony with the hearts of countless individuals, forever etching his name in the annals of inspiration.

FOLLOW YOUR PASSION NOT PASSING FASHION

5. His happiness

His happiness was derived from pursuing his passion with unwavering determination, despite facing socio-economic challenges. Emmanuel had an immense love for cycling, and he wholeheartedly dedicated himself to it.

He pursued his passion and vision with unwavering enthusiasm, undeterred by the initial difficulties. He recognized his talent and pursued cycling with fervor, sacrificing personal pleasures to become the best he could be.

Despite being a shoe shine boy, he was also an accomplished athlete. He possessed multiple talents, but he understood the transformative potential of his passion. He turned his passion into profits. Each one of us carries a unique essence within us; identifying it and harnessing it with relentless determination can propel us to our desired destination.

"Follow your passion, not the passing fashion." Richmond Asare Now, the question arises: What do you bring to the negotiating table of life? What do you possess that others value and are willing to exchange for something you desire? Your bargaining power in life will determine the outcomes you achieve in your transactions.

Your current position in life is a reflection of the investments you have made in the past—academically, socially, professionally, spiritually, psychologically, and more. To a large extent, you cannot reap what you have not sown. This book aims to address these critical questions in your life, inspiring strong negotiation skills as you leverage the limited resources at your disposal to attain the desired results you yearn for.

"Life will give you what you bargain for, not what you wish for."

No matter how gifted or talented you may be, it is crucial to strategically utilize your abilities to maximize your potential. Your perception of your capabilities will determine how effectively you leverage them for personal gain. You possess the power to shape your destiny on this earth, as long as you recognize your capabilities and market them profitably to those in need of your services.

Do not settle for less or accept mere crumbs when you hold the power to influence the course of events around you. Like Captain Planet, the power is yours!!

11. TYRON TRADES TRIUMPHANTLY!

A friend of mine named Tyron was browsing through trinkets at a market in Jamaica. Let me share with you how she skillfully negotiated for an item:

Tyron: How much is this trinket?
Vendor: 20J.
Tyron: I'll give you 10J.
Vendor: 15. Tyron: 9.
Vendor: No, you're supposed to go up!
Tyron: 8.
Vendor: Fine, fine. I'll take 8.

In the end, Tyron managed to secure the trinket for less than half the initial price. Her strong bargaining power was truly impressive. From that day on, we referred to this backward technique as the Jamaican Haggle.

I recently applied for a business credit card. Since I had just opened a business account and didn't have an extensive credit history with the bank, they initially told me, 'We can't give you a card.' However, I highlighted two important points: the card would only be used for small payments, eliminating any credit risk, and if the bank refused, I would have to consider their competitors instead. Within minutes, they granted me the card.

This example demonstrates that you possess the power to negotiate for better deals wherever you go. Recognize your worth and what you bring to the table. If your value is evident, people will be willing to accommodate your requests.

As a business person, it is crucial to know precisely what you bring to the negotiating table. Keep in mind that competition has become more intense and complex than ever before. You need to offer something extra that sets you apart. Never settle for mediocre products or services; aim for the best, regardless of the challenges you may face.

As a young individual aspiring to be in a fulfilling relationship, do not settle for anything less than God's standards for you. Strive for purity, peace, provision, power, and prosperity. Aim for the best in marriage and work towards it. If you negotiate wisely with your positive attributes, you will achieve it.

Political parties vying for power and governance often present their manifestos, aiming to surpass their competitors. However, their ability to win the sympathy of the majority of the electorate relies on their Campaigning or Bargaining Power!

What unique offerings do they bring to the table? How effectively can they market these ideals to the populace? No matter how impressive a manifesto may be, failing to strategically campaign or negotiate will result in electoral defeat. Your bargaining power lies in your ability to possess something distinct and convincingly sell it to the majority of the electorate."

"A policy is a temporary creed liable to be changed,

but while it holds good it has got to be

pursued with apostolic zeal".

Mahatma Gandhi

BECOME A BETTER BARGAINER

In this book, we will address the challenges you need to overcome and the hurdles you must jump over to reach your goals in life. You will learn how to thrive on the negotiating table or the battlefield of life as you bargain to achieve success, even in the face of opposition. One key aspect we will explore is how to identify and seize the great opportunities that surround you. By becoming an expert in your field, you will attract the necessary sales and profitability from the market.

I have outlined twenty-one reasons why this is crucial to your success, whether you're a professional, business executive, or handyman. Furthermore, I have delved into the fundamental principles of bargaining and how to negotiate for long-term benefits rather than settling for short-term gains.

Remember, the impact you make in people's lives is more significant than mere words or material possessions. How you make others feel will be what they remember about you, far beyond any material wealth you may offer.

This manual provides you with essential principles to thrive on the negotiating table, regardless of your background or current circumstances. You will become successful in any negotiation deal you enter into be it formal or informal.

We will explore the different types of negotiators you can expect to encounter and the tactics that exceptional executives employ to win in any negotiation process. Your negotiation style will ultimately determine the level of success you achieve in your bargains.

Additionally, we will highlight the immense benefits of group or team negotiations, as they provide the advantage of multiple minds working together compared to one-on-one exchanges. Furthermore, I have addressed potential hurdles or barriers you may face during the negotiation process and provided practical solutions to overcome them in the sixth chapter.

And now, my dear reader, get ready for the grand finale—the last chapter holds intelligent keys to your ultimate success. Within its pages, you will uncover twelve priceless success strategies that will propel you up the ladder of life. These nuggets have been carefully crafted and honed to perfection, like precious gems awaiting your discovery.

But it doesn't stop there. As you tactically position yourself and embrace these time-tested pillars—faith, integrity, accountability, impeccability, extra ability, imperishability, and loyalty—you will unlock a realm of possibilities that extend far beyond this world. Get ready to transcend the ordinary and achieve extraordinary outcomes.

Believe me when I say that nothing can hinder you. Your desires are within reach, and they will undeniably come to fruition as you

immerse yourself in the profound insights presented in this book. It's time to unleash your full potential and seize the success that awaits you.
Always remember, you possess the ultimate Bargaining Power!

"TRIUMPH IN OUR TROUBLED WORLD"

...Unleashing Your Bargaining Power with Advanced Intelligence

CHAPTER ONE

THE KING IN THE KID: UNLEASHING YOUR INNER POTENTIAL

"When I was a boy

I was told that anybody could become President;

I'm beginning to believe it".

Clarence S. Darrow

It was an August assembly of dignitaries, celebrities, and paparazzi. The news of the nation's Point Man had reached far and near. The atmosphere was electric! A gathering of the Titans. A show of power and bravado! The women would not be left out as they sang and danced to melodious tunes of the time.

'...Even a jazz dancer has beauty,

Dance is grace, dance is beauty,

all wrapped into movement,

I am a dancer; I've taken ballet and jazz,

I love to dance, but...

I'm a dancer you can't trust around glass or fragile trinkets...

Anna Marie Jenema

In the small historic town, a teenager found himself in an extraordinary situation. Surrounded by esteemed elders and influential figures, he carried the weight of a mighty mantle upon his young shoulders. It was as if the universe itself paused to witness this remarkable event, for such an occurrence had never been seen before.

Anointed as the future King, this young Ephrathite of Judah had a divine mission. He was destined to guide his people, steering them away from the worship of false gods and towards the worship of the one true God, JEHOVAH. It was an immense responsibility for someone so young, but his humble nature and unwavering devotion touched the very heart of Heaven.

In a world filled with princes, royals, and influential voices, it was this lad's holy and humorous approach to life that captured the attention of both God and man. He understood that laughter has a unique power to bridge gaps, dissolve tensions, and bring people together. With a quick wit and a contagious sense of humor, he broke down barriers and fostered unity among his people.

Imagine the scenes in the royal court, as this teenage King-to-be used his humor to lighten the atmosphere and dissolve conflicts. His jokes became legendary, bringing smiles to the faces of even the most stoic figures in the land. Through his humility and ability to find joy in every situation, he earned the respect and admiration of all who encountered him.

So, this young lad from the ancient town proved that age is just a number when it comes to touching the heart of Heaven and inspiring those around him. Even though his family did not care a hoot about his exploits, he was relentless until his hour of glorification. His journey as a leader reminds us that a combination of humility, holiness, and dedication can work miracles, bringing people closer to each other and to the divine.

And thus, in the presence of the Major Minister and the entire nation, this teenager was anointed and appointed to embark on a remarkable path, leaving a legacy that would echo through the ages. His story serves as a timeless reminder that a youthful spirit, guided by faith and a good sense of commitment, can change the world in ways unimaginable.

Nevertheless, though he had been anointed and commissioned as the next in line to the lofty throne of the land, he was not King the next day. He carried this heavy and huge responsibility in his somewhat small vessel (spirit) for several years until the fullness of time.

"The King is in a Kid"

Unlike traditional tales of seizing power through political or military means, this lad had a different approach to achieving his destiny as the next King. He didn't rely on flashy displays or extravagant gestures to assert his claim to the throne. Instead, he understood the importance of preparation and honing his skills before stepping into his role.

There were no grand processions with lavish regalia or a fleet of vehicles escorting him wherever he went. No, this future King knew that true power lay not in outward appearances but in his strategic bargaining abilities. He possessed the wisdom to employ the right strategies, skills, and tools to negotiate his way to success.

No need for elaborate ceremonies or press conferences to win over the masses. This young leader recognized the value of what he brought to the table and the significance of his divine calling. He understood that true influence comes from within, and he used his knowledge and conviction to gain support and loyalty.

While others may have sought the spotlight and indulged in extravagant displays, this lad focused on what truly mattered: his mission and the betterment of his people. He didn't need a campaign filled with parties and rallies; he let his actions and words speak for themselves.

So, while the world may be captivated by the pomp and pageantry of political theater, this young King-to-be demonstrated that true negotiation power lies in one's character, skills, and understanding of their purpose. He set an example for future leaders that it's not about the trappings of authority, but about the substance and integrity that one brings to the negotiating table.

And so, armed with wisdom, humility, and a deep connection to his divine ordination, this lad embarked on a journey to claim his rightful place as King, leaving behind a legacy that reminds us all that true power is not gained through showmanship but through the art of skillful negotiation and unwavering dedication to one's purpose.

2. My Meek and Mild Moment

In the early parts of 2014, I had an important meeting with a multi-million dollar company for my final appraisal. I arrived at the company's office dressed in a sharp three-piece suit, expecting to meet high-level executives in formal business attire. Little did I know that the person who would join me would be quite the surprise.

As I sat in the reception area, waiting for my turn to enter the boardroom, a gentleman approached me. He was dressed in a polo T-shirt and short pants, holding what seemed like a Ostack of old newspapers. At first glance, I assumed he was there for a different reason, perhaps seeking assistance or discussing personal matters with one of the managers.

He greeted me kindly and offered his help, noticing that I was sitting alone while the receptionist was occupied with her work. In that moment, I quickly assessed him with a skeptical eye, almost dismissing his offer without much thought. Just as I was about to decline, the bell rang, indicating it was my turn to meet with the panel of executives. I expressed my gratitude and prepared to enter the meeting room.

To my surprise, the gentleman followed behind me, and as we entered, everyone in the room stood up to welcome him. It turns out, this seemingly ordinary individual was none other than Mr. Prince Sarpong, the CEO of ASN Holdings, and the very company I was hoping to join. He was affectionately referred to as Papa Pee by his colleagues, radiating warmth and humility in his speech and demeanor.

In that moment, I realized the valuable lesson I had learned. Despite his unassuming appearance, Mr. Sarpong held a position of great power and influence. His simple attire was a reflection of his down-to-earth nature and his respect for all employees, regardless of their rank or position.

Gratefully, I successfully secured the opportunity to work with this remarkable company. This encounter taught me never to underestimate or look down upon anyone, regardless of their appearance or background. It served as a reminder that true leadership is not measured by outward symbols of authority, but by the way one treats and respects others.

From that day forward, I carried with me the lesson of humility and the importance of valuing every individual I encounter on my journey, knowing that behind any appearance could lie a wealth of wisdom, experience, and potential connections.

Similar to the shepherd boy, the CEO did not distance himself from his old acquaintances and associates or look down upon them after assuming his prestigious role. He remained connected to his roots and continued to care for his former responsibilities with dedication and professionalism. The sheep and goats he once tended were still his valued companions and customers, and he treated them with utmost care, respect, and dignity.

Becoming a king was not an instant transformation for him; it required a journey of growth and preparation. He embarked on a process of royal development, undergoing various stages to acquire the knowledge, skills, and wisdom needed to rule effectively. Just as a caterpillar undergoes metamorphosis to become a butterfly, he too had to undergo personal and intellectual growth to reach his full potential as a king.

Throughout this journey, he remained grounded and focused, understanding that true leadership is not bestowed overnight but is a result of continuous learning and development. He embraced each stage of his journey, acquiring the qualities and experiences necessary to fulfill his role as a wise and just ruler.

His commitment to personal growth and preparation exemplified his dedication to his future role. He understood that leadership is not just about titles or anointing, but about the character, knowledge, and abilities one possesses. By undergoing this process of development, he ensured that he would be fully equipped to serve and lead his people with excellence when the time came.

In essence, his story teaches us the value of patience, perseverance, and continuous self-improvement. It reminds us that true leadership is not about instant gratification or the trappings of power, but about the journey of growth and the commitment to serving others with humility and wisdom.

'We have this treasure in earthen vessels

that the excellency of the power may be of God,

and not of us' -2 Corinthians 4:7.

In today's world, it can be challenging to remain humble and meek after achieving great accomplishments or receiving significant recognition. However, the story of the Group CEO serves as a powerful reminder of the importance of humility and treating others with respect, regardless of one's achievements.

As leaders, whether leading a team, managing a company, or overseeing an enterprise, it is crucial to recognize that leadership is a privilege, not a license to exert power over others. True leadership is about cherishing and appreciating the trust placed in us by our subordinates, colleagues, and even our relatives. It involves identifying with them, understanding their perspectives, and valuing their contributions.

Drawing inspiration from the humility exhibited by the Group CEO and even Jesus Christ himself, we learn that true greatness lies in serving others and remaining composed and respectful in all circumstances. Just as the spiritual genes of the Group CEO and his ancestor David carried traits of humility, we too can strive to embrace and cultivate this quality within ourselves.

The ultimate example of humility can be found in Jesus Christ, who humbled himself and willingly obeyed, even to the point of death on the cross. Despite being called the Son of David and carrying the weight of a mighty mantle, he maintained his composure and exemplified humility in every aspect of his life.

Therefore, let us remember that humility is not a sign of weakness but a mark of true strength and leadership. By cultivating humility, we can create a positive and empowering environment where everyone feels valued and respected, fostering growth, collaboration, and success for all.

Let this mind be in you, which was also in Christ Jesus:

Who, being in the form of God,

thought it not robbery to be equal with God;

But made himself of no reputation,

and took upon him the form of a servant,

and was made in the likeness of men.

And being found in fashion as a man,

he humbled himself, and became obedient unto death,

even the death of the cross.

Philippians 2:5-8

Regardless of the extent of God's blessings and anointing in our lives, it is essential to remain humble and meek. This principle is exemplified by the King of Kings and the Son of Man himself, who walked the path of humility despite their divine status. As followers and servants, we are called to emulate his example.

Even when blessed with abundance in our families, finances, intellect, social connections, physical abilities, and spirituality, we should always maintain a humble disposition. The exaltation of our lives should not lead to arrogance or pride but rather to a deeper sense of humility and honor.

In today's world, there is often a desire to be associated with the external manifestations of blessings and charisma while neglecting the importance of character. However, it is crucial to understand that true greatness is not solely found in external displays but in the inward qualities of humility, meekness, and integrity.

Many young people today want to be associated with the "gymnastics" and the "charismatics" of the blessings but don't want to identify themselves with the *character of the calling*. You must get under (be meek and mild) so you can get to the top.

To achieve true success and reach the pinnacle of our potential, we must be willing to humble ourselves and embrace the posture of a servant. It is by getting under, by being meek and mild, that we can ultimately rise to the top. Humility becomes a catalyst for greatness in all areas of life, enabling us to impact others positively and fulfill our purpose with grace and authenticity.

So, let us not only seek the blessings and favor of God but also strive to embody the character traits that reflect his nature. By walking in humility and honor, we align ourselves with the divine plan for our lives and open doors to even greater blessings and opportunities.

The Black Cleaner Prays

Everybody in this world carries something unique and special inside him or her. It does not matter if you are black or white, short or tall, fat or slim, young or old, schooled or unschooled, popular or unknown, rich or poor, fully abled or physically challenged; God created us equally and deposited talents and gifting in us all.

A notable poet Maya Angelou once said, *'I believe that every person is born with talent'*.

A bunch of rich whites were on a huge cruise boat about to sink.
So they started looking at each other to find someone who could
pray for them, but none of them were suitable.
So finally they see the BLACK cleaner and ask him to pray for them.

He prays:

Lord when I wanted to cross the bridge at the station,
it said:
"Whites only"
When I wanted to sit on the chair, it said:
"White's only"

When I wanted to go to the toilet it said:
"Whites only"
When I tried to enter the front door of the post office it said:

"Whites only"

So Lord as this boat goes down, remember:
"Whites only" Amen!

The Prayer Of An African Pastor

May the Almighty bless you all!

Eternal God, we put our faces on the ground before you today as we beg you to forgive our sins, even though, we black people, haven't sinned. I'm saying this because we are not the ones who killed your only son, Jesus Christ, white people did!

As you know even better than we do, he was betrayed by a white man, they handed him over to another white man who ordered him to be whipped!

Moreover, these same white people ordered him to be crucified! The traitor was called Judas Iscariot. You can check this out, we don't have names like Iscariot here in Africa, we are called: Ikenna, Emem, Yakubu, Achebe, Odige, Ada, Sade, Sola, Halima, Idara, Chidi, Hassana, Nana, Taiwo, Nnamdi, Shehu, Osaro, Funke, Chidera, Danjuma, Doyinsola, Aloaye, etc...

We have no clue where is the Golgotha (that's the place where they crucified your beloved son), we just know how to go from Lagos to Kaduna to Abuja to Ibadan to Enugu to Maiduguri and come back.

We've never been to any of the holy cities in the Bible; therefore we can't possibly be implicated in the crucifixion of our Lord. If you don't believe us, please watch the movie "The Passion of the Christ", and you will see for yourself that no black person, let alone an African took part in that sad event

This is why we beg you, O Lord Almighty, please make black people rich at long last and let white people work for them for a change!

Amen.

Hilarious!!!

Well, friend, you don't have to pray like these two folks; because, whether you are black or white, you have all that it takes to make it in life. The colour of your skin should not determine your destiny. Success in life is not the preserve of 'whites' or people with *light skin.* In the sight of God, you are complete and have enough opportunities to rise to the summit of your potential irrespective of where you find yourself right now.

Before you were formed in your mother's womb, God knew you and gave you a distinct assignment on earth to fulfill before you get back to Him- Jeremiah 1:5. So you can bargain your way to the pinnacle of life.

In you dwells the fullness of the Godhead bodily if you have Christ residing in your heart. You are expected to manifest the great potential in you to the world so people can be blessed through you. There are no limitations except those you put on yourself. Identify your field and cultivate it. Use what you have positively to your advantage!

Rescue The Perishing

You cannot be so selfish to keep what is in you to yourself. Remember, you are blessed to be a blessing to others. Stir up the gift which is in you and put them to good use. You never know how far God could take you with the little he has placed in your hand.

All that you need to break through in life is within you. Don't concentrate on others but, on that which is within you. You carry the master keys to unlock the challenges in your family, business, ministry, community, and generation.

Oliver Wendell Holmes wisely observed, *"I find that the great thing in this world is not so much of where we stand, as in what direction we are moving"*. In other words, it does not matter where you started or your background in life, it is about where God is taking you, and where you intend to go in life that matters. Just say to your soul, 'Arise O my soul, be strong and match forward, in the power of Jehovah!'

Your set time to arise and shine is now! The hour to showcase the glory of the living God to this world is now or never! Generations yet unborn are counting on you and I, if we fail to arise and do something, big dreams, and visions will die and not be achieved; in the end, many will perish because of you and me. Like the popular Methodist hymn goes:

Rescue the perishing, care for the dying

Snatch them in pity from sin and the grave;

Weep o'er the erring one, lift up the fallen,

Tell them of Jesus, the mighty to save

// Rescue the perishing, care for the dying;

Jesus is merciful, Jesus will save //

No matter what challenges lie in your path, now is not the time to give up or grow weary. You've come too far to retreat now. Keep pushing forward until you break through the tape of success. The sky is just the beginning for you.

Have you reached the sky of your potential? If you have, then it's time to embark on the journey to success. But if you haven't, then you still have a long way to go. Rise up, shake off the dust, and keep moving. Keep forging ahead. With perseverance and determination, you will surely reach your destination if you continue pressing forward and refuse to give up.

Dear brethren, let me share a powerful message from Philippians 3:13-14: "I count not myself to have apprehended: but this one thing I do, forgetting those things which are behind, and reaching forth unto those things which are before. I press toward the mark for the prize of the high calling of God in Christ Jesus."

Let these words inspire you to keep pressing on. Leave behind the past, the setbacks, and the failures. Focus on what lies ahead and stretch yourself towards the mark of your ultimate purpose. With unwavering determination, you will press forward towards the prize—the high calling that awaits you.

So, my friend, gather your strength, renew your resolve, and keep your eyes fixed on the prize. Your journey to success is ongoing, and the path may be challenging, but remember that with each step you take, you are one step closer to achieving your dreams. Embrace the journey, embrace the process, and never lose faith in your ability to reach new heights.

The sky is just the beginning. Keep pushing, keep believing, and keep pursuing your high calling. You will triumph, and your success will be a testament to your unwavering spirit. Onward, my brethren, and may your journey be filled with triumph and fulfillment.

No Limit, No Summit
You are absolutely right! The sky is not the limit; as believers, we are seated with Christ in heavenly places, and our potential is limitless. We carry the spirit of a king within us, regardless of our current circumstances or age. It's time to square our shoulders, lift our heads high, and move forward with confidence and determination.

In our society, many successful individuals didn't achieve greatness overnight. They started small, laying one block upon another, learning and growing with each step. Through dedication, determination, and the grace of God, they reached higher heights and made significant contributions. We admire and praise them for their sacrifices, hard work, and unwavering integrity.

As Maya Angelou wisely said, "All great achievements require time." It is through perseverance and patience that you can reach higher heights and accomplish remarkable things. It's a process of continuous growth and development.

Some individuals faced immense challenges, such as not having a proper place to call home or having to endure voluntary fasting to survive. Others risked everything, including their lives, families, and careers, for the sake of their faith or their nation's independence.

No matter what challenges you face or what limitations you perceive, it's time to break out of your shell and pursue something better and bigger in life. Your current situation or physical limitations should not hold you back or make you feel ashamed. In fact, there are people who wish they had the opportunities and abilities you possess right now.

So, step out with boldness, utilize your unique gifts and talents, and pursue your dreams. Embrace the journey of growth and transformation, knowing that with God's guidance and your unwavering determination, you can overcome any obstacle and achieve remarkable things. Your potential is vast, and the world is waiting for you to shine your light and make a difference.

From Shame to Fame

Richard Norris, 39, started a new chapter in his life after a miraculous procedure gave him a new face. The Virginia resident lost most of his face after he accidentally shot himself in 1997. His lower jaw, lips, tongue, and nose were blown off and his face was left disfigured.

For the next 15 years, Norris locked himself inside his parents' home and would rarely step out because of his shame. All the mirrors in the house were covered so he wouldn't have to look at his face. This nightmare continued for Norris until his mother found a Baltimore-based doctor named Eduardo Rodriguez, who specializes in plastic and reconstructive surgery.

Rodriguez was willing to help, and he started by partially reconstructing Norris' face. The recovery began with the doctor creating a nose and chin out of the patient's flesh, but he wanted to go further than that. The ultimate goal was to give Norris a brand new face, which Rodriguez believed was possible using a human cadaver.

The procedure — which would replace the patient's face with that of a deceased donor was extremely risky, as it required removing Norris' face and there was no guarantee he would survive. However, this was a risk Norris was willing to take as this operation could help regain his life back. He wanted to move from shame to regaining his real self-esteem.

With that, the doctor and his team of 150 began the 36-hour-long operation on March 19, 2012. The entire face of the donor was taken off: muscle, blood vessels, nerves, and even bones. The disfigured parts of Norris' face were also removed, and the new face was hammered and sawed in.

Norris made a full recovery, including regaining much of the sensation on his face. His miraculous and one-of-a-kind procedure gained a lot of attention from the media, and he was even approached by a GQ writer to be interviewed and photographed for the magazine's August 2014 edition.

Richard told GQ that after his story went public, he started getting many fan letters. One of those fans even became his girlfriend. *"A drop of hope can create an ocean, but a bucket of faith can create an entire world,"* said Norris regarding his experience.

So, friend, you can reach your aspirations if only you decide to come out of your shell and excel no matter your present conditions.

From Pity to Popularity

Some of the most successful people the world has to offer started with absolutely nothing to call their own. You often hear people whine about how they are destined to always worry about money because they have been 'dealt a bad hand' by life.

After graduating from the University of Exeter in 1986, J.K. Rowling began working for Amnesty International in London, where she started to write the Harry Potter adventures.

In the early 1990s she traveled to Portugal to teach English as a foreign language, but, after a brief marriage and the birth of her daughter, she returned to the United Kingdom, settling in Edinburgh. Living on public assistance between stints as a French teacher, she continued to write.

Rowling battled depression, financial difficulties, grieving over the death of her mother, and having to raise a child by herself while living on benefits. At the end of a pretty difficult journey, she found comfort in working on her writing while her daughter slept.

Once the first few chapters of the book were complete, she sent the manuscripts to publishers that rejected her left, right, and center.

Finally, the Bloomsbury Publishing company agreed to publish the book but warned Rowling that she should get a day job because being a children's author is not enough to feed a family.

When the first book was released, it was evident that no day job would be needed. Rowling was the first author to reach the billionaire mark and her successful series has sold at least 500 million copies across the globe.

The Harry Potter series sparked great enthusiasm among children and was credited with generating new interest in reading. Film versions of the books were released in 2001–11 and became some of the top-grossing movies in the world.

In addition, Rowling wrote the companion volumes *Fantastic Beasts & Where to Find Them* (2001), which was adapted into a film series (2016, 2018) that featured screenplays by Rowling; *Quidditch Through the Ages* (2001); and *The Tales of Beedle the Bard* (2008)—all of which originated as books read by Harry Potter and his friends within the fictional world of the series. Proceeds from their sales were donated to charity.

She later co-wrote a story that became the basis for the play *Harry Potter and the Cursed Child*, which premiered in 2016 and was a critical and commercial success, winning an unprecedented nine Olivier Awards, including best new play. In the production, Harry is a husband and father but is still struggling with his past, while his son Albus must contend with his father's legacy.

A book version of the script, which was advertised as the eighth story in the Harry Potter series, was published in 2016. Two years later the play transferred to Broadway, and in 2018 it won six Tony Awards, including best new play.

The series has made over $7.7 billion with the subsequent movies also bringing in money by the billions. Rowling's journey is summed up in her own words:

"You might never fail on the scale I did, but some failure in life is inevitable. It is impossible to live without failing at something unless you live so cautiously that you might as well not have lived at all – in which case, you fail by default." -J.K. Rowling

Rowling's story is a testament to the fact that our circumstances or the cards we are dealt with in life do not define our destiny. It is our determination, perseverance, and willingness to pursue our passions that can lead us to great achievements.

Instead of dwelling on the belief that we are destined to worry about money or face limitations, let us draw inspiration from individuals like J.K. Rowling. They remind us that with dedication, hard work, and the courage to pursue our dreams, we can overcome any challenges and create our own path to success.

So, let us not be discouraged by our starting point or the obstacles we may face. Instead, let us embrace the opportunities that come our way and have faith in our abilities. With passion, perseverance, and a belief in ourselves, we can turn our dreams into reality, just like J.K. Rowling did with the magical world of Harry Potter

From Poverty to Prosperity

Leonardo Del Vecchio's incredible journey from a difficult upbringing to becoming a billionaire entrepreneur is truly inspiring. Despite facing challenging circumstances, he was determined to create a better future for himself.

After being sent to an orphanage due to his family's circumstances, Del Vecchio started working in a factory. It was during this time that he experienced a life-altering accident, losing part of his finger while working with molds. Despite this setback, he didn't allow it to deter his ambitions.

At the age of 23, Del Vecchio took a significant leap and opened his own molding shop. This marked the beginning of his entrepreneurial journey. Over time, his business grew and evolved, ultimately becoming the world's largest manufacturer of sunglasses and prescription eyewear. The company he founded included renowned brands such as Ray-Ban and Oakley, which have become synonymous with style and quality.

Through his dedication, innovation, and a keen understanding of the eyewear industry, Del Vecchio achieved tremendous success. Today, his net worth is estimated at around $24.1 billion, according to Inc. Magazine.

Del Vecchio's story exemplifies the power of perseverance, resilience, and hard work. Despite humble beginnings and setbacks along the way, he turned his passion and skills into a thriving business empire. His journey reminds us that it is possible to overcome adversity and achieve remarkable success with determination, a strong work ethic, and a relentless pursuit of one's goals.

So, let us draw inspiration from Leonardo Del Vecchio's remarkable story and strive to unleash our own potential, no matter the circumstances we find ourselves in. With perseverance and a steadfast belief in our abilities, we can overcome obstacles and forge our path to success.

Howard Schultz's journey from a humble background to becoming the driving force behind Starbucks is a testament to the power of determination and a relentless pursuit of one's dreams.

Schultz's upbringing in a housing complex for the poor instilled in him a deep sense of longing for something more. He observed the disparity between his own circumstances and those of people with greater resources and happier families. This awareness fueled his desire to transcend societal expectations and achieve something extraordinary.

Despite the challenges he faced, Schultz's talent and perseverance led him to earn a football scholarship to the University of Northern Michigan. After graduating, he began his professional career at Xerox. However, his true calling awaited him when he took the helm of a small coffee shop called Starbucks.

In 1987, Schultz became the CEO of Starbucks, which at the time had only 60 stores. Under his visionary leadership, the company experienced remarkable growth and expansion. Schultz's relentless pursuit of excellence and his commitment to creating a unique coffee experience propelled Starbucks to become a global phenomenon, with over 16,000 outlets worldwide.

Today, Schultz's net worth is estimated to be over $2.9 billion, according to Inc. Magazine. However, he remains grounded, never forgetting his humble roots and the journey that brought him to where he is today. Schultz's success story is a testament to the power of resilience, perseverance, and an unwavering belief in one's ability to overcome obstacles.

Howard Schultz's remarkable achievements remind us that regardless of our background or circumstances, we have the power to shape our destinies and create a lasting impact. His story inspires us to pursue our passions relentlessly and to strive for greatness, no matter where we come from.

The famous American media proprietress, talk show host, actress, producer, and philanthropist is best known for her self-titled, multi-award-winning talk show, which has become the highest-rated program of its kind in history.

Oprah Winfrey's life is a remarkable tale of overcoming adversity and achieving extraordinary success. Born into poverty in rural Mississippi, she faced numerous challenges and hardships throughout her childhood. Despite these difficult circumstances, Winfrey persevered and rose to become one of the most influential media moguls in the world.

Raised by her grandmother in poverty, Winfrey experienced the harsh realities of her situation, wearing dresses made of potato sacks and enduring abuse. However, her grandmother's influence played a significant role in shaping her resilience and self-belief. At a young age, she demonstrated a natural talent for public speaking and found solace in reading and reciting Bible verses.

As Winfrey grew older, she faced further obstacles, including moving to an inner-city neighborhood with her less supportive mother. She endured poverty and prejudice, but her determination never wavered. Despite facing abuse and becoming pregnant at a young age, Winfrey continued to pursue her education and eventually won the Miss Black Tennessee beauty pageant.

Her career in media began to flourish, and she became the youngest news anchor and the first black female news anchor in Nashville. Winfrey's charisma and talent caught the attention of audiences, and she eventually launched her iconic talk show, "The Oprah Winfrey Show," which went on to achieve tremendous success and made her a millionaire by the age of 32.

Throughout her journey, Winfrey remained committed to philanthropy and using her platform for good. She established Oprah's Angel Network, a charity that supported numerous projects and donated significant amounts of her own money to charitable causes. She has been recognized as one of America's most generous philanthropists, giving millions to various organizations and causes.

Today, Oprah Winfrey's net worth is estimated to be over $2.9 billion, making her one of the wealthiest women in the world. Her rise from poverty and adversity to becoming a media icon and philanthropist serves as an inspiration to millions, showcasing the power of determination, resilience, and the belief that anyone can overcome their circumstances and achieve greatness.

So you see, even though Emmanuel, Rowling, Del Vecchio, Schultz, and Oprah all had difficult beginnings, they managed to rise through the storms to become very successful personalities in their fields of profession or business and so can you.

"If You are born poor than this, it's not your mistake,

But if you die poor than this, it's your mistake".

Wildy Karal

Time will not permit me to talk about how the Apostles of old suffered for the sake of the gospel. Today, through their toil and torture in spreading the good news of our Lord and Savior Jesus Christ, we have eternal life and prosperity through the gospel.

Today, many souls have been saved because of their sacrifice and desire to spread the gospel. Beloved, the little gift or talent you have may just be enough to transform a whole generation. Be strong and never give up on your dreams because soon it will yield great dividends and impact your world.

The Magic Mustard Seed

Hello, my incredible reader! Have you uncovered that hidden gem within you yet? It's like discovering the perfect filter for your Instagram photos, except this gem has the power to transform your life and leave a lasting impact on the digital world!

Imagine your mustard seed of greatness as a trending hashtag that starts small but quickly catches fire, spreading like wildfire across social media platforms. Just like a viral meme or a captivating Instagram story, your unique gift has the potential to capture the attention and hearts of people worldwide.

Don't be like Gideon without an internet connection, missing out on the digital revolution happening right before your eyes. While he was offline, his enemies were busy updating their online presence. But fear not, for I'm here to provide you with a digital awakening.

In this fast-paced digital age, your gift could be as groundbreaking as developing the next big mobile app, creating mesmerizing augmented reality experiences, or even launching a successful YouTube channel where you share your talents and inspire millions.

It could be as innovative as leveraging artificial intelligence to solve real-world problems or as influential as becoming a social media influencer, spreading positivity and making a difference in people's lives.

Remember, the KING is still in you, even if you're just a digital newbie, a young content creator, or an aspiring entrepreneur. Your potential knows no bounds in this digital landscape. Embrace the power of technology, tap into your passions, and let your creativity soar!

May your internet connection be strong as you read these words, and may the digital realm be your canvas for expression. Let your talents shine brightly online, and watch as the digital universe embraces your unique voice and contributions. Get ready to make waves, inspire others, and leave an indelible mark on the ever-evolving digital world.

The KING is still in you precious one, even if you are just a amateur or a youth or a "kid"- unpopular, unskilled, unlettered, unappreciated, unnoticed, or rejected. You are who God says you are; and what He says you'll be, you'll certainly become! Nothing can erase that which is written concerning you in the volumes of His Book.

My Humble Beginnings

In the heart of Asawase, a suburb of Kumasi, Ghana, my childhood unfolded like a novel of struggle and hope. The streets of my neighborhood echoed with the footsteps of dreams, while my soul yearned for a chance to break free from the chains of adversity.

As I reflect on those early years, tears well up in my eyes, for they were filled with both heartache and resilience. Picture a young child, surrounded by the dilapidated walls of a cramped room, where the only comfort was the warmth of family. We were packed like sardines, sharing that tiny space with a sense of togetherness that defied our circumstances.

The nights were a battleground, where sleep was elusive and discomfort was our companion. We laid our heads down, limbs intertwined, on that cold, bare floor. Mosquitoes buzzed around us, feasting on our innocence, while the stench of poverty and urine filled the air. It was a cruel symphony that played each night, a constant reminder of the challenges we faced.

Education was a distant dream, fading into the background as survival took center stage. My days were spent navigating the chaos of the streets, selling whatever we could to put food on the table. I roamed the alleys, scavenging for remnants of hope amidst the refuse dumps, knowing that every day was a battle for existence.

But amidst the harsh realities, a ray of light emerged. It came in the form of a loving aunt, who opened her arms and her home to me in the bustling city of Accra. She became my beacon of love, a guiding star in a sea of uncertainty. With her support, I embarked on a new chapter, leaving behind the shadows of my past.

Yet, the scars of my upbringing were not easily erased. I entered a new world, a classroom filled with eager minds and unfamiliar faces. But my academic journey was marred by the gaps in my knowledge and the whispers of self-doubt. I stumbled, I fell, but I refused to let failure define me. With each setback, I found the strength to rise again, fueled by a burning determination to prove my worth.

My life, like the city of Accra itself, became a canvas where resilience painted its masterpiece. I learned that the measure of a person is not determined by their circumstances, but by the fire that burns within their spirit. Every step forward, every achievement earned, became a testament to the power of perseverance.

From the slums of Asawase, through the bustling streets of Accra, destiny carried me on its wings and landed me in the enchanting embrace of the City of London, UK. The contrast between my humble beginnings and the grandeur of this vibrant metropolis evokes a whirlwind of emotions within me.

As I stepped foot onto the foreign soil of London, a city that breathed with possibility, my heart fluttered with a mixture of excitement and nervousness. The towering skyscrapers and bustling crowds serve as a constant reminder of the vastness of the world and the magnitude of the journey I had undertaken.

The transition from my childhood in the slums to the cosmopolitan streets of London is nothing short of a breathtaking metamorphosis. It is as if I have emerged from a cocoon, shedding the remnants of my past and embracing the limitless possibilities that lay before me.

Yet, amidst the awe-inspiring beauty of this international hub, a bittersweet longing tug at my soul. I carry with me the memories of my beloved Asawase, the tight-knit community that nurtured my spirit and taught me the value of resilience. The laughter of children playing in the dusty streets and the warm embrace of neighbors turn family echoes in the chambers of my heart, a reminder of the simplicity and reality I have left behind.

London, with its enchanting allure, presented me with a world of opportunities. The city beat with a vibrant energy, where dreams are chased and ambitions are realized. But in the midst of the hustle and bustle, I often found myself yearning for the familiar faces and the warmth of a community that had shaped my formative years.

Yet, as I navigate the maze of this cosmopolitan haven, I am struck by the beauty of diversity that surrounds me. London is a melting pot of cultures, a tapestry woven with threads of different backgrounds, dreams, and aspirations. It is in this mosaic of humanity that I find solace, for it reminds me that no matter where we come from, we all share a common thread of humanity and the desire for a better tomorrow.

The City of London has become my sanctuary, a place where the dreams of a young child from Asawase continue to blossom and evolve. Each day is a testament to the resilience that courses through my veins, a tribute to the unwavering determination that guided me from the slums to the global stage.

As I walk the streets of this majestic city, my heart swells with gratitude for the opportunities that have been bestowed upon me by divinity. I am reminded of the sacrifices made by my ancestors, the unconditional love of my family, and the unwavering support of those who believed in me. Their unwavering faith in my abilities continues to fuel my pursuit of greatness.

So, here I stand, a product of my past and a citizen of the world. The slums of Asawase may have shaped my character, Accra may have ignited my dreams, but it is in the City of London that I have found my voice. It is here that I strive to make a difference, to contribute my unique perspective to the vibrant tapestry of this global community.

With each step I take on the cobblestone streets, I carry the hopes and aspirations of those who have walked before me. The journey from Asawase to London has been a testament to the resilience of the human spirit, a reminder that no matter where we come from, we can transcend our circumstances and create a life that is truly extraordinary.

And as I look up at the towering skyline of this magnificent city, my heart swells with gratitude. Gratitude for the path that has led me here, for the challenges that have shaped me, and for the unwavering belief in the power of dreams. For in this moment, I am reminded that the journey is not merely about the destination, but about the lessons learned and the person we become along the way.

Today, as I look back on those challenging years, I am grateful for the lessons they taught me. They forged my character, instilled empathy in my heart, and ignited a passion to uplift others. My journey is a reminder that even in the face of adversity, hope can blossom, and dreams can transcend the confines of circumstance.

Beloved, I understand the weight of your current circumstances, living in a cramped space, and feeling overlooked and disregarded by those around you. It can be disheartening and overwhelming. But let me assure you, that there is a glimmer of hope shining through the darkness.

In the midst of your confined living conditions, where it feels like life is closing in on you, there is a divine presence watching over you. God, with His loving arms outstretched, eagerly awaits your surrender and invites you to experience His transforming power. He sees beyond your current situation and knows the potential that lies within you.

Although it may seem like there is no escape from the challenges you face, I want to encourage you to hold on to hope. This difficult season you find yourself in is not permanent. It is just a chapter in your life, and your story is far from over. Embrace the truth that you are loved, valued, and deserving of all the goodness life has to offer.

Picture yourself as more than the circumstances that surround you. Envision yourself as someone who is complete, beautiful, and capable of overcoming any obstacle that comes your way. Let faith guide you towards the Promised Land that awaits you, where dreams are realized, and blessings abound.

Remember, my dear one, your present circumstances do not define you. You have the power within you to rise above them and create a future filled with abundance and joy. Trust in the process, lean on the unwavering love of God, and know that your hour of change is on the horizon.

So, my beloved friend, take heart and keep your gaze fixed on the possibilities that lie ahead. Embrace the truth of your worth and the boundless potential within you. With faith as your guide, step into the fullness of who you are meant to be and embrace the abundant life that awaits you.

> "If you can only conceive it
>
> and believe it, you can achieve it"

The father of faith saw himself in the land of promise even as he walked through the hinterlands. He lived in the Promised Land even before he passed away. His faith was so sharp and strong that he could see thousands of years to come.

While he was childless, he did not consider his body already weary and dead but still believed God for his promised miracle baby. He understood that God was a God of the dead who could bring back to life anything in his life that was dead alive again.

Who against hope believed in hope,

that he might become the father of many nations,

according to that which was spoken, So shall thy seed be.

And being not weak in faith,

he considered not his own body now dead,

when he was about a hundred years old,

neither yet the deadness of Sara's womb:

He staggered not at the promise of God through unbelief;

but was strong in faith, giving glory to God;

And being fully persuaded that,

what he had promised, he was able also to perform.

Romans 4:19-21

It did not mean his body was not physically or medically "dead", but though all indications proved negative and impossible, he refused to accept them by faith and trusted God with all his heart till the spoken promise came to pass. There was nothing that could stand between him and the promise of God. Robert H. Schuller once said,

"Impossibilities vanish when a man and His God confront a mountain".

As you will discover later in this manual, like the many inspiring stories shared earlier, the young lad bargained with the little he had and won great laurels on the negotiating table of life. You will learn how to approach the boardroom of life with confidence, armed with your unique talents and resources, and negotiate your way to victory despite the challenges you may face.

My dear friend, I may not know the exact words that have been spoken over your life, but I urge you to hold on tightly to your confessions and continue moving forward with unwavering faith. Whatever challenges lie before you, face them boldly in the name of the mighty Lord of hosts. For the hour of its full manifestation, the appointed time of God's divine intervention, is drawing near.

It doesn't matter if you don't possess the most impressive qualifications for that job, if you're not at the top of your class, or if you're not the most renowned person in your profession, business or whatever field of endeavour. God has a remarkable way of plucking individuals from the depths of obscurity, cleansing them, and elevating them to astonishing heights that showcase His glory for all to see.

In all of your endeavors, remember that it's not about you, but about magnifying His name. When you reach the pinnacle of success, when you overcome seemingly insurmountable odds, be prepared to humbly give all the glory to Him, for He shares His glory with no one.

So, hold fast to your confessions, move forward with determination, and confront every situation that comes your way. Remember that the power of God is working within you, and the set time for your breakthrough is fast approaching. Embrace the journey of bargaining and leveraging what you have, for in doing so, you will gain immeasurable rewards that transcend any temporary pain or setbacks.

Stay strong, remain steadfast in your faith, and watch as the Lord of hosts orchestrates miraculous transformations in your life. The best is yet to come, and with God by your side, there are no limits to what you can achieve.

I am a King in the making as such;

I cannot live a life of a mediocre.

I possess the spirit of a mighty KING inside me.

I can't be cowed by my present circumstances.

I make a conscious effort to be humble and broken in heart

and contrite in spirit. I have the right character

and attitude of a great leader.

I see myself seated on the throne prepared for me

by the Almighty God and cannot be moved

by current happenings. I may be in a pit or prison today

but will rise to become a Prince or Princess in the Palace tomorrow.

I give you all the glory Heavenly Father that I am seated with

you in my place of prominence in Jesus' name.

Amen.

Summary of points

    i.   You need adequate preparation to become great in life

    ii.   It takes maturity to govern as a 'King or Queen'

    iii.   Your humility will exalt you in due season

    iv.   Charisma without character is a great canker

    v.   Where you are going is more important than where you are now

    vi.   There are no limits except those you place on yourself

    vii.   Identify your gift, talent, or innate abilities and make good use of them

    viii.   Nothing can erase God's plan and purpose for your life

    ix.   Your faith will make the impossible possible

    x.   When all is said and done, give God all the glory

CHAPTER TWO

IN A TROUBLED WORLD, BEEP YOUR BARGAINING POWER

United we bargain; divided we beg!

You are going to be exposed to the central theme of the book. The subject matter of this message seeks to inspire in you fresh hunger and confidence in your bargaining pursuits in this troubled world of ours today.

Many youths are naïve as they are confronted with issues that look daunting amid the myriad of socioeconomic and political challenges. They are limited in the resources to engage with as they face new problems and opportunities day after day.

You are expected to make the best decision in every situation. Sometimes, the decision is very difficult to make but, you have to decide anyway. No matter who you are or where you are right now, you are negotiating or bargaining with one thing or the other in life. It may be in your marriage, academics, business, career, spiritual life, social life, financial life, health, etc.

Like David, who was confronted with a situation and had to make a quick and clever decision in the face of all the daunting problems surrounding him, you must be smart enough to bargain your way through the various issues of life. You need to think and act smart at the negotiating table!

A Smart Blonde

A blonde walks into a bank in Johannesburg and asks for the loans department. She says she´s going to Europe on business for three weeks and needs to borrow R10,000. The bank officer says the bank will need some kind of security for the loan, so the blonde hands over the keys to a new Rolls Royce.

The car is parked on the street in front of the bank, she has the papers and everything checks out. The bank agrees to accept the car as collateral for the loan. The bank manager and its staff all enjoy a good laugh at the blonde for using an R500,000 Rolls as collateral against an R 10,000 loan.

An employee of the bank then proceeds to drive the Rolls into the bank´s underground garage and parks it there. Two weeks later, the blonde returns, and repays the R10,000 and the interest, which comes to R141.66.

The bank manager says, "Miss, we are very happy to have had your business, and this transaction has worked out very nicely, but we are a little puzzled. While you were away, we checked you out and found that you are a multimillionaire. What puzzles us is, why would you bother to borrow R10,000?"

The blond replies ... "Where else in Johannesburg can I park my car for two weeks for only R141.66 and expect it to be there when I return?" Finally, they agree that she is indeed smart!

"If you pay peanuts, you get monkeys" —

James Goldsmith

The key takeaway from this humorous story is that if you want quality results, you must be willing to invest and not settle for peanuts.

David, just like the smart blonde, saw an opportunity and quickly wanted to take advantage of it. His future, the destinies of his family, and the entire nation depended on his action or inaction. He knew he had to be smart.

In chapter seven, we will explore the importance of recognizing and capitalizing on opportunities that may only come once in a lifetime. Quick thinking and making the most of these opportunities at every stage of your life is vital.

David surrounded himself with warriors on the battlefield and didn't merely think about delivering provisions to his brothers and returning home. He engaged with those standing nearby to uncover potential opportunities. He understood his capabilities and sought a chance to showcase them to meet a pressing need.

Success is often said to occur when preparation meets opportunity. The information David needed to succeed was with the men standing right beside him, and he seized that opportunity. They became his destiny helpers before the battle. They also guided him to the King to present his petitions, inspiring him despite his brother's resentment.

Do You Have Helpers In Life's Journey?

Precious one, in life you will need people I call HELPERS. They are all over you from birth till death. There are different types of helpers along the journey to your throne and you must know their roles in your life at a particular point in time.

These include:

✓ Grounders

These are people who keep you set in your values. They keep you grounded. They make sure that while you are reaching high in your goals, you do not lose track. They tell you who you are and the vision you had from the beginning when you were nobody so that you are not carried away.

Success will cause you to rise high but your feet must be stable. You need people who will keep your feet grounded. They could be your parents, husband, sister, brother, wife, or an old lifelong friend. They help you to keep perspective and to keep your feet stable on the ground.

It was said of the Caesars of Rome whenever they run in their parade, that people will hail them saying, "Hail Caesar, hail Caesar, you are a god, you are a god". But someone stood right behind them to whisper to them and say, "Remember you are a man, remember you are a man, remember you are a man". It was meant to keep them focused and grounded.

✓ Mentors

"If you cannot see where you are going,

ask someone who has been there before."

J Loren Norris

The second group of people you need are Mentors. You need mentors in life. They help unleash your potential. You may find them in various areas of your life. You must have mentors in your relationships, career, ministry, social life, etc.

These are normally ahead of you and they coach and critique you. They make you think deeply about your potential and guide you to become a better person of yourself. David's Mentors were Samuel and Nathan. Timothy's mentor was Paul. Who is your mentor then?

✓ **Connectors**

They link you to new levels of your life. Samuel connected David. Sometimes they may use their knowledge, influence, judgment and perception, experience, etc. to link you to your future destiny.

These create vital connections in your life. Nevertheless, you don't have to be opportunistic. Don't ask them, they will create the link themselves.

✓ **Pilgrims**

These are journeymen and women. They are always with you in life. When you are down or up they are there. When you are happy or crying, they are there. When you are betrayed they are there to be with you. They stick with you for life.

They may be absent for a while but they appear suddenly. These defend you and sing your praise even if you are wrong. They don't correct you as mentors do but hail you most of the time.

Stay tuned as we journey through this book, exploring the principles that will empower you to navigate the negotiating table and harness your bargaining power. Remember, being smart and seizing opportunities can make a world of difference in your life.

Keep bargaining, my friend, and watch your life transform!

ADVANCED INTELLIGENCE FOR A GOOD BARGAIN

"If you don't get what you want, it's a sign either that you did not

seriously want it, or that you tried to bargain over the price"

Rudyard Kipling

To bargain to the Cambridge International Dictionary of English is an *agreement* between two people or groups in which each promises to do something in exchange for something else.

Bargaining power is a concept related to the relative abilities of parties in a situation to exert influence over each other. If both parties are on an equal footing in a debate, then they will have equal bargaining power, such as in a perfectly competitive market, or between an evenly matched monopoly and monophony.

In negotiations, bargaining power is the capacity of one party to dominate the other due to its influence, power, size, or status, or through a combination of different persuasion tactics. It also aims at persuading an 'offeror' to revise his or her proposal to better suit one's own needs or desires. This process includes adjusting assumptions and positions, give-and-take, and a certain degree of flexibility.

For a bargain to be well established there has to be a *contract* between the two parties or groups involved. All the necessary conditions of the contract have to be fulfilled for the exchange to be effected successfully and profitably among the parties.

A contract like a bargain is an agreement between two parties or more to create a legal obligation, which may have elements in writing. But contracts can be made orally. In Contract law, it is based on the principle expressed in the Latin phrase, which is usually translated as "agreements must be kept" but more literally means, ''must be kept".

To the Chinese, a contract is a commercial agreement, not a legal document, and should be based on friendship and goodwill. In China, whenever unexpected circumstances arise, they are typically sorted out through the strong relationship bonds that exist.

China is a one-leader-oriented culture and Chinese expect the same approach from foreigners. During negotiation, a team of negotiators is welcomed but the Chinese will look for a leader with authority to make decisions.

It is advisable to bring your technical experts to the bargaining table. Like in any negotiation, you need to be sure that both substantial and relationship issues are considered in terms of the negotiation goals.

While composing your negotiation team, choose delegates who are competent in building relationships, and creating and claiming value. Briefly speaking, if you can create a team that will naturally fit the bargaining context and relationship style you are more likely to achieve an optimal outcome.

How To Become A Better Negotiator

Although for some people negotiating comes naturally, it is a skill that can be improved with time. These skills, are like fine wine or a killer dance move – they get better with time! So, if you want to level up your negotiation game and become an unstoppable force in any field, I've got some tips for you to vibe with in any circumstance:

1. Identify your goals

You must enter negotiations knowing what you want out of an agreement and how much you're willing to compromise. For example, your objective may be to negotiate a salary of £80,000 annually, but you would be willing to settle for £75,000. You may consider asking yourself these questions to identify your goals:

- *What are the minimum terms I need?*
- *How much am I willing to negotiate?*
- *Are my goals realistic for this position and/or industry?*

2. Consider the opinions of others

Although good negotiators are typically determined and decisive people, their ability to empathize and understand people's motivations can massively influence the outcomes of their negotiations.

To learn how to do that, practice looking at a problem through someone else's eyes by taking into consideration their goals, values, and the situation they're in. Doing that can influence others to see you as a reliable and trustworthy person with valuable ideas, which might lead to reaching a compromise that everyone's satisfied with.

3. Understand your strengths and weaknesses

Knowing your strengths and weaknesses can help you understand which approach to negotiating best matches your unique talents and personality. Some negotiators may prefer spending more time analyzing a situation and designing a clear strategy when trying to compromise, whereas others find that improvising and using their communication skills fit their personality better.

To know which approach is right for you, you may want to think about the things you're good at, your values and motivation, as well as your past negotiating experiences and what you'd like to change about them.

4. Build your confidence

It can be challenging to ask for what you want. However, successful negotiation requires self-assurance. Remember to never take things personally or get discouraged by someone's opinion in a discussion. Their goal is to change your mind and achieve their goal, which usually has nothing to do with how they perceive you as a person. By exercising confidence in your negotiation, the other parties can be more inclined to believe in the benefits of your proposal.

5. Don't be afraid to make mistakes

Although striving for perfection can be something that motivates you to improve your skills, it's important to remember that everyone makes mistakes from time to time. If you make a mistake during negotiating, don't be afraid to admit it.

Instead, focus on controlling your emotions and try to look at the situation realistically to come up with a solution to fix it. The ability to do that can be essential at work, even though it takes a lot of courage especially when you're discussing something significant to you.

6. Don't rush

When it comes to negotiating, practice makes perfect. Giving yourself enough time to experiment with different tactics and practices can improve the quality of your negotiation. To achieve that, you might consider entering into role-play situations with friends, family, or co-workers.

It's even possible to find yourself a professional negotiation coach who could help you practice. Going through fictitious situations and discussing them with someone out loud can help you to learn how to influence others and compromise more effectively.

FUNDAMENTAL INTELLIGENCE IN NEGOTIATING ANYTHING

The general elements in negotiating anything of importance with anyone are: *offer, acceptance, intention to create legal relations, and consideration.* However, the most important feature of that transaction is, one party makes an *offer* that another *accepts*. This can be called a *concurrence of wills* or *consensus ad idem* (meeting of the minds) of two or more parties.

An OFFER is something of value given by a *promisor* to a *promisee* in exchange for something of value given by a *promisee* to a *promisor*. Typically, the thing of value is an act, such as making a payment, or a forbearance to act when one is privileged to do so.

In the United States, the general rule is that in "case of doubt, an offer is interpreted as inviting the *offeree* to accept *either* by promising to perform what the offer requests *or* by rendering the performance, as the *offeree* chooses."

Mutual assent is typically reached through offer and acceptance, that is when an offer is met with an acceptance that is unqualified and that does not vary the offer's terms. The latter requirement is known as the "mirror image" rule.

If a purported acceptance does vary the terms of an offer, it is not an acceptance but a counteroffer and, therefore, simultaneously a rejection of the original offer. Offer and acceptance do not always need to be expressed orally or in writing. An *implied* contract is one in which some of the terms are not expressed in words.

CONSIDERATION consists of a legal detriment and a bargain. A legal detriment is a promise to do something or refrain from doing something that you have the legal right to do or doing or refraining from doing something that you don't have to do.

The remedy for breach of contract can be "damages" or compensation of money. In equity, the remedy can be a specific performance of the contract or an injunction. Both of these remedies award the party at loss the "benefit of the bargain" or expectation damages, which are greater than mere reliance damages.

Let's dive into the nitty-gritty, shall we?

From the account below, we unravel some fascinating insights about the treaty between David and King Saul. This agreement was no joke – it laid a solid foundation for a legal and well-considered treaty. The basic principles of bargaining were unquestionably at play, ensuring that both parties entered into the pact with meticulous thought and utmost consideration.

As we embark on this expedition through the intricacies of their contract, get ready to unveil the hidden gems of their bargaining process. Brace yourself for a thrilling ride where ancient wisdom meets contemporary negotiations and contracts.

Together, we'll peel back the layers and discover the valuable lessons that transcend time. Prepare to be enlightened as we unravel the delicate dance between the art of bargaining and the intricacies of human relationships. It's a voyage that will shed light on the pursuit of shared goals and the artful navigation of mutually beneficial agreements.

So, my fellow adventurers, fasten your seatbelts and open your minds to the fascinating world of their agreement. As we explore the depths of their contract, we'll unlock valuable insights that can be applied to the dynamic landscape of modern-day negotiations and contracts. Get ready to witness the fusion of timeless principles with the ever-evolving challenges of our contemporary world.

Together, let's embark on this exhilarating journey where ancient wisdom and modern negotiating tactics collide, revealing the fundamental intelligence to successful bargaining and the art of crafting impactful agreements.

"And David spake to the men that stood by saying,

what shall be done to the man that killeth this Philistine,

and taketh away the reproach from Israel.

For who is this uncircumcised Philistine,

that he should defy the armies of the living God.

And it shall be that the MAN who killeth him,

...the KING will enrich him with GREAT RICHES, and will give him his DAUGHTER,

and make his FATHER'S HOUSE FREE in Israel."

PRINCIPLE #

1. The King- **OFFEROR**

"Where the word of a King is,

there is power, and who can say to him,

'what are you doing"

King Solomon

i.   Authentic source

The first principle adopted by the son of Jesse was all about that authenticity check, my friend - he knew the importance of knowing who's behind the offer, the real deal-maker, the KING himself. When it comes to negotiations, knowing the source of the promise, proposal, or pact is absolutely crucial.

In this epic tale, David, the *promissee*, quickly realized that the challenge had been thrown down by none other than the King himself, the *promissor*. And let me tell you, once that royal signet was on that contract, there was no turning back. The King's word was law, and that made the commitment as authentic as it gets.

Now, here's where things get real, my friend. Too often, people dive headfirst into all sorts of ventures without bothering to check the authenticity of the agreement or contract they're about to step into. Just because someone whispers sweet promises in your ear or shows you something shiny doesn't mean it's legit. Oh no, the source might be as fake as a knockoff designer watch.

So, here's a lesson for the ages: Don't be fooled by appearances or empty words. Before you jump into any deal, do your due diligence and find out if the source is the real deal or just a slick talker. It's all about separating the genuine opportunities from the fakes, my friend. Trust me, it'll save you from some serious headaches down the road.

Find out about the parties involved and be certain of their true nature and character. Who are the dealers and what have been their credentials over time? Do they have a good track record in the field you want to enter? Are they an authority in their area of specialization? Do they exist in reality at all? Can they be taken for their word?

Let's say you're approached by a business partner who presents you with a lucrative investment opportunity. They paint a vivid picture of the potential returns and assure you that it's a reliable way to make a fortune. The offer sounds too good to be true, but you're intrigued.

Before diving in headfirst, you decide to apply the principle of authenticity. You start by researching the credibility of the offeror, in this case, your business partner. You look into their track record, their reputation in the industry, and any previous successful ventures they've been involved in. You also consider if the offer is coming directly from them or through an intermediary.

As you dig deeper, you discover some red flags. You come across reports of their involvement in shady business dealings or instances where promises were made but never fulfilled. You also find out that the offer is not directly from them but through a third-party who has a questionable reputation.

Realizing the potential risks involved, you decide to step back and reconsider the investment opportunity. You understand that even though the offer may sound appealing and exciting, the source is not reliable or trustworthy. You prioritize safeguarding your own interests and opt for a more secure and genuine investment opportunity with a trusted and proven partner.

By applying the principle of authenticity, you save yourself from potentially falling into a scam or engaging in an unreliable venture. You understand that just because something seems attractive on the surface, it doesn't mean it's genuine or worth pursuing. This practical example highlights the importance of verifying the authenticity of the source before entering into any agreement or negotiation.

My Bitter Experience

It was late 2008 when I saw an email in my inbox. It was an invitation to express interest in a job offer from a Metro Hotel in the United States of America. It was the first time I had seen something like this since my graduation from the university.

I was elated and surprised at the same time. All my job applications on the Internet had been to local companies in my country, not to any foreign hotel. This stirred up enthusiasm in me, and I thanked God in my heart for this rare opportunity!

Of course, I decided to apply and show a keen interest in the offer. Who wouldn't want to travel to the United States of America with all travel expenses paid, including the visa and plane ticket? My accommodation was also going to be taken care of by my prospective employer, with the promise of a more extended stay after some time. The offer seemed too good to pass up.

A few requirements were demanded, such as my passport pictures, college certificates, passport details, and other personal data. Then I received a call from one of my schoolmates who was about to meet a relative at the Kotoka International Airport in Accra, the capital city of Ghana. She was from California, USA.

Something struck my heart, and I decided to go to the US Embassy in my country to confirm the job offer, as I had been slated for an interview in a few weeks by my so-called employer in the United States.

As I arrived at the US Embassy, I was taken aback by the sheer size of the building. Many people stood outside, waiting for their turn. They all had appointments and carried a special chit to confirm their date and time. Unfortunately, I didn't have any chit confirming my appointment date and time.

I printed out and carried all the documents sent to me by my 'prospective employer' to prove that I was scheduled for an interview at a later date but needed to confirm the place and time since it was my first time.

However, I was denied access by the tight security officers since I didn't have the proper chit to enter in the first place. I called the helplines, but unfortunately, I was denied entry and advised to do some thorough checks beforehand.

To cut a long story short, my research later confirmed that there was no job offer from any Metro Hotel in the United States, and the whole process was a sham. It turned out to be the work of unknown internet fraudsters. I felt deeply ashamed of myself for falling prey to this fake offer.

Nations, governments, associations, and individuals have all fallen victim to the dubious activities of confident tricksters, con men and women, internet fraudsters, and thieves who promise to deliver a particular product or service, only to realize in the end that these people or companies are nonexistent or fraudulent.

Some may appear well-dressed and polished on the outside but harbor evil intentions. They present you with enticing proposals and agreements, only for you to realize later that it was all a charade.

Avoid such damages.

Countries have signed huge contracts and agreements with other nations or corporate organizations, only to regret their decisions in the end. Sometimes, even entire parliaments or ministries of a nation have been deceived. Huge sums of money are lost in the process, and the reputations of these countries are at stake.

Don't become a victim.

A person seeking a partner may meet someone in the church, at an event, or in town who appears well-polished and ostentatiously wealthy, giving the impression of entering into a promising relationship. However, they later discover that this person was only interested in their body or had ulterior motives.

Similarly, some individuals, particularly women, may parade themselves in churches and attend countless meetings to find their ideal partner, only to realize that it was all pretense. After marriage, their true characters and evil intentions are revealed. They become like "blood-sucking vampires" who drain their partners of all their resources and eventually abandon them. It's important to note that some men can also be equally deceptive in this regard.

Ministers, presidents, parliamentarians, pastors, prophets, top executives, and commoners have all fallen prey to the deception of individuals who initially seemed like "angels" but turned out to be ravaging wolves in sheep's clothing.

I urge those seeking partners to spend quality time in prayer and wait on the Lord. It is essential to thoroughly examine the lifestyles and backgrounds of potential partners to determine if they truly align with their claimed identities.

Many faith based individuals, business executives and leaders have fallen victim to the deception of con men and women. Therefore, great care must be taken when engaging in any relationship, agreement, or contract, whether it be social, financial, or even spiritual in nature.

Numerous individuals have lost their esteemed positions and hard-earned reputations as a result of falling into these traps. Regardless of whether the allegations are true or not, the damage inflicted upon them, their name, their profession, and their families is not easily erased.

For instance, former Prime Minister Silvio Berlusconi was put on trial by Italian prosecutors on charges of having sex with a 17-year-old and attempting to cover it up using his power. Although Berlusconi dismissed the allegations as a smear campaign, the sex scandal garnered extensive media attention and cast a shadow on his ability to govern effectively.

Prosecutors claimed that Berlusconi paid for sex with a Moroccan girl nicknamed Ruby, who later would turn 18. They alleged that he used his influence to secure her release from police custody in an unrelated suspected theft case. It was believed that he feared their relationship would be exposed because though she looked like an adult she was actually less than 18 at the time.

The charge of child prostitution carried a possible sentence of six months to three years, while the abuse of influence charge, which was considered more severe, carried a possible sentence of four to twelve years. The outcome of his trial is well-known to you and me.

Ii. Power to pay

David was curious about the ability of the 'offeror' to fulfill their promises. In this case, the offeror happened to be none other than the King himself, who practically owned "everything and everybody" in the land of Israel.

The King held the reigns of all the mineral and natural resources in the land - gold, silver, bronze, timber, diamonds, coal, crude oil, and more. This meant he had the means to fulfill his promise once the young lad had done his part of the deal: slaying the giant Goliath.

In another scenario, Samuel Bentley popularly known as Sam B. approached the Goodwill Money Lenders Company seeking assistance for his I.T. business. He proudly led the credit officer to 'his office,' showing off a few machines and equipment while making enticing promises of a quick return soon.

The credit officer was impressed by the well-organized office and fell in love with the neatly arrayed machines. Excited, he asked Samuel to fill out the loan application forms, with the machines serving as collateral for the loan.

Bentley then presented a two-page document outlining a lucrative contract he was bidding for, which promised to repay the loan along with interest within a few days of sealing the deal. He had high hopes of securing the contract, although he couldn't recall where he had stored the documents from his previous successful contracts. Despite the imminent contract deadline, the credit officer believed every word his prospective client said.

Within two days, Samuel Bentley received a loan of USD 4,000.00, with a 7% interest rate, payable over three months. The young firm saw great potential in their business prospects. However, it later came to light that the loan was intended to cover another debt Sam B. owed to a nearby financial institution.

Since Sam B. couldn't execute the job within the tight timeframe and his bank account was in the red, he lost the contract he had showcased to the credit officer. Furthermore, the office space he presented to the money lenders belonged to a friend who had gone on a business trip to Europe. Sam B. had only sought the money lenders' assistance due to mounting pressure from the previous financial institution, which was after him for his debt.

The credit officer had failed to do enough due diligence initially and couldn't judge if the business venture had the capacity to pay and sustain its growth after the loan was given. This was a drawback that nearly cost him his hard earned reputation in the institution.

Before entering into any negotiations with a potential partner, it's crucial to ensure they possess the will and ability to deliver as agreed. Conduct thorough background checks before signing any agreements and committing resources. Adequate resources should be available for a considerable period, especially if substantial profits haven't started flowing in yet.

However, it's important to note that not all parties possess the financial goodwill to support you initially. Some may come with the necessary ideas, skills, and experience to help you succeed. Conversely, not everyone who promises monetary returns can steer you toward a safe and successful destination. Know your desires, conduct due diligence, and seek out mutually beneficial deals.

Similarly, one cannot wake up one day and decide to get married without having sufficient savings to cover accommodation, food, utilities, clothing, and daily expenses, let alone the expenses of raising children and their education. Adequate preparation is necessary before embarking on any form of association, venture, or relationship to avoid fruitless waste of time and resources.

Furthermore, possessing a fancy car, a beautiful house, and stylish clothes does not automatically make someone an ideal spouse. It is essential to thoroughly understand and study your prospective partner before saying, "I do." Remember, not all that glitter is gold!

iii.   Legally backed

The deal was not only a verbal agreement but also legally binding. In a land where the word of the King held the force of law, his promises of wealth, his daughter's hand in marriage, and exemption from taxes for the family were all backed by the legal system. The King sealed the agreement with his signet ring, making it a contract accepted and recognized by the constitution and the ruling powers of the time. It was a legitimate arrangement, free from suspicion and societal disapproval.

Dependability was inherent in such a contract, given that it originated from the 'Castle, House of Commons or the White House' and was endorsed by the Head of State of the nation. It was well within the King's powers to fulfill his commitments, unaffected by negative macro or microeconomic factors of the time. The feasibility of the agreement rested on the Head of State's authority, upheld by the legal framework of the constitution and the national budget.

Regrettably, the same cannot be said for many people in our contemporary era. When promised lucrative financial returns, individuals often rush to pursue them without considering the legal implications. Mining companies and corporate entities enter into contracts with communities and groups, neglecting the long-term interests of vulnerable populations within their areas of operation, not to mention the environmental consequences.

In the pursuit of selfish interests, some disregard environmental and social regulations, betraying the less privileged members of society and the laws of the land. It is disheartening to witness individuals accepting substantial bribes to bypass by-laws and sign agreements without any consideration for the marginalized segments of society.

Equally disconcerting is the fact that some football or soccer players sign contracts with teams without fully understanding the details involved. Blinded by the allure of promised wealth, they eagerly sign and begin playing, only to find themselves entangled in legal disputes a few months later.

Many of these issues may have been stipulated in the contract, but due to a lack of thorough reading and interpretation, individuals fall victim to unfavorable circumstances. Football managers or agents often exploit their hardworking clients simply because the clients failed to grasp the legal clauses before signing the contract.

The Football Fantasy

Mirror Football had an exclusive extract from the new book by the Secret Player, the mystery Premier League player who has revealed the ins and outs of life as a top-tier footballer. Here is a portion of his findings:
"Ask any footballer about agents, and they're likely to have a less than complimentary story. Agents manipulate players, especially young ones. They groom them. Agents begin by ingratiating themselves with players, stroking their egos, and promising to look after them like their own children. Agents are salesmen, often with a good business sense, and footballers are their products.

I can see why they exist, but this unregulated, potentially highly lucrative industry attracts all kinds of sharks. Every agent is supposed to be FA and FIFA registered, but that means little. That's just an exam that anyone with half a brain can pass. And some of the most powerful agents in football are not properly registered. They can't call themselves agents, more 'business advisors,' but they are the ones who cut the massive deals.

There are too many agents and not enough of any level of deals to go around. Agents are in it for one thing: themselves. There are some good agents, the ones who have hundreds of contacts, influential contacts. Certain clubs pay agents more than other clubs, so agents favor them and try to propel you towards them, but they are prepared to do you over to keep those clubs sweet.

I had an agent looking after me for a while. I no longer speak to him. He shafted me. He pushed financial advice and products on me that I should never have signed up for, and he cut himself in generously on the commissions.

I strongly suspect – though I can't prove – that he said to one club: 'If I can get him to sign for £15,000 a week, can I get £200,000?' He knew that the club was prepared to pay £20,000 a week for me, but also that I would sign for £15,000. He saved them money and lined his own pockets. It leaves a very bitter taste. I've seen double charging added to that, where an agent concludes a deal and then goes to the player and claims that the club didn't pay him.

A good agent should be an excellent negotiator who is optimistic about his clients. He should have his clients punching above their weight, both in terms of their stature and their wages. He should give hard, no-nonsense advice and keep a player grounded. If he has a player at Sunderland who thinks he's good enough for Arsenal or Tottenham but isn't, then the agent needs to tell him this.

He needs to be like a social worker and speak to his client when he's playing badly, not just when he's doing well and attracting attention.

He needs to be there for his player, offering emotional support and dealing with a player who wants to know why he's not playing, answering questions about why the manager/fans/teammates don't like him, rather than not picking up his calls.

He should have solid contacts and represent good players. If you're a young player, and an agent approaches you and says that he also represents Steven Gerrard, then you'll listen to him. If he has no other players, then you'll be less inclined to do so.

Agents can build up a portfolio with just one big-name player to attract others – and their big-name player will be the one who keeps their agency going. There's a black agent in London with thirty black players on his books – those lads know they can trust him.

Agents manipulate players, but players can also manipulate agents. An agent may approach a player to whom he's not contracted and say that he has a club that is interested in him. They won't be, but the player might raise his eyebrows and feel flattered. But he'll then go to that club and say that the player is interested in joining them.

Some players tell agents to bring offers to them, and they'll take it from there before agreeing to sign with them, but agents naturally don't want that.

Despite attempts to sort things out, the system is flawed, with all sorts of chancers trying to cut in on deals. Clubs use their preferred agents too. One of my former teammates got a big-money move to a top club. He'd used the same agent for years, a reliable fella who negotiated him a decent boot contract and several nice commercial deals.

The buying club told him that they only went through a certain agent – who is widely viewed as a crook throughout football. The agent got a call from the crook, saying that he had to cut him in on the deal, or there would be no deal. The agent cut him in; there was enough money in the pot for two. Or three, given that the team's manager was almost certainly in on it – that's why the crook got the call in the first place. Everyone wants a piece of the pie.

However, I'm not one of those who believe that players can do without agents. Clubs take the piss without them; they did for decades. They'll pay players as little as possible, especially home-grown ones. Footballers indeed go where the money is 90% of the time, but a player should be advised where to go."

A similar phenomenon occurs in the music industry as well. Musicians work tirelessly to come out with nice pieces of music, only for their producers or managers to enjoy the majority of the fruits of their labor. The managers negotiate with corporate organizations such as telecommunication companies while the artists go out there to perform, and they have no clue about the details of the contract.

The Business Development Manager of Empire Entertainment, organizers of the annual 'Ghana Meets Naija' and 'Back In The Day Concert,' Mr. Kevin Adisi advised Ghanaian musicians to be careful when signing ambassadorial deals with telecommunication networks. He counseled them to consider some key clauses in these contracts before signing them, not just the money that comes along with it.

Briefing the press about the annual event "Ghana Meets Naija" concert which took place, Mr. Adisi said, some clauses in the contract restrict the musician from performing at other telecommunication networks sponsored events, affecting the artist negatively.

He stated that "going forward these are some of the challenges the artist might be facing. If the artist doesn't take care, he might hit the rock because you will not get shows to play, and you will now have setbacks coming in your career."

He continued, "The signing of these artists to telcos is creating problems for this industry, and that is why the media has to advise these artists to take a second look at some key clauses before they sign the contract because it depends on them to read the contracts and sign."

Before you agree to any deal, check out the legal details critically before you sign it. You don't want to give your life away by letting someone else enjoy the fruits of your labor.

Artists And Manager Contract Basics

To ensure that the relationship between managers and players, musicians, or other artists flourishes for their mutual benefit, certain legal considerations need to be examined before going ahead to put pen to paper finally.

Here are a few basics to keep in mind about artists and manager contracts:

- It Doesn't Have to be Complicated

Especially if you are a young artiste, skip the fancy talk, and write a simple document that covers money, division of labor, and the length of the agreement.

- It Should be Mutually Beneficial

Even if your manager has been at this longer than you, don't sign your life away for a crack at their expertise. A manager who believes in you won't expect you to do so.

- It Should be Signed in Good Faith

If you are looking for loopholes before you sign, or your manager is, there is a problem.

- The Contract Term

The length of your agreement with the manager is a good place to start. You will need to agree upon a term and a contract cancellation policy. A fair contract term is a one-year agreement, with an option to extend the agreement at the end of the year if both parties agree.

At that point, you can look at negotiating longer agreements, but a one-year term is a good trial term for both parties. Be wary of giving the manager options to extend without your agreement; if you do, you can be forced to stick with a manager you don't want. Be sure your contact specifies how both parties can leave the deal.

- The Job Expectations

What you expect your manager to do depends on where you are in your career. If you're a new artist, your manager should be promoting you to labels, trying to get you a gig, and generally trying to get things off the ground for you.

If you're further along, your manager should be making sure other people are doing their jobs to promote your work. Simply be as clear as possible about what you need from a manager, and what they are willing to do. For instance, do you expect your manager to get merchandise made, or will you take that on? Now is the time to get it all on the table.

- The Management Fee

A standard management fee is usually around 15% - 20% of your earnings. Your manager takes a cut of proceeds from your sales, any label advance, and the earnings from deals they have negotiated.

Some do not get your money from your merchandise sales, your royalties, or from deals they have not negotiated (unless you have a prior agreement saying otherwise).

Keep in mind that if you are new and haven't started making an income yet, 15% -20% of nothing is still nothing. You may want to keep this earning potential in mind when you are nailing down the details of the job expectations.

- The Manager's Expenses

Your manager should not be out of pocket for business expenses for promoting you, but you need to reach an agreement on how expenses will work. You don't have to pay for your manager's phone costs or office costs, in most instances.

You do have to pay for business trips your manager makes on your behalf and reasonable costs like taking label representatives out for drinks. The best way to handle expenses is to pay them at set times, i.e. once a month. The manager should provide you with receipts for expenses. Include a caveat in the contract saying expenses above a certain amount must be cleared with you first.

- Words of Caution

Manager contracts can be very specific to your circumstances, so the advice above is a guide and does not represent hard and fast rules. The best thing you can do is be as clear and specific as possible, anticipating every bump in the road.

If you are young, and your manager is going to grow with you, be sure to re-examine your agreement often to make sure it is still fair to everyone. If you already have a deal in place and have a new manager coming on board, you should seek legal advice to make sure your interests are protected.

Disadvantaged In An Advantaged Economy

Many Ghanaians rejoiced when news of the discovery of oil in commercial quantities in the Western Coastal area of Ghana broke.

The anticipation was that Ghana would soon join the ranks of the world's oil-rich nations, and the revenue generated from the industry would significantly boost the economy.

However, despite the high expectations of increased revenue from mineral resources, Ghana, like many other countries, faced the "paradox of plenty" or the "resource curse." While some countries such as Canada, Chile, Botswana, and Norway have successfully managed their natural resource wealth through prudent and transparent practices, a vast majority of countries, including Nigeria, Ghana, Chad, Liberia, Sudan, Cameroon, Gabon, Angola, Uganda, and the Democratic Republic of Congo, have struggled to escape the cycle of poverty despite their abundance of mineral resources.

Prominent figures like Lloyd George, the former British Prime Minister, have commented on the perceived corruption in the oil industry, suggesting that "oil profits generally seem to find their way by some invisible pipeline into pockets." Such observations only reinforce the notion of corruption within the sector.

A retrospective analysis of over a century of mining activities in Ghana highlights the presence of the "resource curse" and its associated challenges, including corruption. Despite the extraction of various solid minerals over the years, mining communities continue to grapple with poverty and environmental degradation. A stark comparison between Obuasi in Ghana and Johannesburg in South Africa serves as a striking example of the stark disparity between Ghana's deprived mining communities and their South African counterparts.

Recognizing that the exploration and production of oil in commercial quantities were new to Ghana, measures were put in place to ensure that internationally recognized best practices in transparency and accountability were followed. The goal was to prevent oil companies, as well as foreign and local partners, from depriving Ghanaians of the benefits they rightfully deserve.

Former President John Evans Atta Mills emphasized the importance of social, legal, and corporate responsibilities to one of the companies involved in Ghana's oil discovery in the Jubilee Fields of Cape Three Points. His message was clear: local communities must be included in the process and should reap the benefits of oil and gas production.

In addition to the challenges within the oil industry, Ghana also faces issues with foreign individuals who engage in illegal activities within the country, often disguising themselves in various ways. These individuals participate in illicit activities such as prostitution, drug peddling, child trafficking, illegal mining, armed robbery, money laundering, internet fraud, and cybercrime. Disturbingly, political leaders and residents sometimes aid or associate themselves with these criminal acts. All of us must rise and combat these societal ills that corrode the moral and legal fabric of our nation.

Therefore, like David facing Goliath, it is crucial to critically examine the authenticity, legality, capacity, and sustainability of the other party before entering into any agreement. By doing so, we can safeguard our interests and contribute to the development and progress of our society.

2. Enrich with GREAT RICHES- **THE OFFER & CONSIDERATION**

The second principle to consider in the bargaining process is to critically examine the offer itself and also see beyond the immediate monetary returns.

The King was to ENRICH whoever was to partner him in the arrangement he had arrayed before the whole nation. Note here that, he mentioned GREAT RICHES and not just silver, gold, bronze, or diamond.

This meant that the prize was beyond physical cash or money. They were great riches that could not be easily liquidated immediately into cash. These may include large plots of land, farmlands, male and female servants, cattle, sheep, goats, etc. The King was looking beyond today. He sought a lifetime business partner and ally and not just a sucking and greedy individual. He needed a lifelong corporate royal partner or colleague by his side always.

i.   **Bargain beyond borders**

In your negotiations with people, seek for the long-term benefits not only the immediate ones. Watch out for projects that go a long way to benefit you and generations unborn. Our politicians should always take into consideration the welfare of generations unborn and make decisions that will benefit them in the future.

One interesting development worthy of mention in Ghana's oil sector was the agreement signed between the National Vocational Training Institute (NVTI) and Harvard Marine International Ghana Limited. The agreement between NVTI and Harvard Marine is built on the need for a strong partnership to plan, structure, and implement training programs for the offshore oil, gas, energy, mining, and construction industries in Ghana.

The Memoranda of Understanding (MoU) between Harvard Marine and the National Vocational Training Institute (NVTI) also lays out plans for the provision of internationally accredited training in Ghana in partnership with the Australasian Maritime Institute.

The MoU also made provision for the training of Ghanaian trainers and a road map that will eventually see Ghanaians take over the reins of both teaching and management for the certification for occupational health, safety, and environment in the petroleum, mining, energy, construction, and allied industries.

Minority against the use of Heritage Fund

According to a report in the Daily Graphic, the opposition party, led by the Minority Spokesperson on Finance in Parliament, strongly opposed the use of Ghana's Heritage Fund by the ruling government, emphasizing that it should be preserved for future generations. The following extract highlights their concerns:

The Minority expressed its intention to resist any government moves to utilize the fund. The then Minority Spokesperson on Finance, Dr. Anthony Akoto-Osei, described the proposition as "ridiculous." He argued that instead of drawing money from the fund, the government should focus on proper accountability for the 91 percent of oil proceeds that remain unaccounted for. The late Dr. Akoto-Osei acknowledged that the fund's investments were not generating substantial interest but emphasized the importance of not utilizing the money.

He reiterated that Ghana's oil resources, which are projected to deplete in the next 25 years, are meant for future generations. The establishment of the Heritage Fund aims to ensure that there will be something to rely on for future generations. Dr. Akoto-Osei questioned the purpose of utilizing the $117 million currently in the fund, particularly considering the economic challenges the country was facing.

He urged the government to address corruption in the management of the economy and recover embezzled funds from institutions like the Ghana Youth Employment and Entrepreneurial Development Agency (GYEEDA) and the Savannah Accelerated Development Agency (SADA), rather than diverting attention to the Heritage Fund.

Deputy Minority Leader, Dominic Nitiwul, also opposed any attempts to withdraw money from the Heritage Fund, stating that the law prohibits such actions. He suggested that if the government required funds, it could approach Parliament and make a case for using money from the Stabilization Fund, which holds 21 percent of oil proceeds.

Mr. Nitiwul emphasized that the Heritage Fund, which contains only nine percent of oil proceeds, is specifically designated for future generations. He expressed concern about the government's inability to demonstrate effective management of the economy and proper accountability for oil revenues. The Minority had previously advocated for the use of oil proceeds for specific projects, but their recommendations were not implemented.

It is essential to consider the long-term sustainability and growth of businesses. Just as we cannot consume all our eggs today without hatching some to produce more, bargaining and financial decisions should also take into account the well-being of future generations.

Also, it is worth noting that in the present times, relying on a single source of income may not be sufficient for individuals and the younger generation. Even if one's salary is substantial, investing a portion of it for sustainability and future growth is crucial. Adopting a mindset that transcends immediate gains and focuses on generational impact is vital for long-term prosperity.

ii.   Empowered to power peculiar people

GREAT RICHES also meant empowerment of the hands, heart, and head of the individual to bring out the best in him or her for a more productive life. The King was prepared to share his experiences in leadership and governance with any man that could take away the reproach from the land. Thus, he was also going to learn something new and unique from such an individual. It was going to be, hand goes hand come.

Sometimes in life, it is not all about making a lot of money. You need to empower your mind and empower others in society too. You need to sharpen your skills and acquire new ones, learn new technologies, and know more creative ways of doing things better and faster.

In bargaining your way to the top, don't only think of the money you will get today. Look ahead. Sometimes, you may have to serve free of charge to get what you want in the future. You may enjoy certain benefits which go beyond today's salary or pay as you work diligently for others.

There are countless stories of people who started serving or working from a humble background without being given what was due them, but, they ended up with great opportunities and privileges that money could not buy in the long run. When bargaining, look out for the GREAT RICHES of tomorrow not just the immediate riches of today.

You may have to start from a humble background bracing against the odds and pressing on till you realize your dreams in life. The challenges will be obvious but you have to overcome them if you are going to be successful at the end of the day.

She Survived Stroke And Became A Success Story
Behind the great achievements of Wilma Rudolph, the woman who got three gold medals in Athletics was a success story. For those who think that they have disabilities and shortcomings and can't succeed like other winners, please consider this. This is a true encouragement for young people who are desperate for success.

Though born with physical challenges, her mother saw greatness in her baby and was willing to make all needed sacrifice to let Wilma win on the negotiating table of life. She didn't look at the daughter's present limitations but looked at the future prospects of a daughter who will bring great hope the family and many across the world. A trade of today's trials for tomorrow's triumphs.

Wilma Rudolph was born in 1940 in Bethlehem, Tenn. The twentieth of 22 children, she was born with polio and suffered from serious bouts of pneumonia and scarlet fever as a young child. All these ailments contributed to a bad leg that some said would prevent her from ever walking. But Wilma had a loving and devoted family who made sure she got medical attention and who provided physical therapy themselves four times a day.

Rudolph got Pneumonia and a stroke at the age of four. She had to wear a Brace as per medical advice. Everyone believed she could not walk all through life. But her mother was not among them. She believed in hard work and dedication and confidence. She encouraged Wilma to expect good and feel good and work for the best. Her mother was confident that with practice and hard work coupled with divine touch, Wilma can walk again.

Wilma aimed to become the fastest woman in the world!

From the age of nine, she began to walk despite the advice of doctors not to do so. Then from the 13th year onwards, she began to participate in the races. But in all races, she could only manage last places. At the age of 15, she began training under Ed Temple, the trainer at Tennessee State University.

Wilma worked hard under the trainer and her confidence was high. Her greatest weapon was hard work and confidence in herself.

At the 1960 Olympics, her opponent in the 100m race was Jatta Hayden who was never defeated. Wilma defeated her and won the gold medal. In the 200m race also, Wilma defeated Hayden and won the gold medal. In the 400m relay, the baton fell from Wilma, but she took it back and won the race.

In my belief, not all have disabilities and shortcomings like Wilma had. But, we believe we are short of something. We are not like winners. We lack something that winners have. And what could that be? It is the inner self that separates winners and losers. Everyone can be a winner provided one is confident and puts in hard work and dedication to the task.

PRINCIPLE #

3. Give DAUGHTER'S hand in marriage- **THE 'OFFENSE'**

One strategic action of the "offeror" was giving his daughter's hand in marriage to the "offeree". This was a priceless gift to him for his bravery and victory over the adversary. There was nothing that could be compared to this. However, it was a shrewd strategy to get an insider in the other party's camp after the agreement had been successfully signed and executed as planned.

Michal was a source of offense to David, an inevitable trap he bargained for. She was the same woman who despised him after his victory in a fierce battle as he danced before the Lord. The woman who was to bring inspiration and comfort brought pain to his heart.

You see, a good businessman or woman can read the game plan of the opponent or competitors and devise the right strategies and plans to deal with any future occurrences. You need people with insight and trustworthiness in your enterprise. People who will not help your course may come your way, but you must be sensitive enough to know how to handle them.

Furthermore, the offeror sought to raise a *family* together with this intended stakeholder. This was to perpetuate his royal heritage without losing it to a mere individual in society. Giving his daughter's hand in marriage meant he still had a stake in the life of the proprietor, his offspring and the future of his enterprise.

i.   Like begets like

All that the partner was going to have and acquire in the future was also going to benefit him indirectly. As an eagle, he expected to dine and fly with eagles and not chickens. He wanted someone with high business acumen who would also be related very closely. The probability that the business would be stable for some time was assured. And he strategically planted his girl to secure this future interest.

You must do business with people who will be stable for a long time. People you consider to be trustworthy and committed to your vision. You should be able to buy into them as they also buy into you positively. Look out for the sustainability of the venture before you finally agree to it.

"We're never so vulnerable than when we trust someone –
but paradoxically, If we cannot trust, neither can we find love or joy"
Walter Anderson

Saul had a brilliant strategy when it came to handling his properties and hard-earned money. He didn't leave it to chance; instead, he planted his daughter, Michal, right in the camp of his prospective shareholder.

Talk about taking business partnerships to a whole new level! This wasn't just an emotional or social affair, mind you. No, no, Saul was playing the long game here, far beyond the wedding bells and the honeymoon phase that most young people get caught up in these days. He wanted someone he could trust and depend on, an insider he could count on.

Now, my friend, take a lesson from Saul when you're engaged in strategic negotiations. It's no wonder that foreign companies investing in other countries often bring in their nationals and experts to hold key positions. They trust their people more than the locals.

It's all about securing and perpetuating their national or corporate interests, not just looking out for the other partner alone. They've got insiders leaking sensitive information, allowing them to prepare ahead and strategize for their interests. Sneaky, right?

Of course, this can sometimes rub the citizens the wrong way. They feel slighted, and rightfully so. These foreign companies come in, despise the locals' efforts, and even mistreat the vulnerable in society. Some take advantage of the laxity in the system and break the laws of the land with a swagger.

In business, you need like-minded people by your side—those who share your core values and can rally behind your vision and mission statements. Trust me, without this harmony, you'll end up with chaos and schism, like a band playing different tunes at the same time. And trust me, that won't get you anywhere. So, weed out those who have contrary views and ambitions early on. It's like Marie Kondo says, "If it doesn't spark joy or align with your central vision, let it go."

But remember my friend, it's not just about you and your wealth. You've got to spread the love, too. After all, what's the point of amassing all that wealth if your family, friends, and relatives are suffering in abject poverty? Share the blessings, my friend. Make sure your dialogues are profitable enough to benefit others as well. It's like having a buffet—you don't hog all the delicious food to yourself; you let others enjoy the feast too.

And when it comes to bargaining, trust is your secret weapon. If the person you're engaging with can't be trusted, it's like buying a "genuine" Rolex from a shady street vendor. Just walk away, my friend. Don't sign that contract or follow through with the arrangement. And if your potential life partner isn't reliable enough, well, it's time to have a serious heart-to-heart talk. Remember, it's better to sort things out peacefully sooner rather than later.

So, take a page from Saul's playbook, sprinkle some trust, share the blessings, and negotiate your way to success. And who knows, maybe one day they'll write a business strategy book called "Saul's Secrets" with your clever strategies.

"Trust is like a vase. Once it's broken,

though you can fix It, the vase will never be the same"

Weasel Idiot

ii.   **Look up!**

One other point worth noting in bargaining your way to the top is to enter into a good agreement with a partner who is higher than you are in some instances. Over here, Saul was the King of a whole nation, he was older, more experienced, more resourceful, and better positioned to deliver on his promises.

The lad, therefore, saw it as an opportunity and not intimidating to enter into such an agreement. While older people in the army saw the opportunity and were afraid for their lives, he was prepared to take the risk of his life. A story is told of a little tortoise who took a great risk and made a positive move to change its life.

The Brave Little Tortoise and the Monster

Once upon a time, there was a tortoise on a ship, and the ship sank. Sometime later, the tortoise made it to a desert land surrounded by water on all sides except for one. The landward side led up to a big, steep, craggy mountain. To avoid starving to death, the tortoise decided to climb to the top of the mountain, hoping that he would be able to cross to the other side.

When he got to the snow-covered summit he was cold, and then a blizzard (snowstorm) started. He just managed to make out a small pathway leading down the other side of the mountain. But the path was guarded by a big 'MONSTER' that wouldn't stop shouting.

"Uuh uuh uuh!"

Such a sight and sound almost killed the tortoise with fright, and all he wanted to do was hide his head inside his shell. But, looking around him, he saw that many other animals were lying frozen to death with looks of horror on their faces. So the tortoise didn't go into his shell.

He summoned up all his courage to move down the path toward the monster. The closer the tortoise got, the more the monster changed its shape. Then, when he was almost upon it, the tortoise realized that what he had thought was a monster, was only a great pile of rocks, which formed a shape just like a monster.

As for the "Uuh uuh uuh", the tortoise realized this was just the sound of the wind blowing through a small cave. The tortoise carried on and eventually descended into a beautiful valley, filled with woods, and plenty of food. The tortoise lived very happily here and became known everywhere as the Brave Little Tortoise.

Friend, you and I must be prepared to take risks in life like the brave little tortoise. David was prepared to be sacrificed to redeem his nation and people because he saw that the King of the land had his back. This was well calculated and deeply considered by the young shepherd before stepping out to fight the giant.

A great man once said, *"Take risks, If you win you will be happy, If you fail you will be wise"*.

He took a bigger challenge instead of thinking about just his father's sheep at home. Even if he died in the fight, he was going to be given a state burial as one who attempted to save his country. It is no wonder citizens who die in peacekeeping missions in war ton countries are honored and given state burial for their bravery and selfless examples.

Beloved, whenever you want to enter into any agreement with another party, know that which could be a source of 'offense' to you in the future. Prepare for them in advance and handle the situation wisely as they arise.

Make sure you have carefully weighed all the options critically to see if you agree with like-minded people you can also depend on. The agreement should be sustainable for a long time and ideally with an experienced and more resourceful individual, group, or company who will be faithful to the core business agenda.

PRINCIPLE #
4. Father's house exempted from TAXES- **OTHER OFFERINGS**

In a desolate region, four lepers were abandoned at the gate of a bustling city. Cast out because of their infirmities, they were forbidden from reuniting with their loved ones inside. With drought and famine plaguing the land, no one could spare them food or water. They stood at the crossroads of survival or burial, their fate hanging in the balance.

One fateful day, a spark of courage ignited within them. They faced a critical choice: to remain silent, resigned to their current plight, or to muster the strength to venture forth, hoping to find a glimmer of salvation. With nothing to lose, they resolved to push forward, embarking on a treacherous journey in search of a solution to their plight.

As they ventured onward, the lepers found themselves approaching the enemy's camp, the source of their deepest fears. Yet, to their astonishment, their arrival stirred panic among their adversaries. Mistaking the lepers for a formidable army, the enemy fled in haste, leaving behind their weapons, provisions, and precious resources. It was a moment of triumph for the four lepers, who found themselves standing amidst the bountiful spoils of war.

However, amid their jubilation, a twinge of compassion gripped one of the lepers' hearts. They couldn't forget their brethren left behind in the city, suffering without sustenance. With hearts full of empathy, the lepers gathered a portion of the newfound abundance, concealing it for their return. They hastened back to the city, calling out to their brothers and sisters, inviting them to partake in the treasures left behind.

The news spread like wildfire, igniting hope in the hearts of the city's inhabitants. As the hungry and weary gathered to share in the bountiful spoils, a wave of joy swept through the streets. The actions of the four lepers were celebrated far and wide, their selflessness becoming a beacon of light in the darkness of their time.

Their story endured through the ages, a testament to the power of courage, resilience, and compassion. It served as a reminder that even in the most desperate of circumstances, acts of kindness and unity can lead to transformative change.

These lepers did not only consider their welfare but that of the entire nation and took steps to restore hope to them. They had a good opportunity to be selfish and to secure their future but did not forget where they originated from. Their selfless action brought relief and salvation to a starving nation.

i. Consider others too

This story of the four lepers teaches us valuable lessons about taking bold actions, having faith, and considering the well-being of others. Despite their dire circumstances, the lepers made a courageous decision to step out of their comfort zone and seek a solution for the entire state.

Like David who was considering his father's house in the deal, their journey toward the enemy's camp symbolizes the importance of embracing challenges and seeking opportunities even in the face of adversity. It reminds us that progress often requires us to venture into unknown territories, confront our fears, and take calculated risks for the progress of others.

The unexpected outcome, with their enemies fleeing in fear, demonstrates the power of divine intervention and the rewards of stepping out in faith. Sometimes, our greatest breakthroughs come when we trust in a higher power and believe that there are greater forces at work in our lives.

As mentioned, the story doesn't end there. The compassion shown by the lepers towards their fellow citizens is truly inspiring. Instead of hoarding the newfound resources for themselves, they chose to share the abundance with those who were suffering back in the city. This selfless act of kindness not only brought joy and relief to their brethren but also created a sense of unity and community among them.

In today's world, where self-centeredness and individual pursuits often dominate, this story serves as a reminder of the importance of considering the welfare of others. It encourages us to be mindful of the needs of those around us and to use our blessings, resources, and opportunities to uplift and support others.

Ultimately, the story of the four lepers is a testament to the power of resilience, faith, and compassion. It reminds us that in the face of challenges, we can choose to be proactive, have unwavering faith, and extend a helping hand to those in need. By doing so, we not only transform our own lives but also inspire and impact the lives of countless others.

May we all find the courage to take bold actions, the faith to believe in the extraordinary, and the compassion to make a positive difference in the lives of those around us. The legacy of the four lepers continued to inspire generations, a timeless tale of triumph over adversity and the enduring strength of the human spirit.

Do you love your kids? Then make every needed sacrifice for them to enjoy the maximum the world has to offer. Think of their future and sacrifice for them.

A profound statement was made by a mother of two. She was a cleaner and worked hard to give her daughters a better life. "I am working two jobs so Valerie and her sister can go to college with their heads high. That's why I like to do double jobs.

Now I don't think anyone enjoys emptying trash cans and dusting the desks, but it gives me a chance to help my daughters. By day I work as a maid in one of those fashionable houses and by night I work four hours helping clean up this building too. I am giving my children what my parents couldn't give me", she mentioned.

Ii. Bargain beyond borders

"Everything that looks to the future elevates human nature.

Never is life so low or so little as when occupied with the present."

Walter Savage Landor

A Franciscan monk who was a speaker at an international seminar about world peace was asked if successful negotiations between

Israel and Palestine were possible. He called two young people up to the microphone: a Palestinian young man and a Jewish Israeli young man. "Imagine you are brothers," he told them. "Your father has passed away, and he has left you an inheritance with three assets," represented symbolically by three coins, which he placed on the podium.

"Your instructions are that you must share the inheritance fairly but you cannot split any of the assets," the boys were told. "Now you must try to find a creative solution that will get you the maximum possible benefit." When the Palestinian said he would take two coins and give the Israeli one, everyone laughed again and the monk said, "Well, okay, you have the power to do that, but you are sowing the seeds of conflict."

The Israeli said he was thinking of taking one coin and giving the Palestinian two. "Evidently," the monk guessed, "you feel it's worth the risk of investing in your adversary in this way, and hope to somehow benefit in the future from this." The boys sat down.

Next, the monk asked two young women (again one was Israeli, the other Palestinian) to repeat the exercise. It was fairly clear where the monk was going with this, but would the girls get it?

"I would keep one coin and give her two," said the Israeli young woman, "on condition that she donate her second one to a charity, maybe a children's hospital." "Good," said the monk and asked the Palestinian woman if she agreed. She said, "I would keep one for myself, and give one to her, and say that we should invest the third one together." The entire audience stood and applauded for the final solution.

Negotiating is not a game, and it's not a war, it's what civilized people do to iron out their differences. There is no point, the monk said, in figuring out how to get the other side to sign something they cannot live with. A negotiated settlement today is not the end of the story, because "there is always the day after," and a good negotiator should be thinking about the day after and the day after that.

Project into the future and consider the decades ahead. Let the outcome benefit both parties but much more have a positive impact on future generations. Consider the raw materials, the human resources, the financial projections, and the equipment and machinery required to get you to where you want to be. Think deeply before you take a step to agree and sign any pact.

Watch out for the possible leakages and shortcomings of the proposal and try to find solutions to them before signing the contract. Know your strengths and weaknesses and dwell on the strengths. Will your actions today bring a blessing or untold hardships to the country, organization, family, or ministry in the future?

The STX Deal
According to a special report by IMANI on 5th July 2010, the STX-Ghana deal followed a similar logic as President Nkrumah's dealings with the American company Kaiser. To the extent that there were flaws in that deal that progressively lead to its spectacular unraveling a half-century or so later and a near-collapse of our aluminum industrialization plans, through the abandonment of VALCO for instance.

IMANI added that the Parliament of Ghana did not have sufficient information before it to make the right and necessary determinations relevant to the STX-Ghana contract.

For parliament to have even considered evaluating the supplier's credit facility without having been apprised of the actual joint venture documents between the members of STX Engineering & Construction (including incorporation documents) to determine the proportion of risks on the financing side being borne by STX Korea was worrying indeed.

It further questioned; how exposed was the government of Ghana in this risk-fencing vehicle. How assured were we that the terms of future transactions beyond the $1.5 billion shall accord with the strategic principles based upon which Ghana was ready to borrow and spend $1.5 billion (more than a one-third of the domestic budget) immediately in the hope that the remaining $8.5 billion shall be much more concessionary as it was being speculated?

The report also sought to find answers to the following questions regarding the Financing Viability of the contract: who determined that if we get $10 billion even on the most lenient of terms, we would want to splash it all on housing? Who determined that security service personnel should necessarily take precedence over doctors and nurses or teachers and farmers?

Were these determinations, notwithstanding who made them, driven by the *financial imperatives?* Where was the record of analysis then? Who said Ghana wanted to triple its public debt to solve 10% to 15% of its housing problem as opposed to its health, education, or agricultural headaches?

And that it wants to do so in the next 5 years. Where was the cost-benefit analysis that said that returns from housing shall be superior to returns from roads, hospitals, railways, ports, venture capital, schools, irrigation dams, or sanitation systems?

Ghana cannot absorb all the debts it wants, because debt has fiscal implications both in the medium and the long term. We must rationalize and prioritize our expenditures. The key to rationalizing expenditure is to determine the cost-benefit matrix as a requisite framework for accessing the financial viability of any deal.

Could $10 billion spent on housing strengthen our capacity to generate more resources to meet our other needs than $10 billion spent on carriage infrastructure such as roads, irrigation canals, ports, and railways?

What was even more puzzling regarding financing viability was the lack of any fund-raising strategy document before parliament seeing that no Bank guarantee was attached to the supplier's credit facility instrument laid before the august body. How does STX Engineering & Construction Limited, which is by all indications only a few months old, seek to raise $1.5 billion-plus?

Even if it aimed to rely on the credit of its members – supposedly STX Korea and the Government of Ghana – how did it aim to justify to financiers that Ghana had a mortgage market deep enough to absorb such a quantity of houses in such a short time? Where was the analysis? Where were the feasibility studies? Where was the plan?

Or was it a case of "try your luck, what's there to lose"?

In conclusion, the special report reiterated that, far from being implacably opposed to the STX-Ghana deal, IMANI was supportive of the general principle. It argued for greater transparency about the fiscal risks to Ghana.

Once the risks to the country had been substantially mitigated, and duly acknowledged that it was a hit-and-miss deal, the principle should have allowed for the opening up of the scheme for all interested dealmakers to prosper from the same "benefits of the doubt" showered on the proponents of the STX-Ghana deal.

It was therefore not a surprise when the fears among a section of the public that the STX housing project will be a fiasco were allayed when the President Prof. John Evans Mills indicated that the government was looking for alternative sources of funding to bring the project on stream.

At a media encounter in Accra, the late President Mills acknowledged that the STX housing project was beset with legal problems and boardroom wrangling which made it difficult for the contract to be executed as expected.

So whenever nations, companies, and other corporate entities want to sign an agreement, all the necessary terms and conditions must be weighed before going ahead. The best interest of the people on the ground and generations unborn should be sought in all the arrangements before the signing.

"Genuine politics - even politics worthy of the name- the only politics I am willing to devote myself to - is simply a matter of serving those around us: serving the community and serving those who will come after us. Its deepest roots are moral because it is a responsibility

expressed through action, to and for the whole.''- Dr. Martin Luther King

Young people entering into relationships and marriage must approach it with careful consideration. It is crucial to look beyond the present moment if you desire a successful and fulfilling life together. Before committing to a "marriage contract," which I believe is more of a covenant, it is essential to thoroughly understand your intended spouse and their background.

Take the time to delve into important aspects such as financial management, investment strategies, health conditions including chronic diseases, blood group compatibility, HIV/AIDS status, previous divorce or broken home experiences, conflict resolution skills, temperaments, tendencies towards alcoholism or drug abuse, infidelity, and other potential vices.

Conducting a comprehensive assessment of these factors is necessary before taking the step of marriage. It is important to identify what you can handle and what might be beyond your capabilities. Understand which aspects can potentially be changed and those that are unlikely to change, allowing you to make an informed decision before settling down.

Similar to David, consider the influence of your respective family backgrounds. Reflect on what each of you brings to the table as individuals and how those contributions can positively impact your future endeavors, whether it be in business, ministry, or raising children.

By carefully evaluating these aspects, you can lay a strong foundation for a lasting and harmonious relationship that has the potential to thrive and contribute to your shared aspirations.

"Don't settle for less;
Go for the best no matter the test."

iii.   Other benefits

Additionally, David's household was granted the privilege of being exempt from paying taxes to the King as a reward for his victory over the giant. Taxes refer to the monetary contributions individuals or businesses are obligated to pay to the government. They are usually calculated based on personal income or the cost of goods and services.

Certain taxes are deducted directly from the source of income, particularly for civil servants, while others are imposed on the purchase of goods and services. Tax allowances refer to the portion of income that is not subject to taxation, while tax relief involves the system of allowing individuals to exclude a part of their income from taxation.

Jesse and his family were exempted from paying taxes, which meant they would save more financially. It would lead to increased profits from their agricultural produce, thereby alleviating the financial strain on their limited resources.

Beloved, there are instances where entering into certain agreements is not solely for immediate monetary gains. Sometimes, it is strategically beneficial to accept an offer due to the accompanying fringe benefits that may be enjoyed along the way.

I recall the story of a security guard who has dedicated his entire career to a particular commercial bank. Despite receiving better salary offers from other security companies, he has consistently declined those opportunities. Although his salary increment is modest each year, he managed to send one of his children to university and, leveraging his influence and experience, secured a job for his son at the same bank and branch where he is employed.

This is not to endorse complacency or discourage personal growth and advancement when opportunities arise. If one has the chance and ability to progress and attain higher positions, it should certainly be pursued. However, in the case of this security guard (affectionately known as Papa Favor), he made a deliberate choice to remain at the bank to maintain his network with top management and secure his son's future career.

Furthermore, by being employed as the bank's security guard, he and his wife, along with all their children below eighteen years of age, enjoy "free" medical care. Through strategic connections and relationships, he is receiving what he couldn't provide financially. He has effectively leveraged his bargaining power to obtain the necessities of life. Today, he is a contented and fulfilled man.

Similar to this example, you must look beyond immediate monetary rewards and consider the long-term opportunities that lie ahead.

These could include future contracts, the supply of ancillary products, potential expansions, training and evaluation opportunities, provision of cleaning and security services, and networking with other partners. Take into account all these future factors and make the most of them to maximize your prospects.

In conclusion, the story of this shepherd and his strategic negotiations teaches us valuable lessons in various aspects of life, from business dealings to personal relationships. We see the importance of careful planning, assessing risks, and considering long-term benefits before making decisions. Just as the lad secured favorable terms for himself and his family, we too should strive to negotiate wisely and secure advantageous outcomes.

Whether it's in business partnerships, marriage, or any other endeavor, we must look beyond immediate gains and consider the broader implications. By studying our counterparts, understanding their backgrounds, and assessing compatibility, we can make informed choices that align with our goals and values.

Furthermore, we should not underestimate the significance of fringe benefits and indirect advantages that may accompany a particular agreement. Just as David's exemption from taxes brought financial relief to his family, there may be hidden rewards or opportunities that arise from strategic alliances and long-term commitments.

Ultimately, effective negotiations require a blend of foresight, critical thinking, and the ability to identify mutually beneficial arrangements. By applying these principles, we can increase our chances of success and create sustainable partnerships that yield positive outcomes for all parties involved.

As we move forward in our journey in these trying time, let us remember the wisdom of the youngster's negotiations and apply these lessons to our own lives. May we be guided by strategic thinking, integrity, and a vision for long-term growth and fulfillment.

Heavenly father,

please help me to locate my helpers in life

and to keep away from bad influences.

May I attract and maintain good mentors and connectors in my life

Grant me the eye for detail to make the best decision

concerning any offer presented to me today.

May I not fall prey to the cunning ways of the enemy in Jesus' name

I believe with you I can become the best in whatever I set my heart to do.

I declare that I dare to face all my fears and overcome them

As I look beyond the present situation,

I shall leave a legacy for generations unborn

in the mighty name of Jesus Christ I have prayed.

Amen

Summary of points

 i. If you cannot see where you are going, ask someone who has been there before.

 ii. Knowing how to negotiate can save you plenty of money.

 iii. In negotiating devote the necessary time and work to address the details efficiently so that your deal does not collapse

 iv. The most important feature of a contract is that, one party makes an offer and that another accepts.

 v. Your bargaining party should have the willingness and ability to pay

 vi. Check out the legal details critically before you sign it.

 vii. Manager contracts can be very specific to your circumstances but seek legal advice to make sure your interests are protected.

 viii. Funds from the state's coffers should not end in individual pockets

 ix. Bargain beyond the borders of today; think of the future

 x. Take risks, if you win you will be happy; if you fail you will be wise.

 xi. Don't settle for less; go for the best no matter the test.

CHAPTER THREE

STRATEGIC POSITIONING: ACHIEVING PEAK PERFORMANCE

"Victorious warriors win first and then go to war,
while defeated warriors go to war first
and then seek to win"
Sun Tzu

So far, you have uncovered the fundamental elements to consider for a successful bargain—the lasting issues that will make you a true winner and leave an unforgettable impression on the people you negotiate with in life. The ideals which transcend the immediate gains of a deal.

In this chapter, get ready to dive into the realm of advanced intelligence that will make James Bond jealous. We're taking negotiation to the next level with strategies that are sharper than Bond's tuxedo and smarter than his gadgets. These strategies have been battle-tested by the Avengers, refined by Sherlock Holmes, and approved by Tony Stark himself. Get your negotiation game face on!

Life often throws curveballs at us, like a toddler playing baseball. You'll face decisions that make your brain do somersaults and your heart skip a beat. But fear not, my friend, because you have the ultimate bargaining power—the power of your mind, wit, and a healthy dose of sarcasm. You're about to learn negotiation moves in this troubled world of ours that would make even Deadpool raise an eyebrow in awe.

Before we delve deeper, let's take inspiration from the legendary Shepherd, the ultimate underdog negotiator. He didn't rely on swords and shields but on his wit and faith. When faced with a towering giant, David didn't run to the nearest weapons store or consult a team of strategists.

No, he went straight to the source of his power—the brook. Who needs weapons when you have a refreshing brook to rejuvenate your negotiating skills?

Now, I'm not suggesting you bring a water bottle to your next negotiation (although it might not hurt). Instead, take a moment to tap into your inner genius. In today's fast-paced world, where everything is changing faster than you can say "Netflix marathon," it's crucial to position yourself strategically.

Like a master chess player, you need to think ahead, anticipate your opponent's moves, and be prepared to throw in a witty one-liner when needed.

Ignore the naysayers and pessimists who think you're crazy for chasing your dreams. They're probably just jealous that they don't have the guts to negotiate their way to success. Listen to your inner voice, the one that says, "You've got this!" Embrace the unconventional, dare to be different, and be the negotiator that shakes the world.

So buckle up, my friend, because, in this chapter, we're taking bargaining to new heights. We'll blend the wisdom of ancient warriors with the swag of modern influencers. Get ready to negotiate like a boss, laugh in the face of challenges, and come out on top. It's time to unleash your negotiation superpowers and conquer your world, one deal at a time.

"Courage is the most important of all the virtues

because without courage you

can't practice any other virtue consistently.

You can practice any virtue erratically,

but nothing consistently without courage."

Maya Angelou

STRATEGY
1. Drop the Dross

First and foremost, the lad made a bold decision to leave behind any other stones he may have carried in his bag on the way to the war front. He sought something fresh and unique this time. I believe, being a wise person, he always kept a handful of stones as a precautionary measure in the porch of his bag. These stones served as a quick defense against any predator that dared to approach his flock or threaten him personally.

He didn't have to scurry around searching for stones or weapons to strike with; he always had some reserves at hand. However, on this particular occasion, he made the audacious choice to drop them and opt for fresh, smooth pebbles.

This is the hallmark of a successful individual in life. If you aspire to reach the pinnacle of success, you may have to bid farewell to certain individuals or close friends. Some are simply time-wasters and parasites, and those are the ones you must shed along the journey to the top. I'm referring to those who serve as a negative influence or act as a burden on your path to success.

Imagine you're embarking on a journey to climb the tallest mountain in the world. You're determined to reach the summit and conquer all obstacles along the way. As you begin your ascent, you notice a fellow hiker who insists on joining you. Let's call him Bob.

Now, Bob is a well-meaning but not-so-fit individual. He's carrying a heavy backpack filled with unnecessary items like a hairdryer, a blender, and even a pet parrot named Polly. You can't help but chuckle at the sight of him struggling to keep up.

As you continue your trek, Bob starts slowing you down. He constantly stops to take selfies, engages in lengthy conversations about his latest shopping spree, and even tries to make a cup of coffee with his portable espresso machine. It's clear that his priorities are a bit skewed.

At this point, you realize that if you want to reach the summit and achieve your goal, you'll have to bid farewell to Bob. So, in a humorous but assertive manner, you kindly explain to him that you appreciate his company, but you need to focus and travel at your own pace. You even offer to take care of Polly the parrot if he decides to turn back.

With a mix of disappointment and relief, Bob waves goodbye and starts heading back down the mountain. As you continue your ascent, you can't help but feel a sense of liberation and freedom. The weight of unnecessary baggage, both literally and figuratively, has been lifted.

As you finally reach the summit, you celebrate your accomplishment with a victory dance, feeling proud and satisfied. And you can't help but wonder if Bob managed to make it back down without turning his blender into a snowball or using his hairdryer as a makeshift sled.

In this lighthearted example, the humor lies in the exaggerated portrayal of Bob's quirky behavior and his mismatched priorities. It highlights the importance of letting go of individuals who hinder our progress and distract us from our goals. Sometimes, a dose of humor can help us approach challenging situations with a lighter heart and make the necessary decisions to create a path for our own success.

This is the mark of a successful person in life. If you are going to get to the top, you may have to drop certain people or close friends. Some are just time wasters and parasites and these you must drop along the way to the top. I mean those who are a bad influence or baggage to your success in life.

Then there are the self-depreciators, who require delicate handling, as their influence can diminish your chances of acquiring wealth, gaining promotion, and finding happiness. Let's take a look at a couple of types of self-depreciators:

1. *The Belittler*: These individuals take pleasure in putting you down. They relish belittling your accomplishments and achievements. For instance, if you start your own business and make money, the belittler might say, 'Oh, he was just lucky. It's a mere stroke of accidental timing.' These people suffer from severe cases of self-depreciation. By attributing your success to luck or external factors, they attempt to

elevate themselves and appear superior.

2. *The Foul-Language Communicator*: The more a person engages in self-depreciation, the more likely they are to resort to using filthy, putrefied language. They mistakenly believe that such language bestows them with status, makes them feel important, and proves their supposed worldly sophistication. However, the truth is that their excessive use of so-called 'colorful' language reveals their insecurities and lack of self-acceptance.

Instead of engaging with them, it's best to feel compassion for their plight, understand their underlying problems, and simply ignore them. Resist the temptation to seek revenge, engage in a verbal battle, or put them in their place. In a nutshell, "drop the dross and set your sights on the big deal."

STRATEGY
2. Change Your Style

In today's rapidly changing world, it's important to embrace the idea that "out with the old, in with the new." We can no longer rely solely on past achievements or outdated strategies to propel us forward. It's time to adapt, evolve, and stay ahead of the curve.

Take a scene out of Sybase's novella. They recognized that the world was moving towards digital storage and online platforms. By shifting their focus and aligning with existing software giants, they ensured their relevance and success in the market. It's a lesson for all of us to be open to new possibilities and willing to change our approach when necessary.

The digital age has transformed the way we do business. It's no longer about sticking to a rigid 9 to 5 schedule. Global markets operate around the clock, and to thrive in this environment, we must be flexible and adapt our work schedules accordingly.

Embracing a more flexible approach allows us to cater to clients and customers from different time zones, giving us a competitive edge in the global marketplace.

In this fast-paced and interconnected world, being a quick thinker is essential. Continuous learning and staying well-informed are key to making an impact. We must be willing to unlearn old ways of thinking and embrace new knowledge and skills. The ability to adapt and learn quickly sets us apart and positions us for success.

In today's fast-paced world, it's like trying to use a flip phone in a smartphone-dominated era - you'll end up feeling like a dinosaur at a technology convention! We need to keep up with the times and embrace the wonders of modern technology.

Imagine you're at a party, and someone pulls out a cassette tape and asks if you want to listen to some groovy tunes. You can't help but burst into laughter because, let's face it, we've moved on to Spotify playlists and streaming services that bring the party to our fingertips!

It's like going to a restaurant and asking for a printed menu, only to be met with puzzled looks from the waiter. They'll probably hand you an iPad instead and say, "Welcome to the 21st century, where menus are digital and you can even order dessert with a few taps!"

In this digital age, it's important to keep your social media game strong. You don't want to be that person who still thinks *MySpace* is the hottest social platform around, while everyone else is Instagramming their avocado toasts and Snapchatting their adventures. Stay connected and relevant, my friend, because the virtual world is where the party's at!

And let's not forget about those infamous autocorrect fails. You send a text saying, "I'll be there in a few ducks," and your friend wonders if you've developed a newfound obsession with waterfowl. Thank goodness for those hilarious and slightly embarrassing moments that keep us entertained and remind us to proofread our messages!

So, in this ever-evolving world, let's embrace the humor of the digital age. It's a wild ride full of funny tech mishaps, unexpected advancements, and endless entertainment. Just remember, laughter is the best app to navigate through life's quirks and keep our spirits high!

Diversification is another strategy to consider. By expanding your company's interests across multiple sectors or industries, you create resilience and mitigate the risk of downturns in specific areas. Motorola's shift from hardware to software is a prime example. By investing in the Android platform, they tapped into the thriving smartphone market and positioned themselves as a formidable competitor to Apple.

It's a reminder that diversification can open doors to new opportunities and ensure long-term success. So, as you journey towards success, remember to let go of outdated ideas, embrace change, and stay adaptable. The world is evolving, and it's up to us to stay ahead of the game.

In the realm of ministry, it's crucial to recognize that the anointing and power we once possessed may not fully address the challenges of today and tomorrow. As the world changes, so do the needs and concerns of the people we minister to. We must be open to new revelations and seek the guidance of the Holy Spirit to navigate the complexities of the present.

As a CEO, staying informed about modern business trends is essential. It's not enough to rely on past strategies or approaches. The business landscape is ever-evolving, and identifying the best sources of materials, affordable funding, and cost-effective practices is key to maximizing profits. Embracing innovation and staying ahead of the curve will position your company for success in a competitive market.

For students and educators alike, it's important to adapt to the changing educational landscape. What worked in the past may not be sufficient to address the challenges of today's postmodern world. As students, it's crucial to stay updated on current trends, technologies, and methodologies to excel in your studies. As teachers, incorporating relevant and engaging content that resonates with today's learners is vital to ensure their success.

In every aspect of life, we must remember that our ultimate source of success is not ourselves or others, but God. He is the foundation of our faith and the one who guides us through every endeavor. By seeking His wisdom and following His lead, we can expand our mental horizons, tap into divine insights, and unlock the deep secrets of success.

So, as we face the challenges of the present and embrace the opportunities of the future, let us remain rooted in our faith and rely on Jesus Christ as our ultimate source of guidance and inspiration.

You need the extraordinary to do the imaginary!!

STRATEGY #

3. Test the Tactics First

Furthermore, David made a deliberate choice to select the stones *'first for himself'* (NKJV) before placing them in his bag. Despite the imminent threat posed by Goliath, David did not rush to use the weapons he had gathered. He understood that these stones held a significance beyond mere instruments for destroying an uncircumcised man. He recognized the need for a deep and personal connection with these precious pebbles before unleashing them.

'First for himself' also indicated David's desire for a personal encounter and impact from the stones before sharing them with an unbeliever. He understood that it was important to personally experience the transformative power of these stones before exposing others to their influence. David recognized the value of his valuable pearls and was unwilling to cast them before swine without first benefiting from them himself.

In the realm of business and leadership, it's crucial to test and assess the tactics and individuals you engage with before committing to larger-scale implementation. Just as David carefully selected stones that resonated with his heart and stirred his spiritual senses, we should prioritize spending time with individuals who contribute to our organization's productivity and profitability.

In corporate world, it's essential to distinguish between being effective and efficient. Surround yourself with individuals who add value to your ministry or business, while avoiding those who drain your resources and energy. Just like Jesus moved on from His hometown when faced with rejection, we should be willing to seek opportunities and places where our gifts and talents are better received and appreciated.

The stones chosen by David were not only personally appealing but also reliable and trustworthy in his eyes. Similarly, in our enterprises, we must be familiar with and confident in the plans and strategies we adopt. Consulting experienced individuals can provide a sense of comfort and help us make crucial decisions with greater certainty.

Imagine you're starting a new tech company, and you have two potential co-founders. One is a computer whiz who can code with their eyes closed, and the other is a self-proclaimed expert in creating viral cat videos.

While the cat video creator may be entertaining, you'll probably lean towards the coding whiz for a more reliable and valuable addition to your team. After all, as much as the internet loves cats, they can't write your software!

Avoid investing significant resources or money in ventures that carry high levels of uncertainty or risk. Instead, conduct thorough research and analysis to minimize the potential for waste and ensure a solid foundation for success.

Let's say you're considering investing in a restaurant franchise. You come across two options: "The Gourmet Burger Shack" and "The Mystery Meat Emporium." While the name "Mystery Meat Emporium" may pique your curiosity, it's probably best to stick with the more appetizing and reliable option of "The Gourmet Burger Shack." After all, you don't want your customers to wonder if their meals come with a side of detective work.

Furthermore, picture yourself attending a networking event filled with professionals from various industries. You strike up conversations with two individuals: one is a seasoned industry veteran with a proven track record, and the other is a self-proclaimed "idea machine" who has a new business concept every week.

While the idea machine may provide a good laugh and some creative inspiration, it's the industry veteran who will likely offer more valuable insights and guidance for your own professional growth.

STRATEGY #
4. See the Solution Close

One crucial aspect that David considered was the source of his stones—the nearby brook. While others overlooked it as merely a stream for daily tasks, David recognized the potential it held. He saw beyond its ordinary appearance and realized that hidden within that small stream were stones capable of defeating a giant.

Just like David recognized the hidden potential in the nearby brook, we must not overlook the opportunities and resources that surround us. Sometimes, the solutions we seek are right within our reach, waiting to be discovered. It's like searching for your glasses while they're sitting on top of your head! Let's not underestimate the power of what's right in front of us.

Picture a group of executives attending an expensive leadership retreat in a remote exotic location, hoping to gain inspiration and insights for their business. Little did they know that their most valuable ideas will come to them during a casual brainstorming session in their office break room, fueled by an accidental spill of the company's signature gourmet coffee blend. Who knew that the key to their success was right there, in that coffee stain?

Also, think about a CEO who spent hours poring over complex reports and financial analyses, trying to find ways to increase profitability. Meanwhile, his janitor, armed with nothing more than a broom and a sense of humor, suggested a simple and cost-effective solution that saved the company thousands. Talk about sweeping success! This reminded the CEO to value diverse perspectives and to foster a culture where everyone's ideas are heard and considered.

In this fast-paced world, it's easy to become consumed with searching far and wide for answers, thinking that success lies in distant places or extravagant strategies. But the truth is, we possess incredible potential within ourselves, and our immediate surroundings hold treasures that can catapult us to new heights.

Just like David's small stream held the stones that would defeat a giant, the people, opportunities, and privileges in our lives can be the catalyst for our breakthroughs.

We are living in a time of immense significance, where God is raising a generation of believers who will bring about a revolutionary transformation. The impact we will make goes beyond what we can currently comprehend. It's like having a superpower waiting to be unleashed, and when the time comes, the world will witness the extraordinary works of God through our lives.

So, my dear friend, continue to cultivate your relationship with God and embrace the opportunities and people He places in your path. Stay faithful, knowing that the best is yet to come. The world is waiting to be astounded and amazed by the remarkable things God will do through you. Get ready to unleash your hidden potential and make a lasting impact on the world around you!

Indeed, the plans and purposes that the Almighty has for you have not yet been fully revealed on this Earth. There is a hidden aspect of your being, carefully shaped and prepared by God Himself for His appointed time. When it comes to fruition, it will be for His glory alone, and no one else can claim credit for it.

Rest assured that your vision and expectations will not be cut off. Trust in the Lord and patiently wait for His perfect timing. He will exchange your ashes for beauty, and replace your spirit of heaviness with a garment of praise.

Though the fulfillment of the vision may seem delayed, hold on to it, for it will surely come to pass. The glory of what is to come will surpass anything you have experienced before, as declared by the Lord of Hosts.

People may judge you based on your records or shortcomings, and they may overlook your potential for promotion or advancement.

They may even disregard you based on outward appearances or demeanor. But they have not yet seen the magnificent hidden part of you that God is about to reveal. You are on the verge of a breakthrough that will leave them astounded, and it will be solely for the exaltation of His Holy name.

Perhaps what lies within you has remained dormant, untapped, or even seemingly lifeless. But as you reconnect with the divine source, like returning to the brook, everything that appears dead will come alive again in the name of Jesus.

Whether it's physical ailments, the brokenness of the heart, or a sense of emptiness, when you position yourself to connect with the flowing river of God in the spiritual realm, you will receive a divine touch that rejuvenates and restores every part of your being.

Just as the waters in the book of Ezekiel 47:8-9 brought healing and life wherever they flowed, so too will you experience a profound rejuvenation. Your spirit will come alive, and every area of your life will be transformed.

Open yourself up now, wherever you are, to receive that touch from the Lord. Allow His power to permeate your body, soul, and spirit. Receive His transformational touch in the mighty name of Jesus Christ, the Son of the living God.

STRATEGY #
5. Deep calls the deep

Let us consider the story of a struggling entrepreneur named Sarah.

Sarah had been pouring her heart and soul into her business for years, investing countless hours, resources, and expertise into making it a success. However, despite her best efforts, she found herself facing one obstacle after another, unable to achieve the breakthrough she desired.

Feeling disheartened and on the verge of giving up, Sarah came across an inspiring TED Talk by a renowned business mentor. In the talk, the mentor shared personal stories of overcoming challenges and emphasized the importance of perseverance and seeking guidance from higher sources.

Intrigued and desperate for a change, Sarah decided to take a leap of faith and went further. She reached out to the mentor and requested a meeting, hoping to gain insights and guidance for her struggling business. During their conversation, the mentor encouraged Sarah to delve deeper into her purpose, to reconnect with her passion, and to seek divine wisdom in her decision-making.

Taking the mentor's words to heart, Sarah started incorporating moments of reflection and prayer into her daily routine. She sought guidance through meditation, scripture reading and journaling, allowing herself to dive deeper into her own aspirations and values. Through this process, she gained a renewed sense of clarity and focus.

Empowered by her newfound spiritual connection and the guidance she received, Sarah made bold decisions and took calculated risks in her business. She began seeking collaborations with like-minded individuals, embracing the power of community and collective wisdom. As a result, her business started to gain momentum, attracting new clients and opportunities.

With each step, Sarah felt a deep sense of fulfillment and purpose. The challenges she once faced seemed more manageable as she navigated them with a sense of divine guidance. Her business flourished, surpassing her previous limitations and opening doors she had never thought possible.

In this story, Sarah's journey mirrors the disciples' experience with Jesus. By acknowledging the need to launch deeper, to seek guidance beyond her own abilities, Sarah was able to tap into a higher power and experience a transformative breakthrough in her business. Through faith, perseverance, and a willingness to explore the spiritual realm, she unlocked new levels of success and fulfillment.

The brook or stream is further symbolic of the anointing and presence of the Holy Ghost. The deeper you go, the wetter you become, and the more He brings out of your life. The deeper David went, the smoother the stones he picked.

"Like gold which becomes purer when passed through the fire, as carbon, when polished, turns into a diamond, like a tiny seed which passes through the harsh conditions of the earth to become a tree, like learning to swim you have to immerse yourself in water. Human beings have to face competition and challenges to make a difference in themselves and others. So don't wait, take a plunge!" - Siddhart Elhence

If you want to grow in the power and anointing of the Spirit, you must be prepared to take off your foot wares and garments and step into the water of the Spirit. You don't always expect to pick very beautiful and smooth stones at the shore. You must dive deeper to dig out the treasures of the Kingdom. The secret things of God and life in general are with the deep.

"Deep calleth unto the deep"

The disciples of Jesus toiled tirelessly through the night, casting their nets and utilizing their skills and expertise in hopes of a bountiful catch. However, despite their efforts, their endeavors yielded no success. Frustrated and ready to call it quits, they began to pull their boats out of the water.

But just as they were on the verge of giving up, the master fisherman Himself arrived on the scene. With a simple command, He turned their situation around. "Launch out into the deep," He declared, "and let down your nets for a draught."

In obedience to His words, they cast their nets once more, and what happened next was nothing short of miraculous. Their nets were filled to the brim with an overwhelming abundance of fish. In fact, their nets were unable to contain the massive haul, and they began to break under the weight of the catch.

This powerful encounter teaches us a valuable lesson. Sometimes, we may find ourselves exerting all our efforts and skills in pursuit of success, only to come up empty-handed. But when we surrender our own strength and rely on the guidance and direction of the Master, extraordinary things can happen.

To experience a breakthrough, we must be willing to go farther, both in our relationship with God and in our personal lives. It requires humility, a willingness to surrender, and a recognition that there is a price to pay for every good thing we desire. Just as one cannot gather precious pebbles from the brook without getting wet, we must be willing to embrace the process, even if it involves challenges and sacrifice.

So, let us retreat to our closets, kneel in prayer, and seek a deeper connection with our Savior. Let us be willing to be broken and transformed, allowing His love to flow through us. In doing so, we open ourselves up to the abundant blessings and extraordinary miracles that await us.

No pain, no gain!

No shame, no fame!!

No cross, no crown!!!

STRATEGY #

6. Prepare Well- Pure and polished pebbles

One point I want to reiterate about the brook- it is a source of *purity* and *polish*. The stones were smoothened and polished day by day as the waters of the stream passed over them. It carried with it all impurities that were attached to the stones, ensuring a clean and highly polished surface. As we shall learn later on, our hearts could be likened to 'stones' if they are not circumcised and broken unto the LORD.

This means, when we allow the Holy Spirit to fill our hearts and minds daily, He can purify and purge us from all unrighteousness and uncleanness. As He flows through our hearts and minds consistently every chaff and fusty stuff is washed away.

The water of the word of God is a potent way by which we can keep our hearts and minds clean and pure. 'Let us draw near with true hearts in full assurance of faith, having our hearts sprinkled from an evil conscience and our bodies washed with pure water'- Hebrews 10:22.

The more we study the word, the cleaner and newer our hearts and minds become. May we develop a stronger hunger and appetite for the unadulterated *rhema* of the word in our quest to reach higher heights and targets in life?

Business organizations should continuously evaluate or appraise their staff and systems to ensure that, they are always on the right track. The auditing and accounting systems in place must be solid. Strategies not suitable must be reviewed and those unprofitable discarded for better ones. You can't sit and let the business collapse before you find solutions. Put the right mechanisms in place to mitigate any future misfortunes before they occur.

I believe that the brook is also symbolic of the *church or ministry, family, and business;* while the stones represent the people therein. We come in raw, rough, and unclean but God expects us to be cleaned and polished by the power of His word and the Spirit daily. Our knowledge, character, attitudes, talents, and skills need to be sharpened and well-structured in the light of the bible daily.

However, many are in the church, business, and family today who have not allowed themselves to be *trained and trimmed by the power of God* and the corporate philosophies of their organizations for effective use in our various fields of endeavor. There seems to have been no change in our lives all these while in the 'brook'.

In today's rapidly changing technology landscape, there are

employees in various companies who have not embraced digital transformation and new software tools. They resist adapting to new ways of working, relying on outdated manual processes and legacy systems. As a result, they are unable to contribute to the company's digital initiatives and hinder the organization's progress in becoming more agile and efficient.

These employees become a liability, causing delays, errors, and inefficiencies in critical workflows. To drive innovation and stay competitive, organizations may need to provide extensive retraining programs or consider replacing these employees with individuals who are more open to embracing technological advancements and can help drive the organization forward.

STRATEGY #

7. Conquer by Corporate Collaboration

Further, I find it mind-boggling that the lad took just *five* stones instead of *seven, ten, twenty*, or even *one*. I strongly believe there were many of these pebbles at the brook; and yet, he decided to limit himself to just FIVE. This was simply prophetic!

The main crust of the message here is, if he believed God so much and knew he only needed one stone to kill Goliath, then there was no point in selecting five.

This tells us that, David recognized the *power of corporate collaboration* and that, unity is strength. It means, your ideas alone in any corporate organization will not be enough. You need the corporation and the support of others in the company to achieve success. Even though you may have a brilliant idea, you need the efforts of others to realize this great idea. Learn to corporate with people in an organization for success.

Imagine a marketing team tasked with launching a new product for their company. Each team member brings a unique set of skills and expertise, such as market research, graphic design, content creation, and project management.

Instead of working in silos, they adopt a collaborative approach. They hold regular team meetings to brainstorm ideas, share insights, and allocate responsibilities. Through open communication and active listening, they leverage their collective knowledge and experience to develop a comprehensive marketing strategy.

The market researchers provide valuable data on target demographics and consumer preferences, which informs the content creators in crafting compelling messages. The graphic designers bring the brand to life through visually appealing assets, while the project manager ensures that timelines and deliverables are met.

Throughout the process, they collaborate closely, offering feedback and support to one another. They conduct frequent check-ins to assess progress, address challenges, and make necessary adjustments. By working as a cohesive unit, they are able to create a successful marketing campaign that generates buzz, attracts customers, and drives sales for the new product.

This scenario demonstrates how teamwork and collaboration within a marketing team can lead to a more effective and impactful outcome compared to individual efforts. It emphasizes the importance of leveraging diverse skills, pooling resources, and fostering a cooperative environment to achieve shared goals.

As the lad picked one stone and added it to the other, he was picking and piling up different ideas, strength, talents, potentials and synergies from others and filling his *shepherd's bag*- that is, his heart, his mind, and spirit with more and more grace of our savior J-E-S-U-S (The Anointed One, The embodiment of Wisdom and Source of Success in life). A perfect weaponries for success in an epic showdown with the giant of life.

Brethren, may we come to realize that, as we get closer and closer, deeper and deeper in God through his word, good books, fellowship, and prayer; He fills us with His Spirit to the brim and over floods our hearts and souls with beauty, ideas, knowledge, power, and glory for victory.

May you not rest or give up in your longing for the Spirit. We must appreciate the efforts of others and collaborate to achieve greatness. There is so much out there that you have not tapped yet, and so you can't be too content no matter how far you have come. There is always a place called the "other side" in life. Reach out!

STRATEGY #

8. Be Stable- Rough or Smooth?

The story is told of a business owner named Swaniker who runs a successful online retail company. One of the key factors contributing to her success is her stability and reliability in managing her business. Swaniker ensures that her website is consistently operational, providing a seamless shopping experience for her customers. She invests in reliable technology infrastructure, such as robust servers and secure payment gateways, to minimize downtime and ensure the security of customer information.

Moreover, Swaniker maintains stable inventory management practices. She carefully tracks her product stock levels, reorders in a timely manner, and communicates transparently with her suppliers. This stability allows her to meet customer demands efficiently, preventing stock outs or delays in delivery.

In addition, Swaniker is known for her consistent and reliable customer service. She responds promptly to customer inquiries and resolves issues in a timely manner. By being stable and reliable in addressing customer concerns, she builds trust and loyalty, leading to repeat business and positive word-of-mouth referrals.

Outside of her business, Swaniker applies the same principles of stability and reliability in her personal life. She maintains a healthy work-life balance, setting aside dedicated time for her family, self-care, and personal growth. By prioritizing stability and consistency in her daily routines, she is able to manage stress effectively and lead a fulfilling life.

Swaniker's example demonstrates the importance of stability and reliability in both business and personal life. By being stable and reliable, she builds trust, delivers consistent results, and creates a strong foundation for long-term success and happiness.

Indeed, David's choice of smooth stones demonstrates the importance of stability and consistency in various aspects of life, including business, personal growth, and spiritual development.

In business, maintaining stable philosophies and values is crucial for establishing trust and credibility. Continuously changing approaches and strategies can create an image of instability, making it challenging to build lasting relationships with clients, partners, and employees. By adhering to high standards and consistent principles, a business can earn respect and maintain a steady pace of success.

Similarly, in the context of personal growth and development, it is essential to remain committed to a set of values and principles. Constantly shifting attitudes and behaviors can hinder progress and lead to a lack of stability in one's character. By staying true to one's core beliefs and striving for personal excellence, individuals can establish a solid foundation for growth and achieve long-term success.

The analogy also extends to the realm of spirituality and the church. Merely attending church services and participating superficially without seeking transformation and aligning one's heart with the teachings of the Word and the guidance of the Holy Spirit can result in a lack of true growth.

Just as smooth stones are stable and can hit their target accurately, individuals who actively engage with the teachings and anointing of the Spirit can experience genuine transformation and make a positive impact in their lives and the lives of others.

Furthermore, the mention of crooked and rough stones highlights the importance of avoiding lukewarm attitudes and half-hearted commitment. Being lukewarm or indecisive can lead to a lack of direction and unreliable outcomes. Instead, embracing a passionate and wholehearted approach can bring focus, and determination, and ultimately lead to greater success.

In summary, David's choice of smooth stones emphasizes the significance of stability, consistency, and commitment in various aspects of life. Whether in business, personal growth, or spirituality, embracing stable philosophies and values, avoiding lukewarm attitudes, and remaining focused can lead to more accurate and impactful outcomes.

"Happiness is when what you think,

what you say,

and what you do are in harmony."

Mahatma Gandhi

May you be resolute in your faith and profession knowing that you are surrounded by so great a cloud of witnesses. What you pretend to be and are not, can never be hidden forever. In the end, it shall be revealed by fire and if you are a true gem, you will shine; however, if you are a germ, you will surely be consumed with all your works.

===

Be a genuine gem,

Not a gnawing germ among God's goods!

===

The HR, Heaven, and Hell

One day, while walking down the street a highly successful HR Director was tragically hit by a bus and she died. Her soul arrived up in heaven where she was met at the Pearly Gates by St. Peter himself.

"Welcome to Heaven," said St. Peter. "Before you get settled in though, it seems we have a problem. You see, strangely enough, we've never once had a Human Resources Manager make it this far and we're not sure what to do with you."

"No problem, just let me in," said the woman. "Well, I'd like to," replied St. Peter, "but I have higher orders. What we're going to do is let you have a day in Hell and a day in Heaven and then you can choose whichever one you want to spend an eternity in."

"I think I've made up my mind, I prefer to stay in Heaven," said the woman.

"Sorry, we have rules..." And with that St. Peter put the executive in an elevator and it went down-down-down to hell. The doors opened and she found herself stepping out onto the putting green of a beautiful golf course.

In the distance was a country club and standing in front of her were all her friends - fellow executives that she had worked with and they were all dressed in evening gowns and cheering for her.

They ran up and kissed her on both cheeks and they talked about old times. They played an excellent round of golf and at night went to the country club where she enjoyed an excellent steak and lobster dinner. She met the Devil who was a nice guy (kind of cute) and she had a great time telling jokes and dancing.

She was having such a good time that before she knew it, it was time to leave. Everybody shook her hand and waved goodbye as she got on the elevator. The elevator went up-up-up and opened back up at the Pearly Gates and she found St. Peter waiting for her.

"Now it's time to spend a day in heaven," he said. So she spent the next 24 hours lounging around on clouds and playing the harp and singing. She had a great time and before she knew it her 24 hours were up and St. Peter came and got her. "So, you've spent a day in hell and you've spent a day in heaven. Now you must choose your eternity," he said.

The woman paused for a second and then replied, "Well, I never thought I'd say this, I mean, Heaven has been great and all, but I think I had a better time in Hell." So St. Peter escorted her to the elevator and again she went down-down-down back to Hell.

When the doors of the elevator opened she found herself standing in a desolate wasteland covered in garbage and filth. She saw her friends dressed in rags and picking up the garbage and putting it in sacks. The Devil came up to her and put his arm around her.

"I don't understand," stammered the woman, "Yesterday I was here and there was a golf course and a country club and we ate lobster and we danced and had a great time. Now all there is a wasteland of garbage and all my friends look miserable."

The Devil looked at her and smiled. "Yesterday we were recruiting you, today you're staff..."

Well, beloved don't be like this lukewarm HR Manager who could be tossed to and fro without any specific direction or focus. You must let your stand and calling be certain. Be sure of your salvation and never allow yourself to be deceived. In the end, you will pay dearly for it and it may be too late.

Last, but not least, I believe that David took the five stones because; he frankly took into consideration his human fallibility and inadequacy even though anointed, especially seeing such huge crowds before and behind him.

He was wise to pick five and not one or two; because, if he tried the first and failed, he was not going to give up easily, if he tried the second and the third, and still could not work the magic desired, he was not going to throw in the towel so easily. He was resolute and daring enough to continue trying till the giant before him fell flat on his face.

Also, he could not go beyond five because it would have meant that he believed in something besides or above the power and might of Jesus. The five stones were a perfect combination of Jesus in display and not he the shepherd as such, could not look on or depend on someone else for help. If He (Jesus Christ) cannot help you, then who on earth can?

Friend, looking at how far you have come, and the work He has done in your life, you cannot decide to lose hope or give in to the pressures of this world or the attacks of the enemy through the various channels he uses to fight you.

We must continue to fight back till we win the war. Never give up on your dreams; if you fail today, try again, and again, and again, and again till your breakthrough comes.

STRATEGY #

9. Humility and Maturity

Let us consider a team project at work. There's a project manager named Mark who is assigned to lead a cross-functional team to deliver a new software application. Mark understands that each team member plays a vital role in the project's success, just like the stones had to fit perfectly into David's sling.

Mark carefully assesses the skills, expertise, and personalities of each team member to ensure a cohesive and effective team dynamic. He considers the size and weight of their roles, matching individuals with the right tasks that align with their strengths and capabilities. This approach ensures that everyone can contribute their best and work together harmoniously.

If Mark were to assign someone to a role they are not suited for, it would be like putting a stone that is too big or too small into the sling. It would hinder the team's progress and potentially lead to project failure. Mark recognizes the importance of finding the right fit for each team member to maximize their potential and the overall project outcome.

Moreover, Mark understands the value of humility and the need for personal growth within the team. He encourages an environment where team members can learn, adapt, and improve their skills. Just as Joseph had to go through a process of breaking and preparation, Mark fosters a culture of continuous learning and development among his team members. This ensures they are not rigid or overinflated with their own ideas but are open to feedback, collaboration, and personal growth.

By considering the size, weight, and fit of each team member's role, as well as promoting humility and personal development, Mark creates a strong foundation for success in the team project. The team members can effectively work together, complement each other's strengths, and deliver outstanding results.

This modern example highlights the importance of finding the right fit in teams, embracing humility, and fostering personal growth for achieving success in collaborative endeavors.

David's stone needed to fit well into the sling that he was going to use in the battle against the giant. It required the right SIZE and WEIGHT for it to be properly carried and swung by the chap.

If it is too small, it will not swing well and if too big, it will not fit into the sling. The right size and weight were critical to bring victory by the Holy Spirit.

And this is how many of us are in God. In as much as He wants to use us to bring down giants of problems in the lives of people and the world, we do not have the required structure.

Some of us are too big in ourselves. We are so proud and puffy due to our human experiences, education, exposure, and personal ideologies. We make it difficult for God to fit us into his perfect plan and divine agenda. We simply look oversized!

It is time to be broken down! If you are not humble enough, you cannot be used by God. Joseph had to go through various stages of preparation to deal with his pride issues. He was going to become a great deliverer one day but needed to be broken and well-processed before that time.

The torture and torment he went through in the hands of his brothers and Egypt were all meant to prepare him for the great task ahead. His brothers *sold* him, but God *sent* him for a divine agenda in Egypt.

On the other hand, some stones are too small in size and weight to be properly carried in the sling or swung to bring down the giant. We need to grow and develop spiritually, emotionally, and intellectually to handle weighty matters. God will not entrust significant tasks to those who are not prepared and equipped to carry them.

So, we need to examine ourselves and allow God to shape us

according to His purposes. Let go of pride and self-sufficiency, and embrace humility and maturity. Only then can we be effectively used by God to bring down the giants in our lives and make a lasting impact on the world around us.

Your weight determines your freight of maturity.

How deep you are in terms of your knowledge base, wisdom, confidence, courage, patience, integrity, self-discipline, vision, etc. will determine the kind of problems you can solve in life.

You must grow up and develop more muscles in business, your relationships, finances, parenting, ministry, and vital social issues to be able to handle the increasing demands of our time. It will take the more mature psychologically, spiritually, politically, socially, emotionally, and physically to bring down the gargantuan difficulties of our age.

STRATEGY #
10. Know Your Perfect Timing

Elijah stood atop Mount Carmel, his heart filled with the promise of rain. The message had been clear, resonating deep within his spirit. An abundance of rain was coming to Israel. With his track record of calling down fire from heaven and vanquishing false prophets, he expected this to be a swift and effortless victory.

Filled with anticipation, Elijah began to pray. He sought the manifestation of the prophetic word, a sign that would confirm the impending rain. His servant was sent to watch over the sea, awaiting that divine confirmation. But as time passed, the sign remained elusive, slipping through Elijah's fingers like grains of sand.

Undeterred, Elijah persisted in prayer, trying different dimensions and approaches. First, second, third—he fervently sought the fulfillment of the prophetic word. But each attempt yielded no tangible results. Doubts crept into his mind. Was he missing something? Was God ignoring him?

On the fourth and fifth rounds of prayer, Elijah pressed on, hoping for a breakthrough. The fifth round, symbolizing the five stones of David, held a special significance—a reminder of the name of JESUS. Elijah clung to the belief that, even if all else failed, this dimension of prayer would surely bring the answers he sought. Yet, once again, the outcome fell short of his expectations.

In the depths of his soul, Elijah wrestled with confusion. Why was God seemingly deaf to his cries? Was He asleep or indifferent to his plight? But in his struggle, Elijah held onto a profound truth—he understood the perfect timing of God.

Picture a young professional named Sophie who had been searching for her dream job for months. She had put in countless applications, attended numerous interviews, and faced several rejections along the way. Sophie's confidence was starting to waver, and she wondered if she would ever find the right opportunity.

During this time, Sophie decided to invest in her personal growth and development. She enrolled in additional courses, networked with industry professionals, and honed her skills. Although she longed for immediate success, she trusted that her efforts would eventually pay off.

One day, as Sophie was scrolling through job postings online, she stumbled upon a position that seemed tailor-made for her. The job description aligned perfectly with her qualifications and passions. Excitedly, she submitted her application and waited anxiously for a response.

Days turned into weeks, and weeks into months, and Sophie's patience was tested. She questioned whether she had missed her chance or if someone else had been chosen for the role. Doubts started to creep in, but she remained steadfast in her belief that the right opportunity would come at the perfect time.

Just when Sophie was beginning to lose hope, she received an email inviting her for an interview. The timing couldn't have been more ideal—she had just completed a new certification that added value to her skill set. Feeling prepared and confident, Sophie aced the interview and was offered the job on the spot.

Looking back, Sophie realized that if she had secured a job earlier in her search, she might not have had the chance to acquire the additional skills and knowledge that made her a standout candidate for this particular position. The timing of her career breakthrough was perfect, aligning with her personal growth and ensuring she was fully equipped for success.

In life, we often experience moments when things don't happen as quickly as we would like. It's in these moments that we must trust in divine timing. Just as Sophie's dream job came at the right time, we may find that our desired opportunities, relationships, or milestones unfold when we are truly ready to embrace them.

Whether it's a promotion, starting a business, or pursuing a new passion, the perfect timing in our careers and lives ensures that we are fully prepared, equipped, and positioned to make the most of the opportunities that come our way. So, let us remain patient, continue to invest in our personal growth, and trust that the right doors will open at precisely the right moment.

Beloved, there may be moments when you've poured out your heart to the Lord, when your prayers have echoed through the heavens, and still, it seems that your pleas go unanswered. In those times, you might question if it's due to past sins or mistakes you've made. But I come to you in the name of the Lord to offer encouragement and reassurance.

It may not be your past sins or transgressions that hinder your breakthrough. Instead, God is orchestrating all things for your ultimate good. Even in apparent silence, He is working behind the scenes, aligning circumstances, molding you, and setting the stage for a grand manifestation of His glory.

Remember, dear one, that God's timing is perfect. He knows the precise moment to unfold His plans and fulfill His promises in your life. So, hold onto hope, trust in His faithfulness, and continue to seek Him with unwavering faith.

In the fullness of time, the rain will come, the answers will be revealed, and the pieces of the puzzle will fall into place. The waiting may be challenging, but it is in the waiting that your character is refined, your faith deepened, and your dependence on Him strengthened.

Keep praying, keep seeking, and keep trusting. The perfect timing of God is at work in your life, and when it unfolds, it will surpass all your expectations. All things are working together for your ultimate profit and divine purpose.

For ye need patience, that,

after ye have done the will of God,

ye might receive the promise

Hebrews 10:36

God was not incapacitated to perform the request of Elijah; instead, He had a valuable lesson to teach him at this particular stage of his ministry. Despite Elijah's ability to call fire from above with a simple prayer of faith, this time God wanted to teach him the virtue of patience. It wasn't a reflection of Elijah's weak faith or shallow life; it was simply a divine lesson in God's perfect timing.

In contrast, David received an immediate answer to his call with just one stone's throw. But for Elijah, he had to persevere in prayer, going the extra mile, until he witnessed a mere sign of his prophetic promise. This reveals how God deals with each person uniquely in Christ. His ways of working in our lives may vary, tailored to our characteristics, levels, and spiritual journeys.

Some may experience God's leading through dreams and visions, while others through His word or a gentle impression in their hearts. We must discern and embrace how God often communicates and interacts with us individually. Our God is not confined to a single method or time frame. He may respond to one person in the morning and another in the evening. Your breakthrough might come today, while mine might come tomorrow.

Ultimately, what matters most is that we all receive answers to our heartfelt requests. It doesn't imply one person's superiority in holiness, righteousness, prayerfulness, or power. Rather, it highlights the significance of God's perfect timing.

Elijah was transitioning from the permissible will of God to His precise timing. David, being a younger minister, needed training in the permissive timing before advancing to the perfect timing of God. Elijah, as a more mature man of God, understood this and persevered until he prevailed in the seventh dimension of his petitions.

Let us be encouraged never to give up, even when circumstances seem bleak. Instead, let us press on and push forward until we witness the full manifestation of our heart's desires on earth. Patience, combined with faith and obedience, will position us to receive the promises of God in His perfect timing.

The seer sensed this and gave a caution to all his enemies saying:

"Do not rejoice over me, my enemy;

When I fall, I will rise;

When I sit in darkness,

the LORD will be a light to me"

Micah 7:8

Weeping may endure for the night but joy comes in the morning. The righteous may fall seven times and seven times will rise again. Thank God for the prophetic insight of David; he picked only five stones and by this, he was saying that, there is no power above the power of Jesus Christ.

If He couldn't do anything about the situation at the mention of His name (5th stone); then, no one else and nothing could be of help to him a shepherd, hence the five stones.

To end with, just as the staff and sling meant so much to the shepherd boy; the stones he selected further symbolized and typified so many other things to him in person and the situation at hand. We shall thus highlight more of its significance and relevance in the final chapter.

We have explored the importance of understanding and aligning with the perfect timing of God. Through the stories of Elijah and David, we see different examples of how God works in the lives of His people.

Elijah learned the valuable lesson of patience and perseverance, even as a mighty prophet, as he waited for the manifestation of God's promise. On the other hand, David experienced a more immediate answer to his call, demonstrating the diversity of God's timing in different individuals' lives.

The chapter has demonstrated among others, the need to be well-positioned to take advantage of the myriads of opportunities around us. That God's timing is not necessarily determined by our holiness, righteousness, or power, but by His sovereign plan and purpose for each person. It encourages us to discern how God communicates and interacts with us individually and to trust His timing, even when things seem uncertain or delayed.

By embracing patience, we acknowledge that God's ways and timing are higher than ours. We surrender our agendas and desires, trusting that He knows what is best for us. Through faith, we believe that God is faithful to His promises and that He will fulfill them in His own time and way.

And by obeying His will, we demonstrate our love and devotion to Him, positioning ourselves to receive His blessings and experience His faithfulness.

As we walk in patience, confidence, and obedience, we open ourselves up to the full manifestation of God's plan and purpose for our lives. We can rest assured that His timing is perfect, and when His promises come to pass, they will exceed our expectations and bring glory to His name.

So, let us persevere, pressing on and pushing forward in our walk with God. Let us trust His timing, knowing that He is orchestrating everything for our good. And as we align ourselves with His will and wait expectantly, we will witness the fulfillment of His promises and experience the richness of His blessings in our lives.

I position myself today to deal with all challenges

that come my way.

I shall maximize the opportunities around me.

Heavenly Father, help me to depend on you for fresh ideas always.

Please grant me a special heart of love for all and even for my enemies.

I shall not give up on my dreams no matter the difficulties.

From today, I make a solemn pledge to live a life of purity before God.

I declare that every dead or dormant gift be quickened by the

power of the Holy Spirit in Jesus' name I pray.

Amen

Summary of Points

i. You must position yourself well to take advantage of opportunities

ii. Life at times presents both opportunity and a challenge at the same time.

iii. You can practice any virtue erratically, but nothing consistently without courage."

iv. Drop the dross and go for the big deal.

v. You must spend more time with those who are more profitable in the organization.

vi. Sometimes we look far away for solutions while we may be sitting close by one.

vii. Be a genuine gem, not a gnawing germ among God's goods!

viii. Never despise your humble beginnings

ix. When you fall, you can rise again

x. Happiness is when what you think, say, and do are in harmony

xi. Make mature decisions in the face of difficult situations

CHAPTER FOUR

NEGOTIATE INTELLIGENTLY IN A TURBULENT WORLD
"Let us never negotiate out of fear.

But let us never fear to negotiate."

John F. Kennedy

OUR TROUBLED WORLD TODAY

In a troubled world, there is an underlying sense of unrest and turmoil that permeates different spheres of existence. It is a world where economic instability prevails, marked by financial crises, rising unemployment rates, and growing income inequality.

Many individuals struggle to make ends meet, facing poverty, limited access to basic resources, and inadequate healthcare services. The pursuit of financial security becomes a constant challenge, causing stress and anxiety for individuals and families alike.

On a social level, a troubled world is characterized by divisions and conflicts. Prejudices and discrimination based on race, ethnicity, religion, gender, and other factors create a fragmented society. Inequality and social injustice manifest in various forms, such as systemic racism, gender disparities, and marginalization of certain groups. Trust between individuals and communities may erode, leading to a breakdown of social cohesion and a sense of isolation.

The weight of despair hangs heavy in the hearts of despondent youth. Their dreams, once vibrant and full of hope, now seem elusive and distant. They navigate a landscape scarred by economic uncertainty, limited opportunities, and a pervasive sense of disillusionment.

For these young souls and many others in the world today, the path to success appears obscured by layers of adversity. They face relentless competition, societal expectations, and the fear of failure. The pressures of academia, the demands of technology, and the constant comparison of social media further exacerbate their anxieties.

Mental health stands as a vital thread intricately woven into every aspect of their existence. Academic and professional pursuits, once filled with promise, are hindered as anxiety and depression take hold, undermining focus, productivity, and educational attainment.

In the realm of relationships, many people grapple with the complexities of modern love and the quest for genuine connections. The vibrant connections that once sustained them grow strained. Social withdrawal and isolation become companions, eroding bonds with friends and loved ones, leaving them feeling disconnected and alone.

The fear of rejection and the emotional toll of heartbreak loom large, leaving them yearning for solace and understanding in a world that often feels cold and detached.

Overall well-being becomes shrouded in darkness, as the joy and fulfillment they once experienced fade away. Energy levels wane, sleep patterns are disrupted, and physical health bears the weight of emotional turmoil, leaving many emotionally and physically exhausted.

Their mental and emotional well-being bears the brunt of this troubled world. The constant bombardment of negative news, social unrest, and a pervasive sense of uncertainty takes a toll on their psyche. Anxiety, depression, and a sense of hopelessness become unwelcome companions, casting a shadow over their once-optimistic outlook.

This troubled world perpetuates a cycle of interdependence, where mental and physical health intertwine. The toll of mental health issues manifests in physical symptoms, further exacerbating their struggles. Individuals may struggle to maintain their emotional well-being amidst the challenges of the world, leading to a sense of hopelessness and helplessness.

The ripple effects reverberate throughout society, burdening communities as strained support systems struggle to provide adequate care. Increased healthcare costs, decreased productivity, and social consequences manifest, perpetuating a cycle of societal challenges.

Yet, amidst the darkness, a flicker of resilience remains. Within the hearts of these despondent youth, there exists a yearning for change, a longing for purpose, and a desire to transcend the limitations imposed upon them. They seek inspiration, guidance, and the tools to navigate the tumultuous journey ahead.

It is within this troubled world that the significance of successfully negotiating life's challenges becomes paramount. Empowering these young minds with strategies, resilience, and a sense of purpose can ignite a spark of hope and help them rise above the trials that surround them.

As we delve deeper into this book, we share more light on the transformative power of negotiation amid adversity. By equipping the despondent youth and individuals from all walks of life with the tools to navigate a troubled world, we believe in their ability to create positive change, find fulfillment, and ultimately forge their path to success.

In terms of governance and politics, a troubled world may experience political instability, corruption, and abuse of power. Citizens may feel disconnected from their leaders and institutions, leading to a lack of faith in the democratic process. In some cases, authoritarian regimes suppress freedoms and violate human rights, further exacerbating the troubled state of the world.

The environment also bears the brunt of a troubled world. Climate change, deforestation, pollution, and resource depletion threaten the delicate balance of ecosystems. Natural disasters become more frequent and severe, displacing communities, destroying habitats, and contributing to a sense of environmental insecurity.

INTELLIGENT NEGOTIATIONS IN A TURBULENT WORLD

As we explore deeper into the concept of the negotiating table of life, it becomes clear that this isn't limited to a specific age group or demographic. It encompasses individuals from various walks of life, including despondent youth who are grappling with their own set of challenges and uncertainties. These young individuals find themselves at a critical juncture, seeking guidance, direction, and a way to overcome their struggles.

For them, the negotiating table represents a platform where they can confront their fears, doubts, and insecurities head-on. It's a space where they must summon the courage to advocate for themselves, leveraging whatever limited resources they have to achieve their goals. The emotional weight they carry is significant, as they yearn for a breakthrough that will transform their lives and offer a glimmer of hope in uncertainty.

In a troubled world, the challenges faced by humanity are multi-faceted. They grapple with issues such as unemployment, societal pressures, educational setbacks, mental health concerns, and a general sense of disillusionment. The weight of their circumstances often leaves them feeling overwhelmed, devoid of hope, and unsure of how to navigate the complexities of the negotiating table.

However, it is precisely during these moments of vulnerability that the lessons drawn from the youngster's journey become even more relevant and impactful. Just as the youngster's dad provided him with the necessary support, ideas, and resources, God, our Heavenly Father, stands ready to extend His hand to the despairing youth. He offers guidance, inspiration, and strength to overcome the challenges they face.

In the forthcoming pages, we will explore these vital tools that are indispensable on the negotiating table of life. These tools encompass not only practical strategies but also emotional resilience and a deep sense of self-belief.

Through the lens of faith and the wisdom gleaned from biblical teachings, we will uncover valuable insights that will empower many especially the despondent youth and equip them to navigate the troubled world they find themselves.

So, let us embark on this journey together, delving into the critical lessons and essential principles that will equip you to successfully negotiate in a troubled world. Brace yourself for the transformative insights that lie ahead, for they have the potential to shape your mindset, ignite your spirit, and pave the way for a brighter future.

"Then Jesse said to David,

"Take NOW for your brothers an EPHAH of this DRIED GRAIN

and these TEN LOAVES, and RUN to your brothers at the camp.

And carry these ten CHEESE to the CAPTAIN of their thousand,

and SEE how your BROTHERS FARE and BRING BACK NEWS of them"

1 Samuel 17: 17-18

INTEL #

I.   Take NOW!

Once upon a time, there was a man named Robert who was tired of living a mundane and unfulfilling life. He worked a job that didn't excite him, had no hobbies or passions to pursue, and felt stuck in a rut. One day, while scrolling through social media, he came across an advertisement for a local community college offering evening classes in web development.

The ad sparked something within Robert. He had always been fascinated by technology and had a natural curiosity for coding. At that moment, he realized that this could be his chance to make a change and pursue a career that truly excited him.

Without hesitation, Robert picked up his phone and called the community college to inquire about the web development program. He enrolled in the classes immediately, even though he had no prior experience in coding. He knew it would be a challenging journey, but he was determined to give it his all.

Over the next few months, Robert immersed himself in learning web development. He spent countless evenings studying and practicing coding, sometimes staying up until the early hours of the morning. He faced numerous challenges and moments of frustration, but he never gave up.

As he gained more knowledge and skills, Robert started working on small web development projects for friends and acquaintances. His passion and dedication were evident in the quality of his work, and soon word started spreading about his talent. He began receiving offers for freelance projects and even landed a part-time job as a web developer with a local tech startup.

With each success, Robert's confidence grew. He continued to expand his knowledge, attending workshops and conferences, and networking with professionals in the industry. Within a few years, he had established himself as a reputable web developer, working on exciting projects and earning a comfortable income doing what he loved.

Looking back, Robert realized that taking immediate action to enroll in those web development classes was the turning point in his life. By recognizing the opportunity and seizing it without delay, he was able to transform his life and find true fulfillment in his career.

Robert's story serves as a reminder that sometimes all it takes is a single moment of inspiration and the courage to take immediate action to change your life for the better.

Opportunities need to be taken NOW!

Many people see the need to act on their present situations but fail to take action now! They see an opportunity to change their lives and to come out of any predicament but lack the willpower to act on it.

Whenever you see an opportunity to do something worthwhile, take immediate action. According to Jim Rohn, a legendary motivational speaker and businessman, "You will learn more from failing than you will from winning" so take action.

Don't be afraid to make mistakes or to fail at anything new. Give it your best shot and by all means, start anyway, anyhow, and from anywhere. Whatever you have been dreaming of doing or achieving in the future start today and start now!

Take a piece of paper and write down your vision and goals right now. What do you want to have or achieve in say ten years? Ask yourself all the little things you can do in the short and long run that will gradually take you to where you want to get to and start immediately.

Now begin by reading and researching your ideas, talking to the right people about it, gathering the right information, and planning towards it. Whatever little thing you need to do to kick start, do it, and do it now!

Remember, a journey of a thousand miles begins with a step, not a wish. So act before you think and don't be afraid to fail. It's better to take 100 steps and fail than not trying and having these great plans in your head and not implementing any. You will learn so many ways things do not work so you can be a better person or entrepreneurial than going to the grave with your great idea. So take action now!!

INTEL #

II.   **GRACE-** An *ephah* of dried grain

In the first place, Jesse sent his sons *a measure* (ephah) of grain on the war front. The *ephah* was a measure for dry grain in those days. So, in your hour of pain or difficulty, God will give you the measure of grace you need to succeed in that situation. Like Jesse, He will provide you with the right amount of assistance (an ephah) as you navigate through any negotiation process.

God's grace is tailored to your specific needs. He will never burden you with more than you can bear. When you face challenges or discouragement, His grace is there to sustain you. In the realm of business, no corporate organization can rise to the top and maintain its success without the favor and blessing of God. Even in this modern age, businesses recognize the importance of invoking the powers of a supreme being in their daily activities.

Some institutions have established dedicated prayer teams to seek the face of God continually, seeking His favor and goodness. They understand that success goes beyond mere planning and marketing strategies. On the contrary, some resort to occult practices and sacrifices to lesser gods in the pursuit of breakthroughs and victories in the market.

Beloved, you cannot underestimate the significance of God's grace in your life. He will provide you with the right ideas, resources, and plans to navigate through your circumstances. You will have the strength and skills necessary to endure and overcome the challenges as long as you trust Him.

Remember, every temptation or challenge you face is common to humanity. But God is faithful, and He will not allow you to be tempted beyond what you can handle. He will provide a way of escape so that you can bear the trials and emerge victorious.

When Jesse sent dried grains to his sons instead of preparing sumptuous meals, it may not have been what they expected. However, every circumstance works together for your good if you do not lose heart. Even though Jesse could have provided more luxurious provisions, he chose to give them dried grains. It was a test of their resilience and faith, just as your trials are meant to strengthen you and reveal the depth of your trust in God.

Our Upper Room Experience…

In the depths of my senior high school years, a vacation unfolded that left an indelible mark on my soul. My roommate and I found ourselves clinging to the shelter of our school's campus, seeking solace from the tumultuous storms brewing in our respective homes. The weight of our emotional and psychological burdens pressed upon us relentlessly, while financial struggles and the aftermath of broken family ties cast a shadow over our lives.

We were not alone in our struggles. My companion served as the assistant chaplain for the prestigious Presbyterian Boys Senior High School- Legon, while I held the esteemed position of vice president in the Scripture Union.

Together, we sought refuge in a small, secluded cubicle tucked away in the upper reaches of the school's Assembly Hall. It became our sanctuary, a place we affectionately named "The Upper Room." It was a refuge, but little did we know that it would become the backdrop for a grueling battle against hunger and desperation.

As days turned into weeks, our meager food supplies dwindled to nothingness. The once comforting aroma of hearty meals gave way to the harsh reality of survival. Raw *gari* became our staple, accompanied by moldy bread and stale *'shito'*(chili sauce)—a feeble attempt to appease our rumbling stomachs. But even that failed us in the end, and we found ourselves staring into the abyss of hunger, grappling with the gnawing emptiness that consumed us.

In those moments of desperation, our prayers became our lifeline. Fasting became our source of sustenance, as we clung to the belief that our present afflictions were but fleeting shadows, soon to be replaced by a brighter tomorrow. Yet, amid our prayers and fasting, questions echoed in the depths of my being. Why were our homes marred by imperfections? Why were we left emotionally and financially destitute? Why did our parents' broken paths become our burden to bear?

During this turmoil, I came to realize that our Heavenly Father was orchestrating a unique journey for us. He was testing our mettle, molding our character, and preparing us for a future laden with greater responsibilities. Like dried grain, He presented us with challenges and disappointments, a seemingly endless stream of obstacles designed to refine our spirits and fortify our resolve.

These dried grains were more than mere trials; they symbolized the arduous decisions we had to make. As students, we sacrificed precious hours of sleep to conquer academic mountains. To shed unwanted pounds, we pushed ourselves to the brink, forgoing indulgences and enduring grueling exercise routines.

As young individuals navigating a treacherous world, we held onto our moral compass, resisting the temptations that threatened to derail us from our destined path. Even parents and children faced the need to tighten their belts, cut back on luxuries, and navigate the precarious tightrope of financial stability.

It is during these seasons of dried grain that we discover our strength, our resilience, and our unwavering determination. Our Heavenly Father knows the depths of our hearts, and in His infinite wisdom, He uses these challenges to mold us into vessels of greatness. He plants seeds of hope within us, assuring us that these trials are not meant to break us but to shape us into instruments of His divine purpose.

So, dear one, when you find yourself surrounded by the harshness of dried grain, take heart. Embrace the discomfort, for it is within these struggles that your character is refined and your spirit is strengthened.

Remember that your Heavenly Father sees the grand tapestry of your life, and He knows the beauty that lies ahead. Hold on tightly to the flickering flame of hope, for change is on the horizon, and a bountiful harvest awaits those who endure.

INTEL #

III. **SHARE-** *Ten* loaves

> *"We make a living by what we get,*
>
> *but we make a life by what we give.*
>
> *A gift, though small, is welcome".*

Greek proverb

Even though his sons were three, he sent *ten loaves* which meant if they shared them equally among themselves, there will be *one* left with each getting three. The surplus was meant for the eldest son or another person in need in the camp.

So in your hour of pleasure or pain think about others too. You are not the only one going through one problem or the other. Others may even be in a worse situation than yours. You cannot close your eyes to those around you who may need your help.

Two men, both seriously ill, occupied the same hospital room. One man was allowed to sit up in his bed for an hour each afternoon to help drain the fluid from his lungs. His bed was next to the room's only window.

The other man had to spend all his time flat on his back. The men talked for hours on end. They spoke of their wives and families, their homes, their jobs, their involvement in the military service, where they had been on vacation.

Every afternoon, when the man in the bed by the window could sit up, he would pass the time by describing to his roommate all the things he could see outside the window. The man in the other bed began to live for those one-hour periods where his world would be broadened and enlivened by all the activity and color of the world outside.

The window overlooked a park with a lovely lake.

Ducks and swans played on the water while children sailed their model boats. Young lovers walked arm in arm amidst flowers of every color and a fine view of the city skyline could be seen in the distance. As the man by the window described all this in exquisite detail, the man on the other side of the room would close his eyes and imagine this picturesque scene.

One warm afternoon, the man by the window described a parade passing by. Although the other man could not hear the band – he could see it in his mind's eye as the gentleman by the window portrayed it with descriptive words.

Days, weeks, and months passed.

One morning, the day nurse arrived to bring water for their baths only to find the lifeless body of the man by the window, who had died peacefully in his sleep. She was saddened and called the hospital attendants to take the body away.

As soon as it seemed appropriate, the other man asked if he could be moved next to the window. The nurse was happy to make the switch, and after making sure he was comfortable, she left him alone. Slowly, painfully, he propped himself up on one elbow to take his first look at the real world outside. He strained to slowly turn to look out the window beside the bed. It faced a blank wall.

The man asked the nurse what could have compelled his deceased roommate who had described such wonderful things outside this window. The nurse responded that the man was blind and could not even see the wall.

She said, 'Perhaps he just wanted to encourage you.'

There is tremendous happiness in making others happy, despite our situations. Shared grief is half the sorrow, but happiness when shared, is doubled. If you want to feel rich, just count all the things you have that money can't buy.

Today is a gift, which is why it is called The Present.

You may have the solution to someone's problem and no matter the challenge you may be going through, you have to lend a helping hand. God helps us so we can also lend a helping hand to others. Share the little you have and it will come back to you multiplied.

You are watered so you can also water someone. You are blessed to be a blessing to someone. As you assist others out of their predicaments, you will find more peace and relief in your own heart. Soon, you will be able to overcome the hurdle that stands before you on your voyage to success.

What you take into your system in times of trouble will make or break you in the long run. While some go in for sympathy others go for the solution. Whiles others commit suicide others still press on to succeed in the end. What you feed your spirit will determine the outcome. You will reap what you sow into your life. GIGO- Garbage in garbage out!!

Like Jesse, God has sent us Jesus, who is the *bread* of life that whosoever eats (accepts Him as Lord and personal Savior) will not die but have eternal life-John 6: 48-51. The word of God is food for your soul and spirit to strengthen and revive you in the battles of life.

Many are the things you will hear, see, or experience in times of difficulty, but you must stick to the unadulterated word of God concerning your life. In the end, you will become a better person as you feed on and share the word of God.

INTEL #

IV.   PROCESSES- Ten *Cheese* to their...

Even though milk was in abundance in the home of Jesse, he did not simply send his sons raw milk. No, he took the time and effort to process it into cheese. He knew that cheese was more portable and could be preserved for longer periods. Jesse added that extra value to the raw milk before dispatching it to his sons' captain. It was a gesture of love and care, ensuring that they would have sustenance and nourishment on the battlefield.

In life, opportunities are like raw milk. They come to us in their initial form, unrefined and unprocessed. It is our responsibility to learn the art and skill of proper preparation, processing, precision, and planning. Just as Jesse turned raw milk into cheese, we must refine and process our ideas to fit into present-day situations or for future purposes.

Don't be hasty to jump into implementation the moment you have a great idea. Take the time to sit down and think it through. Research, gather information, conduct a SWOT analysis, and learn from the experiences of others. This is the process of turning your raw milk into cheese—a product that is well-crafted and relevant to the current global trends. You don't want to present an idea that is outdated and irrelevant, as it may be easily dismissed or ignored.

Moreover, adding extra value to your brilliant ideas or opportunities is crucial. The preferences of customers are complex and ever-evolving. To stand out and succeed, you must go the extra mile.

Just like the paperless transactions that have replaced the cumbersome paperwork in banking halls, or the creatively packaged coconut juice and breakfast items, you need to find ways to add value to your offerings. It could be through innovative packaging, unique combinations, or incorporating cultural elements that resonate with your target audience. These value additions delight customers, create a positive impression, and can bring you additional income.

So, remember to take time to process your fresh ideas and opportunities. Refine them, polish them, and add that extra value. By doing so, you will capture the attention and loyalty of prospective customers and your endeavors will be rewarded with success and prosperity.

INTEL #

V.   COMPETITIVE URGENCY- *Run* to brothers

In this fast-paced and competitive world, cultivating a sense of competitive urgency is crucial for your success. Drawing from my experience working at Merchant Bank Ghana Limited, now known as Universal Merchant Bank (UMB), I witnessed firsthand the value of responding promptly and accurately to the needs of customers.

The concept of competitive urgency revolves around satisfying the desires and demands of our valued customers with a sense of promptness and efficiency. We strived to handle their complaints with the utmost professionalism, ensuring we followed the necessary processes to meet their needs without wasting their time. Our goal was to leave them delighted, all while minimizing their time spent in the banking hall or any interaction with our services.

In today's rapidly changing and fiercely competitive global economy, every entrepreneur must instill in their team a sense of urgency and lead by example. It's not about frantic activity or simply reacting to emergencies; it's about adopting proactive measures and a mindset of swift action. John P. Kotter, in his book "A Sense of Urgency," emphasizes the importance of urgency as a series of proactive activities rather than a reactive stance.

This mindset is vital if you want to thrive and achieve success in the negotiation process of life, whether it's in business, ministry, or family matters. You must approach your endeavors with seriousness and a sense of alacrity.

Remember, you are not only competing with external factors such as limited resources, competitors, and the socio-economic landscape, but also with yourself—your purpose, vision, and personal growth.

What you fail to do quickly may be seized by your competitors, and they could claim what rightfully belongs to you. You need to act smart and swift. No longer can bankers rely on customers flooding their halls just to save their hard-earned money. The landscape has evolved, and you must adapt.

To stay ahead of the competition, you must be agile, proactive, and capable of attracting potential clients with exceptional, tailored, and efficient services, even from the comfort of their own homes.

In any business, ministry, or relationship, address issues promptly before they escalate. Seize opportunities with a sense of urgency. Avoid wasting time when there's work to be done or deadlines to be met. Act swiftly, perform excellently, and take action now. By embracing competitive urgency, you position yourself for success in the ever-evolving world of negotiations and competition.

INTEL #

VI.   MENTORSHIP-Ten cheese to their *Captain*

Jesse understood the significance of acknowledging and honoring the captain of his sons' battalion. He recognized the captain's leadership and the positive impact he had on his children. Despite the absence of a clear deliverer to confront the formidable Philistine giant, Jesse had faith in the captain's ability to keep his sons safe and protected.

Jesse's act of blessing the captain was not merely a formality, but a genuine display of appreciation for his role in guiding and mentoring his boys. He held the captain in high regard and respected his position as the leader of their battalion. By honoring the captain, Jesse aimed to reinforce the bond between him and his sons, while also instilling in them a sense of admiration and respect for their leader.

The captain, in turn, embraced his role as a role model and mentor to Jesse's sons. He took on the responsibility of instructing, reproving, protecting, and inspiring them throughout the challenges they faced. Jesse recognized the importance of this influence and desired to nurture it even in his absence. He wanted the captain to continue being a source of inspiration and guidance for his children, ensuring their growth, development, and ultimate success.

By fostering a strong relationship between his sons and their leader, Jesse believed that his children would not only navigate the immediate battle with the Philistine, but also learn valuable lessons in leadership, resilience, and character. Through the captain's guidance, they would be equipped to face future challenges and emerge victorious in their own right.

Jesse's act of blessing the captain exemplified his wisdom and foresight as a father. He understood the significance of strong leadership and the impact it could have on his children's lives. By valuing and encouraging the relationship between his sons and their captain, Jesse ensured that his boys would have a source of inspiration and guidance even in his physical absence.

"The mediocre teacher tells. The good teacher explains.

The superior teacher demonstrates.

The great teacher inspires."

William Arthur Ward

You see beloved, many people have trodden the path you are treading. Many have gone through the challenge or situation you may be going through right now. Some have messed up while others made it to the very pinnacle and even made names for themselves. We celebrate and sing their praises for their guts and acts of dexterity and courage.

Jesse was proverbially saying to his boys to draw inspiration and courage from their captain in the camp. He was challenging them to look up to him as a role model and mentor. He may not be there physically, but he had not left them as orphans on the battleground. They needed to become good mentees to the Captain, their mentor.

You can have mentors in various aspects of your life. Even in the corporate world mentors help to make a great mark. There are different types of mentors, some of which include:

1. The Professional or Trade mentor
    I. Industry mentor
    II. Organization mentor
    III. Career Development mentor
    IV. Customer mentor
    V. Work process mentor
    VI. Technology mentor

These mentors are experienced individuals in your field of interest or expertise. They provide guidance, share their knowledge and skills, and help you navigate your career path. They can offer valuable insights, advice, and networking opportunities.

One can have mentors who advise him or her about the right career path to chart. The needed skills and tools you may need to become a success in a chosen field of work. Modern industries and organizations can also have mentors to help them reach the top.

2. Parental mentor
    These are people you look up to for advice in making critical decisions in marriage and relationships. Your parental mentors are people who inspire you when you have a challenge in marriage or life in general. These could be your biological parents or any parent figure in your life.

3. Pastoral mentor
    These are those you look up to as a faith based person. Matured people of common faith who inspire you and prop you up when you fall or become weak in faith. They support you spiritually and can also give you directions in many instances.

4. 'Prophetic' mentor
    People come into your life for a short while but can advise or inspire you on specific issues. These come at the right time to shake up or shape up your life for a period and then move on. They usually do not stay close for a long time.

5. Life Coaches
    Life coaches are professional mentors who help you clarify your goals, overcome obstacles, and make positive changes in your life. They provide guidance, accountability, and

support in various areas such as career, relationships, personal development, and total well-being.

Precious one, there are people close to you who have very good intentions towards you and you must be smart enough to tap positively into their experiences. There are brothers, sisters, aunties, uncles, cousins, nieces, nephews, grandparents, and well-wishers biological or non-biological all around you. Take time to talk to someone who you believe will be in a good position to assist you.

The President of a medium-sized bank in Chicago was interviewed on the secret of his success even though he was in his early thirties, and this was how it went.

Interviewer: Mr. George A., I am astonished at your youth. Forgive me but I expected someone much older.
Mr. George A.: He laughed and said, "It happens every day. I will be thirty-three next week and maybe I will soon be old enough so I'll stop shocking people"
Interviewer: George, very few people make it to the top of a bank at such a young age. Tell me, how did you do it?

Mr. George A.: "It took a lot of hard work and dedication" he explained, "but the real secret is that I selected a mentor."
Interviewer: What do you mean by a mentor? I asked.

Mr. George A.: "Let me explain," George continued, "During my senior year at the university, a retired banker addressed the class. He was in his seventies. His parting remark was, 'If I can ever help any of you, just call.' It sounded as though he was just being polite, but his offer intrigued me. Though nervous initially, I got the courage to call him finally."

Interviewer: "What happened?" I asked.

Mr. George A.: "Frankly I was amazed," the young banker responded. He was very friendly and invited me to meet him. I did and got a vault of advice. He gave me some good pointers on how to choose a bank to work for, and then how to sell myself so I'd land a job. I called him my coach and developed an excellent relationship." He continued, "My coach is genuinely grateful for letting him help me because it keeps his mind young as well"

Interviewer: We need all the help we can get I guess.

Regardless of what kind of work or field, find a mentor. It will help you maximize your ability and chances are that it will bring satisfaction to your coach too.

Someone loves you, honey!

Sometimes a problem shared is half solved. Some experts and professionals are well vexed in their various specialties to assist and support you come out of that problem you may be going through now. So don't always stick and stay by yourself without getting a professional or experienced hand.

No matter the problem; in your academics, relationship, health, finances, career, or profession, talk to someone who can help you by the grace of God. He or she is your captain to protect and help you in that battlefield and that is what Jesse sought to instill in his sons in the camp.

His gift to their Captain was also an act of seed sowing into the future of his sons. As he did for the captain, one day someone will also do for his sons if they became leaders in the land. He was making a strategic investment in their future careers.

Beloved, there are others you must draw inspiration from when you go through the battles of life. No matter how great the crisis, someone has gone through it before. It means you can also go through and be victorious. Recognize that, at a point in time, you need someone to help you. You can't continue all by yourself when you can get help from a higher authority.

So get involved before you are dissolved.

INTEL #

VII.   EMPATHIZE- *Welfare* of sons

The Ephratite of Bethlehem sought to know how his *sons fared* on the war front. He shared in their pain and predicaments like Jesus who left his heavenly throne to take the form of man to die for you and me. He can identify with your feelings of infirmity

For we have not a high priest which cannot be

touched with the feeling of our infirmities;

but was in all points tempted like as we are,

yet without sin.

Hebrews 4:15

Friend, your welfare is very much at the heart of your creator. He knows whatever you go through and will come in at the right time for your rescue. Your change may seem slow or delayed but, with God, He is not too late or too early, He is just on time. A very present help in times of need, the Psalmist puts it.

It is pathetic that most employers do not care so much about the welfare of their employees but only think of the profits to be made at the end of the day. They will squeeze all the juice out of their hardworking employees by setting unrealistic targets and some even refuse to rightly remunerate their staff even when they perform satisfactorily.

Taking a personal interest in people was one of the secrets of Theodore Roosevelt's astonishing popularity. Even his servants loved him. His valet, James E. Amos, wrote a book about him entitled: "THEODORE ROOSEVELT, HERO TO HIS VALET." In that book, Amos relates this illuminating incident:

My wife one time asked the President about a *bobwhite*. She had never seen one and he described it to her fully. Sometime later, the telephone at our cottage rang. Amos and his wife lived in a little cottage on the Roosevelt estate at Oyster Bay.

My wife answered it and it was Mr. Roosevelt himself. He had called her, he said, to tell her that there was a bobwhite outside her window and that if she would look out she might see it.

Little things like that were so characteristic of him. Whenever he went by our cottage, even though we were out of sight, we would hear him call out: "Oo-oo-oo, Annie?" or "Oo-oo-oo, James!" It was just a friendly greeting as he went by. How could employees keep from liking a man like that? How could anyone keep from liking him?

Roosevelt called at the White House one day and his honest liking for humble people was shown by the fact that he greeted all the old White House servants by name, even the scullery maids. "When he saw Alice, the kitchen maid," writes Archie Butt, "he asked her if she still made cornbread. Alice told him that she sometimes made it for the servants, but no one ate it upstairs.

"'They show bad taste,' Roosevelt boomed, 'and I'll tell the President so when I see him.' "Alice brought a piece to him on a plate, and he went over to the office eating it as he went and greeting gardeners and laborers as he passed. . .

"He addressed each person just as he had addressed them in the past. Ike Hoover, who had been head usher at the White House for forty years, said with tears in his eyes: 'It is the only happy day we had in nearly two years, and not one of us would exchange it for a hundred-dollar bill.' "

The same concern for the seemingly unimportant people helped sales representative Edward M. Sykes, Jr., of Chatham, New Jersey, retain an account. "Many years ago," he reported, "I called on customers for Johnson and Johnson in the Massachusetts area. One account was a drugstore in Hingham. Whenever I went into this store I would always talk to the soda clerk and sales clerk for a few minutes before talking to the owner to obtain his order.

One day I went up to the owner of the store, and he told me to leave as he was not interested in buying J&J products anymore because he felt they were concentrating their activities on food and discount stores to the detriment of the small drugstore.

I left with my tail between my legs and drove around the town for several hours. Finally, I decided to go back and try at least to explain our position to the owner of the store.

"When I returned, I walked in and as usual said hello to the soda clerk and sales clerk. When I walked up to the owner, he smiled at me and welcomed me back. He then gave me double the usual order; I looked at him with surprise and asked him what had happened since my visit only a few hours earlier.

He pointed to the young man at the soda fountain and said that after I had left, the boy had come over and said that I was one of the few salespeople that called on the store that even bothered to say hello to him and the others in the store. He told the owner that if any salesperson deserved his business, it was I.

The owner agreed and remained a loyal customer. I never forgot that to be genuinely interested in other people is a most important quality for a salesperson to possess - for any person, for that matter."

I have discovered from personal experience that one can win the attention and time and cooperation of even the most sought-after people by becoming genuinely interested in them.

As a husband, you have to empathize with your wife when she comes home tired and needs help. You have to be there to support your spouse when they need you most. You cannot leave all the chores in the kitchen to your wife all the time.

She can't be cleaning the bathroom and dusting the entire house while you sit and watch TV or go and hang out with your friends all the time. Give her a helping hand in the kitchen and with the kids.

You must be smart enough to know when you are needed most in your relationship because you must complement each other if this is to work successfully. Support your partner emotionally, financially, and physically by putting yourself in their shoes all the time. Just as you want to be treated, you must do the same to them.

"Your partner is not your subordinate
but your co-ordinate."

INTEL #

VIII.   RESPONSIBILITY- *Bring back* news of them

There is always an expectation in your period of temptation or confusion. People around you- friends and loved ones are always waiting to see how you will react to the situation you find yourself in. Your growth or downfall will be made known to others at the end of every challenge; as such, you cannot afford to behave anyhow and think you can go scot-free.

Heaven is counting on you to survive the situation at hand. There is a company of witnesses in Heaven watching to see your end in the condition you find yourself in. As a parent, your children will judge at the end of the day if the decisions you make today will inure to their benefit or not.

You are not the only person who is going through rough times, others have been murdered for no wrong and yet, they did not curse God nor commit suicide. The fact that someone promised to marry you and ended up breaking your heart does not mean it is the end of the world! Life must still go on.

You have wonderful people around you and you must enjoy their company. You have a future career and ambitions to pursue. Don't stop here because of someone's negative actions towards you. Within you lay great potential, so, rise and move on with your life.

You never know what you have or can get till you lose something or someone dear.

"So don't fold in the cold;

Be bold and go for gold!!"

Corporate institutions will be accountable to society at the end of the day for all their activities. Students will always have examinations to write to prove themselves at the end of the day if they deserve to be graduated to the next level on the academic ladder or not.

A story is told of a great King who had four daughters. He wanted to see what responsibilities he could give to each of them. So he gave some wheat grains to each one of them and asked them to come back after a year.

After a year he called all the four daughters and inquired about the wheat.

First daughter: On the same day I fed it to sparrows thinking that they were meant for that. King did not give any responsibility to her.

Second daughter: I mixed them in the Bhandara thinking that they are sacred and so that everyone could have it.

King: Ok you take care of Bhandara.

Third daughter: I saved them safely along with my jewelry and here they are.

King: OK you take care of the treasury

Fourth daughter: I need two bullocks and two men to get the wheat.

All of them laughed and asked why? So she said, "I sowed the grains and now it's grown so big that I need to harvest it and get it on carts.

King: Good you are the best. You take care of the whole house and so saying he gave her the keys.

Friend, you and I have no excuse but to survive the storms and make it in life. You have come too far to retreat or give up even though your expectations have not been met. Indeed, we must not let the challenges we face deter us from our goals and dreams. Life may not always unfold as we expect, but that doesn't mean we should give up or lose hope.

You are surrounded by a great cloud of witnesses, those who have gone before you and faced their trials and tribulations. They serve as examples of resilience and perseverance, showing us that it is possible to overcome obstacles and achieve greatness. Let us draw inspiration from their stories and experiences.

To move forward, we must let go of the weights that burden us. These weights can be in the form of negative thoughts, self-doubt, fear, or unhealthy habits. We must lay them aside and free ourselves from anything that hinders our progress. Additionally, we should strive to overcome the sins that easily entangle us, for they can hinder our growth and lead us astray.

The race set before us requires patience, endurance, and steadfast focus. It is not a sprint but a marathon, and we must run with perseverance, keeping our eyes fixed on Jesus, the source and perfecter of our faith. He endured the cross, despising its shame, because He saw the joy that awaited Him. Likewise, we should consider His example and not grow weary or faint in our minds.

Remember, you are accountable for your actions. Take responsibility for your choices and decisions. Seek guidance from God, trust in His plan, and align your actions with His will. Be mindful of the impact your actions have on yourself and those around you. Strive to be a source of inspiration and encouragement to others on their journeys.

In conclusion, my friend, press on with determination and unwavering faith. Embrace the challenges as opportunities for growth and development. Trust in God's provision and guidance.

With His strength and perseverance, we can navigate through the storms of life and emerge victorious. Keep your focus, run the race with endurance, and let nothing hinder you from reaching the destiny that awaits you.

I thank you Heavenly Father

for the many opportunities you have made available to me.

I thank you for opening my eyes and mind

to identify and maximize the opportunities around me.

I believe I have enough grace to survive every storm

that comes my way from today.

I know you are with me always even to

the end of the age so I fret not.

With you, I survive every stormy weather because,

I am more than a conqueror in the

mighty name of Jesus Christ.

Amen.

Summary of points

    i.   Bargain with the little resources you have and win the deal

    ii.   God will give you the measure of grace you need to succeed in any situation

    iii.   You are being tested and prepared to face more responsible situations in future

    iv.   In your pleasure or pain think about others too

    v.   You are watered to water others; blessed to be a blessing

    vi.   Act with a sense of competitive urgency always

    vii.   Have mentors in various aspects of your life

    viii.   Your partner is not your sub-ordinate but your co-ordinate

    ix.   So don't fold in the cold, be bold and go for gold!

    x.   You are accountable to God, then yourself, and after that to others

CHAPTER FIVE

SEALING THE DEAL: LEVERAGING ADVANCED INTELLIGENCE

"Whatever it takes to finish things, finish.

You will learn more from a glorious failure

than you ever will from something you never finished."

Neil Gaiman

I am extremely happy that you have come along with me to this juncture of this piece of work and trust that you have learned to adopt the right tools in your negotiation process. You have navigated your way through some of the principles to consider in bargaining up the ladder of life –professionally, academically, socially, emotionally, spiritually, and so on.

It is vital to critically evaluate the *offeror* and the *offer* itself, any strings or *offense* attached to it, as well as other *offerings* or future benefits that come along with the deal before you endorse it. The most important of all is to remain in the hearts of the people you engage and to make a lasting impression on their lives.

However, in the midst of a troubled and rapidly changing world, the art of negotiation has taken on a new dimension. Gone are the days when traditional approaches could guarantee success. Today, negotiators must rise above the chaos and uncertainty, armed with a unique set of traits and strategies that I refer to as "advanced intelligence." This concept represents a fusion of astute judgment, strategic thinking, and adaptability in the face of complex challenges.

Negotiation in the modern world requires more than just basic skills and techniques. It demands a higher level of awareness, a deeper understanding of human dynamics, and an ability to navigate the intricate web of interconnected interests. It is within this context that advanced intelligence emerges as a guiding principle for negotiators seeking to thrive amidst the turmoil.

Advanced intelligence as a concept in this manual is the power to tap into one's inner potential and reach out to those in-built traits and capabilities that enable you to navigate successfully any opportunity or deal you face. This concept equips negotiators to not only survive but to excel in negotiations, even in the face of unprecedented challenges.

At its core, advanced intelligence empowers individuals to navigate the troubled waters of our modern reality with clarity, conviction, and finesse. It enables you to transcend conventional limitations and leverage your intellectual, emotional, and interpersonal capacities to drive successful outcomes.

In this chapter, we will probe into the key traits, skills, and strategies that constitute advanced intelligence and explore their application in the context of negotiation within our distressed modern world. By mastering these skills and strategies, anyone can unlock their full potential and become effective agents of change, fostering positive outcomes in the most daunting situations.

I hope that you will be inspired to embrace my concept of advanced intelligence and integrate it into your negotiation endeavors. By doing so, you will unlock a new realm of possibilities, enabling you to navigate the troubled modern world with strategic wisdom, forge meaningful connections, and achieve extraordinary results.

We shall consider the various negotiating styles to employ for quick and successful results as you are confronted with issues on the negotiating table. Also, we shall explore the types of negotiation and the various types of negotiators we have in the world today.

The phases or stages of the negotiation process have been highlighted along with some winning tactics to employ to get the most from the other party also vividly expounded. We will also attempt to look at the common pitfalls and barriers which can derail and diminish our success on the negotiating table and proffer some solutions and winning tactics to these.

Join me as we unravel the secrets of winning any deal using advanced intelligence and embark on a transformative exploration of negotiation in our troubled modern world. Together, we will discover how to navigate the complex maze of conflicts and seize opportunities that lie hidden within the tumultuous landscape of life.

The Negotiation Styles

"Negotiation is the process of two individuals or groups reaching joint agreement about differing needs or ideas." The word "negotiation" originated in the early 15th century from the Old

French and Latin expressions *"negociacion"* and *"negotiationem."* These terms mean "business, trade, and traffic."

By the late 1590s negotiation had the definition, "to communicate in search of mutual agreement." With this new introduction and this meaning, it showed a shift from "doing business" to "bargaining about" business.

Animals do not negotiate or bargain with themselves. They use violence or threat of violence, and various forms of 'dominance' and 'display' to get what they want, be it food, mates, or territory. Theirs is a 'red in tooth and claw' instinct and intentions."

Human beings negotiate, though not all of them use this method. Negotiation has been defined by various people in history. The process by which we search for terms to obtain what we want from somebody who wants something from us. A joint decision made by two or more parties is referred to as Negotiation.

Reaching a consensus is the basic idea behind negotiating. Kenneth W. Thomas identified 5 styles of negotiation. These five strategies have been frequently described in the literature and are based on the dual-concern model. The dual concern model is a perspective that assumes individuals' preferred method of dealing with issues based on two themes or dimensions:

1. A concern for self (i.e. assertiveness) and
2. A concern for others (i.e. empathy)

In the fascinating realm of negotiation, individuals skillfully navigate the delicate balance between their own needs and interests and the needs and interests of others. Drawing from the dual-concern model, we uncover five distinctive negotiation styles that individuals adopt based on their personal preferences and goals.

It's important to note that these styles are not fixed and can evolve, and individuals may demonstrate a predisposition towards multiple styles. Let's dive into each style and explore their characteristics, strengths, and adaptability:

1. Accommodating:

Accommodators are like the friendly neighborhood mediator who always has a knack for understanding people's emotions and finding common ground. They excel at resolving conflicts and preserving relationships. They might be the ones who offer a shoulder to lean on and go the extra mile to solve the other party's problems. But be careful, as they can sometimes feel like they're being taken for granted if the other party doesn't reciprocate the same level of concern.

Imagine you're negotiating with a co-worker over a project deadline. As an accommodator, you prioritize maintaining a good relationship and solving their problems. You might say, "I understand you're overwhelmed. I'm willing to take on some of your tasks to help lighten your workload and ensure our team succeeds."

2. Avoiding:

Avoiders are negotiation ninjas who prefer to dodge confrontation whenever possible. They have a talent for gracefully sidestepping tense situations and choosing their battles wisely. They're the ones who know how to delay a negotiation until the timing is right or delegate the decision-making to a neutral party. They're often seen as tactful and diplomatic, but beware, as important issues can be left unresolved if avoidance becomes a habit.

You're at a car dealership negotiating the price of a vehicle. Being an avoider, you might shy away from confrontation. You could say, "I appreciate your offer, but I need some time to think it over. I'll get back to you once I've reviewed my options and made a decision."

3. Compromising:

Compromisers are the deal-closers who believe in fairness and equality for all parties involved. They're the ones who find a middle ground and make concessions to reach a mutually agreeable outcome. When time is of the essence, they're the heroes who can swiftly strike a compromise. But beware, as their eagerness to wrap things up quickly can sometimes lead to hasty decisions and unnecessary sacrifices.

You're negotiating a contract with a vendor for your business. As a compromiser, you aim for a fair agreement that satisfies both parties. You might propose, "Let's meet halfway on the price and delivery terms. This way, we can maintain a good working relationship while still ensuring profitability for both our companies."

4. Competing:

You're negotiating a salary increase with your employer. As a competitive negotiator, you focus on your achievements and the value you bring to the organization. You might assert, "Considering my exceptional performance and the current market rates, I believe a higher salary is justified. I'm confident that my contributions deserve recognition."

Competitors are negotiation warriors who love the thrill of the game. They possess a strategic mindset and are determined to achieve their goals. They're not afraid to assert their position, and they have a keen instinct for leveraging their strengths. However, their relentless pursuit of victory can sometimes overshadow the importance of building and maintaining relationships.

These negotiators do not give much importance to the relationship with the opposite party. Other characteristics include:

- There is suspicion and hostility in attitude toward the opposite party.
- They use assertive and tough language.
- They would not prefer to bargain over it.
- There may be the use of tools like coercion, threat, or deception.
- They will subtract certain items from the deal to get more profit.
- They will listen less to the opposite party, and they talk more.
- There will be the use of domination over the weaker party.
- The competitive negotiator will close the negotiation by giving a final offer.
- They believe they know best, they may also make a display of authority, which they may not have

5. Cooperative Negotiations

Cooperative negotiations are characterized by agents working together to achieve a common objective that benefits the entire system. Instead of focusing solely on individual interests, cooperative negotiators understand the value of collaboration and strive to find mutually beneficial solutions. Here's an example to illustrate cooperative negotiations:

Imagine a team of architects, engineers, and contractors working on a construction project. Each professional has their expertise and perspective on the project. In a cooperative negotiation, they come together to address any conflicts or challenges by pooling their knowledge and finding the best solutions for the project as a whole.

During the negotiation process, each party expresses their concerns and viewpoints, but instead of competing or trying to dominate the discussion, they actively listen to one another and seek common ground. They understand that by cooperating and sharing information, they can achieve a more optimal outcome.

For example, the architect might emphasize the importance of aesthetics, while the engineer focuses on structural integrity, and the contractor considers cost-effectiveness. Through cooperative negotiations, they engage in open dialogue, consider different perspectives, and work collaboratively to find solutions that meet all of these requirements.

In the end, the cooperative negotiators reach a consensus that balances the priorities of each party. They may modify the initial design, adjust the construction timeline, or find alternative materials that satisfy both the functional and aesthetic aspects of the project. The result is a collaborative effort that maximizes the overall success of the construction project.

Cooperative negotiations emphasize the power of working together, leveraging collective intelligence, and finding win-win solutions that benefit all parties involved. By prioritizing cooperation over competition, negotiators can achieve outcomes that surpass individual interests and contribute to the success of the larger system or project.

Some characteristics of cooperative negotiators are as below:

- The negotiators give importance to the relationship with the opposite party.
- They would communicate with honesty.
- They would use soft language in communication.
- The attitude towards the opposite party is friendly and cooperative.
- They will be ready to compromise and sacrifice.
- They will add certain items to the deal, even if they incur a loss.
- They may talk less and listen more.

TYPES OF NEGOTIATORS

Three basic kinds of negotiators have been identified by researchers at Harvard University. These types of negotiators are:

1. Soft Bargainers,
2. Hard Bargainers
3. Principled Bargainers.

- **Soft**. These people see negotiation as too close to competition, so they choose a gentle style of bargaining. The offers they make are not in their best interests, they yield to others' demands, avoid confrontation, and they maintain good relations with fellow negotiators.

  Their perception of others is one of friendship, and their goal is agreement. They do not separate the people from the problem but are soft on both. They avoid contests of wills and will insist on the agreement, offering solutions and easily trusting others and changing their opinions.

Example: Imagine two business partners negotiating the terms of a contract. A soft bargainer would approach the negotiation with a friendly and cooperative attitude. They would be open to concessions and compromises, seeking to maintain a positive working relationship between the partners.

- **Hard**. These people use contentious strategies to influence, utilizing phrases such as "this is my final offer" and "take it or leave it." They make threats, are distrustful of others, insist on their position, and apply pressure to negotiate.

They see others as adversaries and their ultimate goal is victory. Additionally, they will search for one single answer and insist you agree to it. They do not separate the people from the problem (as with soft bargainers), but they are hard on both the people involved and the problem.

Example: In a business acquisition negotiation, a hard bargainer would push for the best possible deal for their company, using tactics like strong negotiation positions, demanding concessions from the other party, and leveraging their strengths to gain favorable terms.

- **Principled**. Individuals who bargain this way seek integrative solutions and do so by a sidestepping commitment to specific positions. They focus on the problem rather than the intentions, motives, and needs of the people involved.

They separate the people from the problem, explore interests, avoid bottom lines, and reach results based on standards (which are independent of personal will).

They base their choices on objective criteria rather than power, pressure, self-interest, or an arbitrary decisional procedure. These criteria may be drawn from moral standards, principles of fairness, professional standards, tradition, and so on.

Example: Suppose two countries are negotiating a trade agreement. Principled bargainers would strive to understand the underlying interests and concerns of both nations. They would explore potential trade-offs and creative solutions that address the needs of both economies, fostering cooperation and mutual benefits.

It is important to note that negotiators can exhibit a combination of these styles, and their approach may vary depending on the specific situation and their personal preferences. The key is to adapt and employ different strategies based on the context of the negotiation and the desired outcome.

Common Pitfalls To Avoid In Your Negotiations

Negotiation, my friend, is a delicate dance, and even the most skilled negotiators can stumble and leave opportunities on the table if they aren't careful. Let's explore some common pitfalls to watch out for and ensure you don't miss that silver lining:

1. Poor Planning:

   Imagine you are negotiating a salary raise with your employer. However, you haven't researched industry standards, comparable salaries, or the company's financial performance. As a result, you may not have a strong argument or supporting data to justify your request, putting you at a disadvantage during the negotiation.

Successful negotiators don't just wing it; they plan meticulously. Know your priorities, alternatives, and your bottom line—the point where you'll walk away. Time constraints and future negotiation possibilities should also be considered. Don't forget to understand your opponent's agenda too—know their preferences, alternatives, and bottom line. Test your propositions to gauge their priorities.

2. Failing to Pay Attention to Your Opponent:

In a negotiation for purchasing a property, you focus solely on the price without considering the seller's underlying interests. Unknown to you, the seller is motivated by a desire for a quick sale due to financial constraints. By failing to explore their interests, you miss an opportunity to negotiate favorable terms, such as a faster closing timeline or waived inspection contingencies.

You can't just focus on your interests; understanding your opponent's biases and evaluating how they perceive your offers is crucial. Use the technique of "framing" to shape the issues in a way that influences their attitude and risk tolerance. Guide them to see the starting point from your perspective and highlight the unique advantages your proposal offers.

During a negotiation for a business partnership, the other party expresses concerns about the proposed timeline for project completion. Instead of actively listening and addressing their concerns, you dismiss them or fail to fully understand their perspective. This can lead to misunderstandings and hinder progress in reaching an agreement.

3. Assuming That Cross-Cultural Negotiations are less important:

Cultural differences can either be a source of immense benefits or significant problems if ignored. Embrace the differences, as they can enhance your position and create fruitful collaborations. Tailor your services and negotiation strategies to align with the cultural context of the other party.

4. Thinking the Pie is Fixed:

In a negotiation for a business partnership, you assume that the available resources or benefits are limited and fixed. As a result, you compromise too quickly, settling for a less favorable agreement because you believe both parties cannot achieve their desired outcomes. By adopting a mindset of abundance and exploring creative solutions, you may discover options that allow both parties to get more of what they want.

The pie isn't always fixed, my friend. Don't fall into the trap of assuming that both parties can't achieve what they want. In situations where both parties desire the same thing, like negotiating salary, bonus, and vacation, don't compromise unnecessarily. Don't assume you have to settle for the middle ground. Explore creative solutions and seek mutually beneficial outcomes.

5. Paying Too Much Attention to Anchors:

Anchoring and adjustment play a significant role in negotiations. The initial offers set the parameters for bargaining. Don't get fixated on the first offer, whether it's too low or too high. Respond thoughtfully, considering the range between the initial offer and your target. Beware of where the anchors are set, and skillfully navigate the negotiation landscape.

During a negotiation for a used car, the seller starts with an extremely high asking price, setting a high anchor. Despite recognizing the inflated price, you still focus on it throughout the negotiation. As a result, you may overlook other aspects of the deal, such as the condition of the vehicle or potential discounts, which could have allowed you to negotiate a better overall price.

6. Caving in Too Quickly:

Accepting a good deal too quickly can leave both parties dissatisfied. Even if the offer seems fair, always start with a slightly lower counteroffer. This allows your opponent to feel like they've accomplished something in the negotiation. You can always come up to the full price later, but at least they'll appreciate the effort you put into it. Remember, never give anyone their first offer—it drives them crazy!

You're negotiating the terms of a contract with a vendor for your business. Due to time constraints and pressure, you agree to their initial proposal without fully exploring alternative options or negotiating for more favorable terms. Later, you discover that you could have secured better pricing or additional benefits if you had taken the time to explore alternatives and negotiate further.

7. Don't Triumph:

When you've sealed the deal and achieved success, resist the temptation to gloat or revel in your victory. Dancing with joy and boasting about getting a better deal can backfire. Maintaining professional relationships with your negotiating opponents is essential in today's world of corporate alliances and frequent job changes. You never know when you'll be sitting on the same side of the table again.

By being aware of and avoiding these negotiation pitfalls, you can navigate the negotiation process more effectively and increase your chances of achieving favorable outcomes. Remember to prepare thoroughly, actively listen, consider cultural differences, think creatively, and avoid being overly influenced by initial offers or anchors.

Avoiding these common drawbacks, my friend, you'll be well-equipped to navigate the negotiation minefield and emerge with successful outcomes. Keep these lessons in mind as you embark on your negotiation journey, and may the art of negotiation always be in your favor!

THE FIVE PHASES OF NEGOTIATIONS

Knowing how to negotiate can help you out in many situations. For example, the next time you go looking for a sales job, negotiation skills can get you a better commission or a few extra fringe benefits. And when you find yourself on the purchasing side of a transaction, knowing how to negotiate can save you plenty of money.

The first step in any negotiation is knowing what you want to get. This may sound pretty basic, but amid a heated discussion, it's easy to lose track of your original goals. Always attack the easiest issues first.

Each time you and the other party agree on something, it makes him more willing to agree on other points. So if you can reach a consensus on several minor issues then it will be easier to get him to agree on the more difficult points.

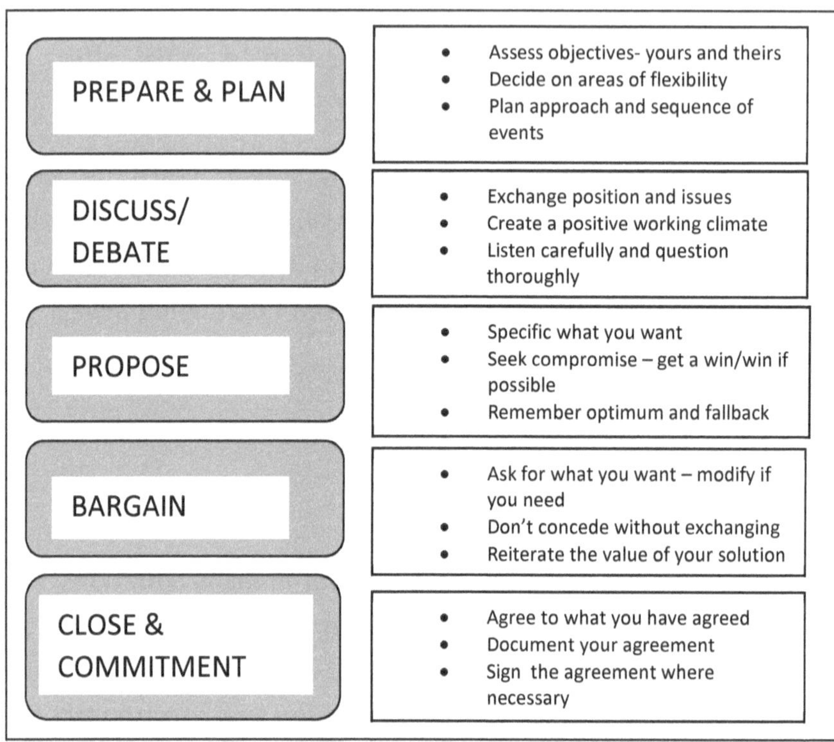

1. PREPARATION AND PLANNING

It is the first step in the negotiation process. Here, both parties will organize and accumulate the information necessary to have an effective negotiation. Information can be powerful in negotiations and help add validity to claims. Both companies should investigate each other's history and try and figure out what the opening offer will be. One party will have to find out the lowest his partner will be willing to pay and the other, the highest amount of benefits involved.

Consideration will be given to questions, such as:

- Where will negotiations take place?
- Will time constraints exist?

2. DISCUSS/DEBATE

In this step, rules and procedures will be established for the negotiation. Consideration will be given to questions, such as:

- Will any issues be off-limits?
- What happens if there's not any agreement?

In addition, both parties will try and figure out what price should be the starting point for the negotiation. Also, demands and expectations should be disclosed honestly. A discussion needs to take place regarding the specifics of the offer. The positions of both parties are discussed at length. Each side will get a chance to explain, justify and support their original request.

This part of the negotiations should not be argumentative, but instead, it should provide the opportunity for each side to educate and inform each other about their position.

3. PROPOSE

Specifically, ask what you want and negotiate for it. As the discussion proceeds, each party may wish to suggest or propose changes to the initial positions, either to their initial position or to the initial position of the other party. The discussion continues in this way, with the parties trying to maintain an element of flexibility until they can reach an agreement that is acceptable to both.

4. BARGAIN

Discuss the problems of implementing the partnership realistically, so that it is both, viable and workable. Hammer out the details as they relate to production, scheduling, handling delays, task responsibility, and authority. You have to use your own technical and management people to streamline the process so it works smoothly, and meets your standards and requirements.

5. CLOSE & COMMITMENT

When an agreement has been reached it is most helpful to make a written record of it, including how the implementation of the agreement will be monitored. Both parties should agree to the content of the written record and sign it.

The final portion of this process is then left to your respective legal experts, to put the agreement into a written form of documentation, and to describe the contractual obligations to which both parties have agreed.

Settling the details correctly and meticulously is extremely important. Many negotiations have collapsed because the parties failed to devote the necessary time and work to address the details efficiently. Until these are properly ironed out, we can't celebrate our success.

o   FOLLOW-UP

Just because you have signed on the dotted line doesn't mean that it ends there. You cannot toss the contract into your files and forget about it. It seldom ends there as problems always arise.

Any aspect of any contract may need to be re-negotiated, or the details altered to counter a broad variety of changing circumstances. Expensive and embittered legal battles can be skipped simply by keeping the lines of communication open with your counterparts. You should be experienced enough to understand, that nothing is ever as simple as it seems today.

Team Negotiations

Due to globalization and evolving business practices, team-based negotiation is increasingly prevalent. Collaborative negotiation by teams allows for the breakdown of complex issues and benefits from the collective knowledge and wisdom of multiple individuals. The diverse expertise within a team enhances problem-solving capabilities and minimizes errors, leading to more favorable negotiation outcomes.

Selecting the appropriate members for your negotiation team is crucial. Genuine and effective bargaining requires the presence of individuals who possess the necessary authority, knowledge, and expertise to engage in productive discussions and make informed decisions. By assembling a well-qualified team, the chances of achieving success in negotiations are significantly heightened.

The team-based approach offers several advantages. Firstly, it enables a broader range of perspectives and insights, which enhances the team's understanding of the negotiation dynamics and the interests of all parties involved.

Secondly, the collective capacity of the team ensures a more comprehensive evaluation of options and potential trade-offs. This enables the team to develop creative solutions that align with the interests of all stakeholders. Additionally, team members can support and complement each other, providing diverse skills and perspectives to tackle different aspects of the negotiation process.

Furthermore, team negotiation fosters familiarity and trust among team members. Regular collaboration and shared experiences strengthen relationships and facilitate effective communication and coordination during negotiations. The team's collective knowledge and shared understanding contribute to smoother interactions with the opposing party and increase the likelihood of reaching mutually beneficial agreements.

In summary, team-based negotiation is a valuable approach in today's globalized business environment. It harnesses the collective intelligence, expertise, and authority of team members, enabling more comprehensive analysis, innovative problem-solving, and effective decision-making. By assembling the right team, organizations can enhance their negotiation outcomes and successfully navigate complex business challenges.

The bargaining team is most likely to be successful if the team members have the authority, knowledge, and expertise to engage in genuine bargaining about the issues involved. This includes:

- Understanding the needs of the business, or businesses, and of the workforce

- Understanding the issues that will arise and the reasons for, and likely effects of, what might be proposed

- Understanding the obligation to bargain in good faith, including the need to make sure the people they represent are kept accurately informed of the direction being taken in the bargaining process

- Being credible advocates for the process among those they represent

- Having the authority to make decisions and clear decision-making processes in place

- Being a representative of and able to communicate with people involved in the different types of jobs and/or work areas covered by the bargaining

- Everyone on the team knows what their roles are (who will take the offers at the bargaining table, who will take notes of what is said, who will communicate to the people they represent and when)

- Investing in the team by appointing members with the appropriate authority and by providing training

- Considering who is on the other party's bargaining team and whether there are relationships that can be drawn on to aid in effective bargaining

- Ensuring that your team has enough time away from the workplace to conduct the bargaining successfully

Providing training for your bargaining team will ensure they are familiar with the legal obligations associated with negotiation and assist your team to operate by the duty of good faith.

Placing Proposals on the Table

The terms parties wish to see in a proposed agreement are referred to as a party's "claims", for instance, a desired pay increase or profits in sales. Clear presentation of claims ensures parties understand what has been offered and it also reduces the risk of conveying the wrong message. It will help if the claim is in writing (along with any external data to support the claim) and a rationale can be provided for advancing or rejecting a claim.

Trust and confidence between the parties can be undermined by changing the basis repeatedly or without good reason or by tabling new claims without warning or late in the process.

Bargaining is generally a process of give and take. This can have implications for a party's claims. It is sensible to leave room for flexibility. If your initial claims are presented on a "take it or leave it" basis, you risk being accused of not genuinely considering what the other side has to say.

Parties in bargaining should engage in genuine dialogue and discussion about needs, restrictions, and challenges. Each party must consider with an open mind what has been claimed and, if a proposal is not accepted, explain so that everyone understands why there is disagreement.

Delaying a response merely for tactical advantage or dismissing a proposal without any consideration may be inconsistent with the obligations of good faith. If a claim is not accepted you should explain why. The extent to which a party explains its decision may be relevant to whether the issues involved have been genuinely considered, and whether the behavior is judged to have been in good faith.

Reporting back

Bargaining representatives have a responsibility to advance the interests of those they represent, and also to the bargaining process itself. This includes doing all they reasonably can to ensure the process is orderly, efficient, and effective.

Part of a successful process is reporting back to the people you represent accurately and comprehensively. Simplistic or incomplete explanations of the other party's position can both mislead and inflame the situation, as can anecdotes when taken out of context.

Although bargaining representatives are always entitled to give their views to those they represent, what is said must not be misleading or deceptive. Focusing on one component of the negotiation to the detriment of others could be seen as misleading.

A report back may be undertaken jointly or separately by the bargaining partners but good-practice options include agreeing on the facts to be released, or a written record of the bargaining.

Parties to the bargain must act in good faith and that means not doing anything to deceive or mislead each other. Parties should not:

- renege on agreed positions such as agreements during the course of negotiations or agreements to endorse proposals for settlement
- refuse to sign a negotiated settlement.

When an agreement is reached at the table it is still only a proposal until the parties have ratified it. Be sure to commit that proposal to writing and have all parties sign the document. This is called a *Terms of Settlement* and it can smoothen the process between the negotiators at the table.

Some Common Barriers To Your Bargaining Power

Bargainers or negotiators are human. They are subject to being distracted by personal problems, other matters, and even exhaustion. To a lesser extent, bargainers can be distracted by delays in a meeting, the hostile behavior of someone in the room, or by some form of external stimuli.

Being comfortable is an essential ingredient to being effective as a negotiator or bargainer. Before entering into any agreement meeting, put aside your issues and clear your mind. If the other issues are such that you can't do this, don't start the negotiation. Ask for a postponement or send someone else.

You need to have all of your faculties focused to do the job properly. Such distractions are barriers or obstacles that stand in the way of a successful negotiation. Better put, barriers are obstacles to effective bargaining. These are some great insights into the barriers and obstacles that can arise during negotiations. Here are some suggested solutions to overcome these challenges:

1. INTERPERSONAL ISSUES: Before entering into a negotiation, it is crucial to settle any personal differences with the other party. Addressing these issues beforehand can prevent confrontations that might hinder the negotiation process.

2. POOR COMMUNICATION: Maintain professionalism in your language, tone, and gestures during negotiations. Effective

communication is key to a successful negotiation. Listen actively to the other party and strive to understand their perspective.

3. 'HARDBALL' ATTITUDES: Recognize that negotiation is not about winning at the expense of the other party. Be flexible and open to compromises. Avoid making unreasonable offers and instead focus on finding mutually beneficial solutions.

4. LIMITATIONS: Limited resources can create challenges in negotiations. If both parties share a desire to reach a compromise, engage in collaborative problem-solving to overcome these limitations. Brainstorm creative solutions and encourage active participation from all parties involved.

5. NEGATIVE EMOTIONS: Negotiations can be stressful and emotions can run high. Acknowledge that diverse perspectives and interests exist and address them openly. Instead of reacting with escalating emotions, try expressing empathy or offering a sincere apology to defuse tense situations and create a more collaborative atmosphere.

6. NEGOTIATION STRATEGY: Thoroughly prepare for negotiations by understanding your objectives and researching the interests of the other parties involved. Anticipate arguments and arm yourself with alternative solutions. Be willing to compromise and make concessions while considering factors like timing and other circumstances that might impact the negotiation.

7. LACK OF TRUST: Building trust is essential for successful negotiations. Establish open and honest communication with the other party. Emphasize the importance of reliability and ask for documentation to support the data presented. Consider using

enforcement mechanisms, such as financial penalties or security deposits, to ensure compliance with contractual terms.

8. CULTURAL AND GENDER BARRIERS: Avoid making assumptions or jumping to conclusions based on cultural or gender differences. Take the time to analyze the situation thoroughly and step outside of preconceptions or biases. Foster an environment of understanding and respect for diverse perspectives.

9. SPOILERS: Be prepared for spoilers who may try to sabotage negotiations. Identify their motivations and understand their fears. Counter their resistance by highlighting the benefits they stand to gain from the proposed agreement. Offer them active roles and assure them of their importance in the negotiation process.

By addressing these barriers and implementing the suggested solutions, negotiators can improve their effectiveness and increase the chances of reaching mutually beneficial agreements.

Counter their resistance and explain 'why' this change will benefit them. Illuminate their gains and explain that they may profit from the proposed venture. Offer them roles so that they will be able to retain control over their business and be more proactive in the negotiation process. Assure them that they will be active and productive members of a partnership.

ADVANCED BARGAINING: UNLEASHING WINNING TACTICS

Tactics are always an important part of the bargaining process. But tactics don't often jump up and down shouting "Here I am, look at me." If they did, the other side would see right through them and they would not be effective.

More often than not, they are subtle, difficult to identify, and used for multiple purposes. Tactics are more frequently used when the focus is on taking as much value off the table as possible.

Many bargaining tactics exist. Below are a few commonly used ones:

Anchoring:

The tactic of anchoring involves making an initial offer or setting a reference point that strongly influences the negotiation range. For example, when selling a used car, the seller might start with a higher asking price, anchoring the buyer's perception of the car's value and influencing the subsequent negotiation toward a higher selling price.

Auction:

The bidding process is designed to create competition. When multiple parties want the same thing, pitch them against one another. When people know that they may lose out on something, they will want it even more. Not only do they want the thing that is being bid on, but they also want to win, just to win. Taking advantage of someone's competitive nature can drive up the price.

Brinksmanship:

One party aggressively pursues a set of terms to the point at which the other negotiating party must either agree or walk away. Brinkmanship is a type of "hard nut" approach to bargaining in which one party pushes the other party to the "brink" or edge of what that party is willing to accommodate. Successful brinksmanship convinces the other party they have no choice but to accept the offer and there is no acceptable alternative to the proposed agreement.

Bogey:

Bargainers use the bogey tactic to pretend that an issue of little or no importance to him or her is very important. Then, later in the negotiation, the issue can be traded for a major concession of actual importance.

Chicken:

Bargainers propose extreme measures, often bluffs, to force the other party to chicken out and give them what they want. This tactic can be dangerous when parties are unwilling to back down and go through with the extreme measure.

Defense in Depth:

Several layers of decision-making authority are used to allow further concessions each time the agreement goes through a different level of authority. In other words, each time the offer goes to a decision maker, that decision maker asks to add another concession to close the deal.

Deadlines:

Give the other party a deadline forcing them to make a decision. This method uses the time to apply pressure to the other party. Deadlines given can be actual or artificial. This tactic involves creating a sense of urgency by setting deadlines or time constraints.

For example, a supplier may offer a discount on a product but only if the buyer agrees to the terms within a limited timeframe, creating pressure to make a quick decision.

Flinch:

Flinching is showing a strong negative physical reaction to a proposal. Common examples of flinching are gasping for air, or a visible expression of surprise or shock. The flinch can be done consciously or unconsciously.

The flinch signals to the opposite party that you think the offer or proposal is absurd in hopes the other party will lower their aspirations. Seeing a physical reaction is more believable than hearing someone say, "I'm shocked."

For instance, during salary negotiations, a job candidate might flinch in response to the initial salary offer, signaling that it falls below their expectations and prompting the employer to reconsider and improve the offer.

Good Guy/Bad Guy:

The good guy/bad guy approach is typically used in team negotiations where one member of the team makes extreme or unreasonable demands, and the other offers a more rational approach.

This tactic is named after a police interrogation technique often portrayed in the media. The "good guy" will appear more reasonable and understanding, and therefore, easier to work with. In essence, it is using the law of relativity to attract cooperation. The good guy will appear more agreeable relative to the "bad guy." This tactic is easy to spot because of its frequent use.

In a real estate negotiation, a buyer's agent acts as the "good guy" and expresses understanding and empathy toward the seller's concerns. Meanwhile, the buyer, represented by a different agent, takes a more aggressive approach by making unreasonable demands and presenting lowball offers. The seller is more likely to perceive the first agent as easier to work with and may be more willing to compromise.

Highball/Lowball:

When selling a used car, the seller starts by asking for an unreasonably high price, well above the market value. This is a highball offer designed to set a higher anchor point for negotiation. The potential buyer, in response, counters with a significantly lower offer, the lowball, which is below the expected market price. This tactic aims to create a perceived "middle ground" where the final agreed-upon price will still be favorable to the seller.

Depending on whether selling or buying, sellers or buyers use a ridiculously high, or ridiculously low opening offer that will never be achieved. The theory is that the extreme offer will cause the other party to reevaluate his or her opening offer and move close to the resistance point (as far as you are willing to go to reach an agreement).

Another advantage is that the person giving the extreme demand appears more flexible he or she makes concessions toward a more reasonable outcome. A danger of this tactic is that the opposite party may think negotiating is a waste of time.

The Nibble:

Nibbling is asking for proportionally small concessions that haven't been discussed previously just before closing the deal. This method takes advantage of the other party's desire to close by adding "just one more thing."

For example, a customer purchasing a new computer may negotiate the price, warranty, and accessories and then proceed to nibble by requesting a free software upgrade or an extended service plan.

Snow Job:

Negotiators overwhelm the other party with so much information that he or she has difficulty determining which facts are important, and which facts are diversions. Negotiators may also use technical language or jargon to mask a simple answer to a question asked by a non-expert.

For instance, imagine a software company selling a sophisticated data analytics tool to a potential client. During the negotiation, the sales representative bombards the buyer with an extensive presentation that includes intricate technical specifications, complex algorithms, and in-depth case studies.

The intention is to create an illusion of superior value and complexity, making it harder for the buyer to evaluate the software objectively. By overwhelming the buyer with information, the seller aims to steer the negotiation toward the perceived complexity of the product rather than focusing on its actual cost and value.

It's important to approach negotiations with transparency and ensure that information is shared clearly and concisely. Falling for a snow job can lead to making decisions based on confusion rather than a thorough understanding of the terms and values at hand.

In conclusion, effective bargaining and negotiation are not only about strategies and tactics but also about the individuals involved and their unique character and personality traits. While the negotiation process can be influenced by various barriers and challenges, it is the people at the negotiating table who ultimately determine the outcome.

Successful negotiators understand the importance of building rapport and establishing trust with the other party. They are aware that interpersonal dynamics play a significant role in shaping the negotiation process. By addressing personal issues and clearing their minds before entering into negotiations, negotiators can create a comfortable and conducive environment for productive discussions.

Moreover, skilled negotiators possess excellent communication skills and understand the impact of their language, tone, and gestures on the negotiation outcome. They are not only professional in their approach but also empathetic, recognizing the diverse perspectives and interests of all parties involved.

By actively listening to opposing viewpoints and demonstrating understanding, negotiators can foster a collaborative atmosphere and facilitate constructive dialogue.

Characteristics like flexibility, adaptability, and resilience are also vital in the negotiation process. Successful negotiators anticipate and navigate obstacles, whether they are limited resources, negative emotions, or cultural and gender barriers. They approach negotiations with an open mind, willing to consider alternatives and make concessions when necessary.

Their ability to remain calm and composed under pressure enables them to find creative solutions and reach mutually beneficial agreements.

Furthermore, negotiators who exhibit integrity and honesty can establish trust and credibility, which are crucial for successful negotiations. By acting as good-faith partners, negotiators can foster an atmosphere of cooperation and transparency.

They demonstrate reliability by providing supporting documentation and enforcing agreements through mechanisms such as financial penalties or security deposits.

Lastly, negotiation is a dynamic and evolving process that requires continuous learning and growth. Successful negotiators invest time in thorough preparation, researching the interests of the other parties, and arming themselves with alternative solutions. They are lifelong learners who recognize the value of self-reflection and improvement in honing their negotiation skills.

In essence, negotiation is not solely about the technical aspects; it is about the people involved and the qualities they bring to the table. By weaving character and personality into the negotiation process, negotiators can enhance their effectiveness, build stronger relationships, and achieve mutually satisfactory outcomes.

Through the right mix of strategies, interpersonal skills, and individual strengths, negotiators can master the art of negotiation and forge successful agreements.

I have the mind of a good negotiator.

I declare that I will not be distracted by my personal

problems on the negotiating table.

I walk in the wisdom of God and cannot be deceived by crooks.

Any barrier that stands in my way is brought down

by the power of the Holy Spirit.

I will not be a weak negotiator with any

negative tactics of my opponent.

I am favored in whatever deal that I get involved

and will nail every deal in Jesus' name.

Amen

Summary of points

i. "Negotiation is the process of two individuals or groups reaching joint agreement about differing needs or ideas."

ii. Competitive negotiators have strong instincts for all aspects of negotiating and are often strategic

iii. Cooperative negotiators put together an optimized partial view and cooperate to reach a common object.

iv. Hard Negotiators make threats, are distrustful of others, insist on their position, and apply pressure to negotiate.

v. Negotiators are human and are subject to being distracted by personal problems or other matters

vi. Some barriers to effective negotiations are poor communication, hardball attitudes, negative emotions, lack of trust, etc.

vii. There is more knowledge and wisdom dispersed in a team than in a single mind.

viii. Bargaining representatives have a responsibility to advance the interests of those they represent

ix. Brinkmanship is a "hard nut" approach in which one party pushes the other to the "brink" or edge of what that party is willing to accommodate.

x.   Nibbling is a method that takes advantage of the other party's desire to close by adding "just one more thing."

CHAPTER SIX

BARGAIN TO GAIN, BETTER TO SUSTAIN AND REMAIN

"Don't bargain for fish which are still in the water."
Indian Proverb

You have learned about the basic principles in your bargaining quest in life. No matter who you are or where you find yourself now, you are negotiating your way through one thing or the other. It may be in your relationship with friends or loved ones, profession, or business environment.

You have discovered basic factors to look out for in the previous chapter like the authenticity of the *'offeror'* or source of the deal. The willingness and ability of the other party to deliver on what is in the contract and the legal framework to look out for. One major key to anticipate is the trustworthiness and loyalty to the objectives spelled out.

In addition, you must be ready to take well-calculated risks in the fulfillment of your objectives as a partner and never be afraid of what might never happen. Take a plunge and finally be prepared to share your successes with other people especially those less privileged in the society and generations unborn. The sacrifices you make today have great dividends in the future.

As earlier intimated, my main aim in writing this book is to stir in your heart a fresh hunger and desire to rise above all odds and bargain your way through the many daunting challenges of our time and make headway towards the realization of your dreams. This I believe you can achieve successfully by knowing and activating YOUR BARGAINING POWER!

In this chapter, you will learn about a man who was confronted by the elders of his fatherland to lead them in war after he had been cast away and banished from the land through no fault of his.

Though the son of a "prostitute", he did not allow the circumstances surrounding his birth keep him down. He was presented with a *blank cheque* and he needed to rewrite his destiny by negotiating for a better price at a juncture in his life.

He needed to sign a contract with older people but, due to his ability to bargain, he got more than what he wanted and ended up becoming the President of the entire nation. I have thus entitled this chapter, BARGAIN TO GAIN, BUT IT'S BETTER TO REMAIN.

He could have asked for lots of material things including silver, gold, and modern garments but realized that to GAIN all these things were good but to REMAIN in the hearts of the people was better. The material things you gain today can be lost, but those graces and inner qualities you allow to remain with you and in others are forever.

"I've learned that people will forget what you said,

people will forget what you did,

but people will never forget how you made them feel."

Maya Angelou

He wanted those inner qualities which no one could take away from him and these lasted longer and brought more fulfillment and joy to him as a person. Let us, therefore, take a more critical look at the ensuing proposal that he tabled before the partners as he was tended with the contract of leading the battle.

And Jephthah said unto the elders of GILEAD,

"if ye bring me HOME again

to FIGHT against the CHILDREN OF AMMON,

and the Lord deliver them before me,

shall I be YOUR HEAD?"

Judges 11: 9

PRINCIPLE #

1. **IDENTIFICATION** -Reinstatement as a son of the land

Jephthah's foremost motivation stemmed from the denial of his birthright, the inheritance and recognition as a true son of Gilead, the patriarch of the land. Being a son meant more than just lineage; it signified a connection to his roots and a sense of belonging. Jephthah longed to reclaim his true identity, as he felt that something significant was missing in his life, despite his achievements as a wilderness champion.

Carrying a specific name in society often comes with inherent benefits and privileges. Some individuals are fortunate to receive kindness and favor based on the positive legacy established by their ancestors. A good name carries weight and commands respect. Even after their passing, the mention of their family name continues to evoke admiration and attention. Unfortunately, Jephthah lacked this advantage, despite his father's prominent role as the founder of the entire lineage or clan of Gilead.

The desire to restore his rightful place and gain the recognition associated with his family name served as a driving force for Jephthah. It symbolized not only a personal quest but also the restoration of his heritage and the reinstatement of his family's honor.

Some people have been shown kindness due to the good legacy left behind by their forefathers. They may not know it but, the mere mention of their family names attracts special attention to them. The name speaks volumes even after death.

This was lacking in the case of Jephthah, even though his father was the founder of the entire lineage or clan of Gilead. A good name sells big!

Identify your identity

Many individuals in today's world can relate to the experiences of Jephthah, where their sense of identity feels lost or fragmented. They carry a deep emptiness and hopelessness due to the absence of a mother or father figure in their lives, whether biological or adoptive. Some have been orphaned from a young age, while others are aware that their biological parents are alive somewhere but remain unknown to them.

I have a friend who, for most of his life, believed that his cousin was his mother. She had taken care of him since his birth, fulfilling the role of a mother. However, his world was shattered when, at the age of fifteen, he discovered that his biological mother, who had abandoned him at birth, was actually present before him. The revelation left him furious and deeply upset, as he had never known her.

Similarly, my younger brother, Ebenezer, had no knowledge of our biological mother until he was about five years old. She had returned from Europe one day, having left us as infants to seek a better life. During her absence, we were raised by our grandmother and other family members.

Our mother had made the difficult decision to leave us behind due to challenges in her marriage and her desire to take control of her own life. She embarked on a journey to find greener pastures, hoping to provide us with a better future someday.

These stories reflect the struggles faced by many individuals who grapple with a fragmented or absent sense of identity due to the absence of a parental figure. It highlights the complexities and emotions that arise when one's true origins and family connections are revealed later in life.

Mum died without realizing many dreams

It was 4:30 am on February 19th, 2014, when the piercing sound of my ringing phone startled me awake. Reluctantly, I pulled myself out of bed, anticipating yet another distress call from one of my clients in the financial sector. However, this call was different. In the background, I could hear loud cries, a male adult's voice filled with agony and despair.

To my surprise, it was my stepdad on the other end of the line, his voice hoarse and broken as he struggled to convey the heartbreaking news. "Rich, your mother just passed away!" he repeated, his words weighed down by the weight of his grief. The world seemed to stand still as I processed the shocking revelation.

I couldn't believe it. I questioned how it could have happened. 'Just an hour earlier, she had complained of chest pains, and before we could rush her to the nearest hospital, she was gone', said my step dad. My hand trembled, and I almost dropped the phone as the reality of the situation sunk in.

The night before, I had spoken to her at 8:30 in the evening, and she was perfectly fine, bidding me goodnight as we always did. And now, she was gone. The tragedy of it all engulfed me, and my voice echoed through the quiet morning, awakening my neighbors to the news.

But even in the face of such devastating loss, there is hope. Beloved, you may find yourself in a similar situation, grappling with profound challenges and uncertainties. Yet, you have the power to negotiate your way through this troubled world and emerge victorious.

One person who inspires me greatly in Ghana is Mr. Emmanuel Dei-Tumi, the CEO of the Foundation for Future Leaders Group (FFLG). He, too, experienced the loss of his parents at a young age, yet he has risen above his circumstances to become one of the most successful people coaches and personality development trainers in the country.

Through his motivational programs, especially among the youth, which have been aired on national television, he has touched countless lives and earned national recognition for his work. Despite his humble background, he has proven that with determination and resilience, one can overcome adversity and achieve greatness.

So, dear reader, take heart and remember that even in the midst of tragedy and challenges, there is always a way forward. You have the ability to negotiate your path to success and create a bright future for yourself.

John Luthuli

You can make it with or without your biological parents. John Luthuli was born near Bulawayo on a Seventh-Day Adventist mission, in South Africa. His father died when he was an infant, and so his mother sent him back to the family's traditional home at Groutville in Natal. Luthuli lived in the household of his uncle several kilometers away from his mother.

Through thin and thick and despite a difficult childhood he rose to become the President-General of the African National Congress from December 1952 until he died in 1967, and recipient of the Nobel Peace Prize in 1960, Luthuli was the most widely known and respected African leader of his era.

In 1920 he received a government bursary to attend a higher teachers' training course at Adams College and subsequently joined the training college staff. For 17 years he immersed himself in the local problems of his people, adjudicating, mediating local quarrels, and organizing South African cane growers to guard their interests.

Through minor clashes with white authority, he gained his first immediate experience with African political predicaments. Beginning his career in national politics, Luthuli defeated Selby Msimang in a by-election for a successor to Dube on the Natives' Representative Council. John Luthuli was returned unopposed to the semi-defunct council in 1948.

Luthuli issued a statement, "The Road to Freedom is via the Cross," perhaps the most famous statement of his principles. A belief in non-violence, a conviction that apartheid degrades all who are party to it, and an optimism that whites would sooner or later be compelled to change hearts and accept a shared society.

The notoriety gained by his dismissal, his eloquence, his unimpeachable character, and his demonstrated loyalty to the ANC all made Luthuli a natural candidate to succeed ANC President James Moroka, who at his trial during the Defiance Campaign had tried to dissociate himself from the other defendants.

At the annual conference of December 1952, Luthuli was elected ANC president-general by a large majority. Bans imposed in early 1953 and renewed in the following year prevented him from giving direction to the day-to-day activities of Congress, but as a country-bred "man of the people," combining the most inspiring qualities of Christian and traditional leadership, he provided a powerful symbol for an organization struggling to rally mass support.

He was re-elected president-general in 1955 and 1958. Although bans confined him to his rural home throughout his presidency, he nevertheless was able to write statements and speeches for presentation at ANC conferences, and occasionally circumstances permitted him to attend conferences personally.

In December 1956 he was included in the treason arrests but was released with 60 others in late 1957 after the pre-trial examination. He always defended the rights of people of all ideological persuasions to play their part in the struggle for African equality.

In 1960, Luthuli sought to rally Africans to resistance by publicly burning his pass in Pretoria, by an ANC decision, and calling for a national day of mourning. On March 30, he was detained and held until August, when he was tried and sentenced to a £100 fine and a six-month suspended sentence.

He was allowed to travel to Oslo to receive the Nobel Peace Prize in December 1961, an award that Die Transvaler labeled "an inexplicable pathological phenomenon."

No matter the challenges of your background, you can make it to the zenith of your life. Your lack of biological parents should not be an excuse for you to lament and limit yourself. Like John and Jephthah, learn to bargain with the resources and innate potential you have.

Yours could be singing, cooking, drumming, rapping, a particular sporting activity, motivation, reading and writing, cracking funny jokes, modeling, playing a particular musical instrument, selling, preaching, praying, etc. Put them to good use and you never know who will need your services one day. You may end up in the Castle one day if you do not give up.

From limbless into nimbleness

Meet Hirotoda, a remarkable man who defies all odds. Despite being born without hands and legs, he has refused to let his physical limitations define him. Instead of succumbing to a life of begging on the roadside, Hirotoda has chosen to rise above his circumstances and achieve extraordinary things.

Using his chin and shoulders, he has mastered the art of writing and completed his education. But he didn't stop there. Hirotoda went on to write an autobiography called 'GOTAI FUMANZOKU,' which became a bestseller in Japan. His story of resilience and determination captured the hearts of readers, inspiring them to look beyond their own limitations.

Not content with just personal accomplishments, Hirotoda pursued a career in teaching. With his education degree in hand, he embarked on a journey to impart knowledge and empower others. He has become a teacher, defying expectations and proving that a disability does not limit one's potential.

Reflecting on Hirotoda's achievements, we are reminded that our excuses pale in comparison. We have been blessed with fully functioning bodies and countless abilities. If Hirotoda can accomplish so much with his challenges, then we, too, have the power to make a difference in our own lives and the lives of others.

So, let Hirotoda's story serve as a powerful motivator. Let it be a call to action, urging us to seize the present moment and take steps towards our goals. There is no time to waste. Embrace your abilities, embrace your potential, and make a meaningful impact in the world today. The choice is yours.

" You block your dream when you allow

Your fear to grow bigger than your faith"

Mary Morrissey

PRINCIPLE #

2. **DOMESTICATION-** A home, not a house

In the pursuit of success, it is easy to accumulate material possessions and achieve external accomplishments. However, true satisfaction and fulfillment go beyond mere material wealth. Jephthah's story teaches us this valuable lesson.

Despite his achievements in the wilderness, Jephthah felt a deep longing for something more. He yearned for a sense of belonging and a loving family who would accept him unconditionally. Material possessions alone could not fill the void in his heart.

Jephthah's desire to come home to a caring and loving family stemmed from his need for emotional connection and acceptance. He longed for a place where he could be embraced for who he truly was, where his worth was not measured by his accomplishments but by the love and grace bestowed upon him.

This aspect of Jephthah's story reminds us of the importance of relationships and genuine human connection. No amount of material possessions can substitute for the warmth and love found within a family that accepts and cherishes us for who we are.

It serves as a reminder to prioritize nurturing meaningful relationships, fostering love, and creating a sense of belonging in our lives. Ultimately, true contentment and fulfillment come from the bonds we form with others and the love we share, rather than the accumulation of material wealth alone.

"I long, as does every human being,

to be at home wherever I find myself."

Maya Angelou

Indeed, the importance of family cannot be overstated. While financial success and material possessions may bring temporary happiness, true fulfillment lies in the love, support, and care of our loved ones.

No matter how successful or wealthy we become, without a loving and supportive family, we may still feel a sense of emptiness and loneliness. Our homes may be grand, but it is the presence of family members that truly makes it a warm and comforting place.

Family provides a sense of belonging, unconditional love, and emotional support. They are the ones who stand by us through thick and thin, offering guidance, encouragement, and understanding. In times of hardship, they are there to lift us up and provide solace.

Friends may come and go, but family remains a constant presence in our lives. They share our joys, sorrows, and achievements, providing a solid foundation of love and connection. They celebrate our successes and stand by us during challenging times, offering strength and reassurance.

As we navigate the challenges and obstacles on our journey to success, it is essential to prioritize and nurture our relationships with family. By cherishing and valuing our loved ones, we create a strong support system that sustains us through the ups and downs of life.

So, in your pursuit of success and as you bargain your way through life's challenges, always remember to prioritize your family and loved ones. Cultivate meaningful connections, invest time in building strong relationships, and express your love and gratitude for the people who bring joy and meaning to your life.

As Olivia Newton-John wisely said, "Family, nature, and health all go together." Family is an integral part of our overall well-being and happiness. Embrace and appreciate the blessings of family, and they will be a constant source of strength and happiness on your journey to the top.

Who was coming to visit me...?

During my time at Presbyterian Boys Senior High School (PRESEC, Legon), I found myself resorting to unconventional means to find solace. I would discreetly make my way from the dormitory to the secluded classrooms known as 'Sodom and Gomorrah' during my weekend rest periods. There, I would study or sleep, seeking refuge from the emotional turmoil that accompanied visiting hours.

From my top bunk bed, I had a clear view through the windows of the dormitory. I observed with a heavy heart as parents and guardians visited their children, their cars brimming with bags of provisions and mouthwatering homemade food. The sight of their luxurious vehicles and the excitement that filled the air only intensified my feelings of longing and isolation.

PRESEC was a prestigious school, attracting students from affluent families, including children of prominent leaders. These privileged students received frequent visits from their loved ones, greeted with great fanfare and affection.

As I pretended to be asleep, I would hear the senior on duty call out the names of my peers, beckoning them to meet their visitors. Peering through the windows, I witnessed the embraces, kisses, and smiles that accompanied these cherished family reunions.

And there I was, engulfed in a profound sense of despair. No one came to visit me. Not a single farewell message or provisions to sustain me. As I watched the joyous celebrations of my classmates' families, I wept silently, my pillow becoming soaked with tears. The stark contrast of their experiences only amplified my yearning for a loving and caring family of my own. It was this poignant realization that led me to forgo the solace of siestas during my time in boarding school.

I craved a home, a place where I would be embraced and supported by a family that cared deeply for me. It is crucial to recognize that as we strive for financial success and chase worldly achievements, we must prioritize the well-being of our families, especially our spouses and children. Numerous accomplished individuals have faltered, sacrificing their familial bonds in pursuit of wealth. Let us learn from their mistakes and avoid repeating them.

Providing financial stability and meeting material needs is not the sole responsibility we have towards our families. True fulfillment lies in nurturing the bonds of love, spending quality time together, and creating a supportive and nurturing environment. Let us not overlook the profound impact that genuine care, attention, and emotional support can have on our loved ones.

As you navigate the pursuit of wealth and success, remember that the true measure of abundance lies in the strength and happiness of your family. Treasure the moments shared, the laughter, and the conversations that forge lasting connections. Invest your time, energy, and love into building a home that becomes a sanctuary of warmth, acceptance, and unwavering support.

"A man should never neglect

his family for business."
Walt Disney

Indeed, peace is a vital ingredient in truly savoring our accomplishments. The adage that states we can select our friends but not our family holds wisdom.

It is crucial to devote our lives to demonstrating to our loved ones that they will forever have their family to provide care and unwavering support, regardless of the circumstances they encounter. These enduring connections are what withstand the test of time and hold great significance.

As Jet Li aptly expressed, perceiving the world as one vast family reminds us of our shared humanity and the importance of extending assistance to one another.

Embracing this perspective allows us to foster compassion, empathy, and unity among all people. By working together and offering support to those around us, we contribute to the well-being of our global family and create a world where care and cooperation prevail.

PRINCIPLE #

3.   RESTITUTION- Inheritance restored

Jephthah also wanted all his inheritance restored to him. All that he had lost since his expulsion needed to be given back to him. To inherit is to receive money or property from someone after he or she is dead. It also means to be born with a particular physical or mental quality that a parent, grandparent, or other relatives in the family have.

Jephthah's desire to regain his inheritance goes beyond material possessions. He recognizes the importance of the intangible qualities passed down from his parents. These qualities, such as moral upbringing, courage, respect, and truthfulness, hold great value and cannot be bought or acquired through money alone. They are the foundation of his identity and the key to restoring the greatness of his lineage.

In our own lives, we too have inherited certain qualities and traits from our families. Some may be positive, while others may be negative.

It is important to recognize and embrace the good qualities we have inherited and work to cultivate them further. At the same time, we must be aware of any negative patterns or behaviors that have been passed down and actively strive to break those cycles.

Bargaining our way to success involves not only leveraging our external resources but also developing and honing our inner qualities. It requires self-improvement, continuous learning, and personal growth. By investing in ourselves and acquiring new skills and knowledge, we enhance our bargaining power and increase our value in the marketplace.

While material possessions may come and go, the qualities and skills we develop remain with us for a lifetime. They are the true assets that can propel us to greater heights and open doors of opportunities.

So, instead of dwelling on past pain or complaining about our circumstances, let us focus on building ourselves, negotiating for the things that truly matter, and striving for excellence in all aspects of life.

PRINCIPLE #

4. **CONTENTIONS-** Fight against the opposition
Jephthah needed to defeat the enemy before he could enjoy all the privileges he was enumerating. They were not going to come on a *silver plata* though. Life does not give you what you deserve but what you fight for.

"He who is not courageous enough

to take risks will accomplish nothing in life."

Muhammad Ali

No matter the good intentions you have, if you fail to fight the opposition and win, you will remain unsuccessful. As far as this earth is concerned, you are in charge here so take charge! Fight the fight of faith and win.

Hard Work Pays

Always bear in mind that your resolution to succeed is more important than any other thing. The dictionary is the only place where *success* comes before *work*. Hard work is the price we must pay for success. You can accomplish anything if you're willing to pay the price.

Hollywood loves to dramatize the lives of great boxers. But it has so far ignored the most incredible ring story since Muhammad Ali. Then again, it would be difficult to make a movie about Bernard Hopkins—both because his career had seemed like it would never end, and because if someone wrote a script about Hopkins's journey, no Hollywood producer would believe it was true.

Hopkins began boxing after leaving prison, gained fame first as a knockout artist and later as a crafty defensive fighter, and is now one of the oldest successful pro boxers ever.

But if Hopkins had fought in the 1950s, when boxing on TV was part of mainstream American culture, he would have been a household name. As it is, old Hopkins had to settle for a few million devotees who tuned in to see what could well be his last fight along with several thousand ringside at Brooklyn's Barclays Center when he faced the International Boxing Federation light-heavyweight (limit 175 pounds) champion Tavoris Cloud, who was 17 years his junior.

Bernard Humphrey Hopkins, Jr. was born on January 15, 1965, in Philadelphia. He grew up in perhaps the most crime-ridden projects in Philly. By the time he was 11, he was already into petty theft; within two years, he was mugging people and had been to the emergency room three times with stab wounds.

He joined a gang and graduated with higher crimes. By the age of 18, he had accumulated a rap sheet longer than his left arm. In 1982, after racking up nine felonies, he was sent to Graterford Prison for 18 years.

As he once told a reporter for the *Philadelphia Daily News*, "I saw worse stuff inside prison than I ever saw in the streets. I saw guys raped, beaten, and tortured. When I saw a guy murdered for a lousy pack of cigarettes, something in me snapped. I knew that I had to be responsible for turning my own life around."

Around his 21st birthday, he discovered boxing. A cliché about fighters is that many are violent men who come out of the pugilistic trade more violent than they went in. According to legend—which Hopkins helped create himself—the warden of Graterford Prison told him upon his release after five years, "You'll be back." To which Hopkins supposedly replied, "No, I ain't ever coming back here again."

Whether or not the exchange ever happened, the important part is that Hopkins kept his vow. He became a convert and swore off drugs, alcohol, and even junk food. He lost his first fight in 1988, got discouraged, and then refocused; resuming his career nearly 16 months later and earning his first win.

Over the next two years, he scored 21 victories in 21 fights, 16 by KO and 12 of those in the first round. He gave himself the nickname "The Executioner." "I know it sounds kind of dumb," he told a boxing writer, "but I couldn't think of anything else to call myself, and it got me noticed. I got on TV a lot."

In 1993, five years after leaving Graterford, Hopkins had his first big fight, against middleweight champion Roy Jones, regarded by analysts as the best pound-for-pound fighter in the world. Hopkins had yet another setback, losing badly, though he finished the match.

Discouraged and disgusted, seven months later he pulled it together for another big fight, meeting the IBF number one contender Segundo Mercado in Quito, Ecuador. Dizzy from the 10,000-foot altitude, Hopkins was knocked down twice and nearly counted out. He pulled himself up to win a decision.

In April of 1994, re-matched with Mercado in Landover, Maryland, he won on a seventh-round KO and became the middleweight champ. Some writers were calling him the best fighter in the game; he certainly looked it, making 12 consecutive title defenses. Finally, he got his revenge against Jones, spectacularly knocking him down en route to a unanimous decision. Some people said that Jones, age 37, was over the hill.

Since then, Hopkins has lost a couple but won many more, compiling a ring record of 52 wins, six losses, and two draws. When he turned 40 in 2005, he seemed to lose much of his fabled knockout power but replaced it with ring craft and guile.

The late, great boxing historian Bert Sugar said during a TV broadcast that "younger, stronger fighters would try to bull rush Hopkins only to find that he could tie them up tighter than Willie Nelson's headband." He developed into a superb defensive fighter; some compared him to "The Mongoose" himself, Archie Moore.

"Younger guys would think that an old boxer must be an easy target," Sugar said, "Only to find out when they stood in front of him they couldn't hit him with a handful of stones."

At 46 years, four months, and 10 days old, Hopkins broke George Foreman's record to become the oldest fighter ever to win a world championship. A few months later, in perhaps the crowning achievement of his career, he won a unanimous decision over Pascal to take *The Ring's* version of the light-heavyweight title.

At 46 years, four months, and 10 days he broke George Foreman's record to become the oldest fighter ever to win a world championship.

Many things will oppose you, ranging from your social life to your financial life, down to your health as well as some spiritual wars too. You must be strong to deal with all these along the road to your future glory. There will be times of discouragement, and ridicule from close pals as well as disappointments from loved ones but, you must press on till you overcome.

"Greatness is not in where we stand, but in what direction we are moving. We must sail sometimes with the wind and sometimes against it- but sail we must and not drift, nor lie at anchor." (Anonymous)

As a businessman, don't expect everything to go all smoothly with you. There will be ups and downs. People will doubt your dream of making it in that business, friends will betray you, economic factors like inflation and price hikes will come hard at you, competition in the market will be keen, suppliers will disappoint you, etc.

Be strong because you have to face and fight these before you rise to your throne. So, in the event of any trial, don't be discouraged, seek help from an experienced person. Be resilient and face the opposition till you win.

"People of mediocre ability sometimes achieve success

because they don't know when to quit.

Most men succeed because they are determined to"

George Allen

Tackle the Little Issues

Fighting the children of Ammon also meant that, the problem had been with them for a long period. It had been carried from generation to generation and this particular generation of children also came to have their pound of flesh. This was what the elders of the land of Gilead sought to cease by negotiating with Jephthah the warrior.

This means that the little problems you fail to address today will grow to hunt you tomorrow. This time, it had begotten other offspring. So whenever you have a difficulty in any venture, make time to address and solve it as quickly as possible to avoid escalations and possible disasters.

Melcom is a supermarket chain in Ghana consisting of over 24 shops spread all over the country. It was started in 1989 by Indian Magnate Bhagwan Khubchandani. His late father, Ramchand Khubchandani, had arrived in the then Gold Coast in 1929 from Hyderabad, Sindh, post-partition India but now part of Pakistan as a 14-year-old to work as a store boy. Melcom consists of four companies under the Melcom Brand Name.

In the year 2012 Melcom suffered two major accidents: on 7 November 2012, Ghana suffered a major accident when Melcom's five-story Shopping Mall at Achimota near Accra collapsed trapping many people inside. The Government of Ghana organized a rescue mission. In all 82 people including 14 dead, were pulled out of the rubble.

Melcom had been operating in the building which it said it had rented only since January 2012. Reports suggested that the building had structural defects owing to a lack of adherence to building codes and the use of improper materials.

Some of the staff interviewed gave an account that they saw cracks in some parts of the structure but all efforts to address this were ignored by management.

Furthermore, the fire incident at Melcom's mall in Agona Swedru (C/R, Ghana) serves as a poignant reminder of the importance of addressing even the smallest problems in our fast-paced and interconnected world. In an era where information travels at lightning speed and trends evolve rapidly, neglecting to tackle issues promptly can have disastrous consequences.

Just like a viral social media post or a trending hashtag, problems have the potential to spread and gain momentum if left unchecked. In the case of Melcom, the fire that broke out after business hours may have seemed like a minor issue at first. However, its impact on the adjoining warehouses and the loss of valuable Christmas merchandise highlighted the need for proactive problem-solving.

In today's digital age, relationships, marriages, ministries, and businesses face unique challenges. Social media, online platforms, and virtual connections have transformed the way we interact and conduct our affairs. While these advancements offer tremendous opportunities, they also expose us to new risks and vulnerabilities.

A seemingly insignificant disagreement or miscommunication can quickly escalate in the digital realm. A small issue left unaddressed can be amplified through the power of social media and online networks, potentially damaging reputations, relationships, and bottom lines.

In a world where news spreads rapidly and public perception can make or break an individual or an organization, attending to problems promptly is essential.

By embracing modern trends and technologies, we can also leverage them to our advantage in problem-solving. Online collaboration tools, communication platforms, and data analysis can help us identify and address issues in real-time. Monitoring trends, gathering feedback, and actively engaging with stakeholders allow us to stay ahead of potential problems and make informed decisions.

Moreover, the interconnected nature of our modern world provides opportunities for learning and growth. Sharing experiences, seeking advice from experts, and leveraging the collective wisdom of online communities can help us navigate challenges more effectively. By staying attuned to the pulse of the digital landscape, we can adapt and respond to emerging issues swiftly and decisively.

In conclusion, in our fast-paced and interconnected world, it is crucial to blend traditional problem-solving approaches with modern trends. By being proactive, harnessing the power of technology, and leveraging digital resources, we can address even the smallest problems before they escalate into major crises.

Embracing a mindset of agility and adaptability allows us to thrive in an ever-evolving landscape while safeguarding the well-being of our relationships, marriages, ministries, and businesses.

PRINCIPLE #
5. TRANSFORMATION- Divine reformation and renovation

In today's fast-paced and technologically driven world, it is easy to get caught up in the hustle and bustle of everyday life. We are bombarded with information, distractions, and the constant pressure to achieve more. However, amidst all the modern trends and advancements, the timeless truths found in the stories of Jephthah and Nineveh still hold great significance.

Just as Jephthah sought the restoration of his inheritance, we too must strive to reclaim what is truly valuable in our lives. In a society that often values material possessions and external success, it is important to remember that our true inheritance lies in the intangible qualities that shape our character and relationships.

Traits such as integrity, compassion, and love for others cannot be bought or acquired through technological advancements. They are nurtured through genuine connections and meaningful interactions.

In the case of Nineveh, their repentance and turning away from wickedness hold a powerful lesson for us today. While we may not be facing the exact same sins as they did, we are confronted with moral challenges and societal issues that require our attention.

In the age of social media and instant gratification, it is easy to fall into the trap of compromising our values for the sake of popularity or personal gain. Yet, the story of Nineveh reminds us that true change and transformation start from within, as we align our lives with the timeless principles of justice, compassion, and respect for others.

Furthermore, the message of relying on God and His Word remains as relevant as ever in our modern context. In a world that promotes self-reliance and the illusion of control, we are reminded of our need for a higher power.

Technology may provide us with convenience and efficiency, but it cannot replace the peace and fulfillment that comes from a deep connection with our Creator. As we navigate the challenges of the digital age, we must remember to seek guidance and strength from God, allowing His wisdom and truth to guide our decisions and actions.

In summary, while the world around us may be evolving rapidly, the timeless principles of faith, morality, and reliance on God remain steadfast. By integrating these principles into our modern lives, we can find a sense of purpose, direction, and fulfillment amidst the ever-changing trends and advancements. Let us not be swayed by the fleeting desires of the world, but rather hold fast to the eternal truths that bring true peace and lasting joy.

PRINCIPLE #

6.   **LEADERSHIP-** Head of the Nation

Jephthah's aspiration extended beyond being a ruler; he sought to become a leader and commander over the people. To accept the offer of going to war, he knew he needed to be the head of state, assuming the role of Commander in Chief of the army. This position granted him the highest authority in the land, enabling him to fulfill his duties without undue interference or obstacles.

Being the head of state also meant that his words carried the weight of law, making them difficult to challenge during his administration. Jephthah desired increased security and loyalty, recognizing the importance of these factors in his leadership.

His quest for leadership resonates with the principles of modern leadership and the pursuit of positive change. In today's world, effective leaders are not solely focused on personal gain or power;

they understand the importance of serving their people and promoting ethical governance.

Just like Jephthah, modern leaders aspire to set higher standards and bring about positive transformation in their organizations, communities, or nations. They recognize that true leadership is not about authoritarian control, but about influencing others through integrity, transparency, and a commitment to the greater good. By assuming positions of authority, they have the opportunity to shape policies, enact reforms, and establish a culture of fairness and justice.

In the context of Jephthah's story, his aspiration to become the head of state reflects the importance of strong leadership in promoting social harmony and legal reforms.

Today, leaders play a crucial role in addressing social issues, eradicating corruption, and ensuring that the legal system operates fairly and justly. They have the power to enact laws and policies that are socially friendly, taking into account the well-being and rights of all individuals within society.

Moreover, Jephthah's experience of being unjustly expelled by his brethren highlights the need for leaders who can bring about positive change and rectify past injustices. Modern leaders who have faced adversity or discrimination can draw inspiration from Jephthah's determination to overcome challenges and bring about a fairer and more inclusive society. They understand the importance of reforming systems and structures to prevent the recurrence of past injustices.

In conclusion, Jephthah's pursuit of leadership aligns with the principles of modern leadership, emphasizing the importance of serving others, promoting ethical governance, and enacting positive change.

Leaders today strive to create a better future, establish higher standards, and rectify past wrongs through their influence and positions of authority. By embodying the values of integrity, transparency, and fairness, they can inspire and empower others to work towards a more just and equitable society.

"Leadership is influence, it is nothing more, nothing less"
J. Oswald Sanders

A Good Role Model

Jephthah's desire to be a role model and provide inspiration to the young people reflects the contemporary understanding of leadership as a source of guidance and mentorship. In modern times, effective leaders are not just focused on their own success or authority; they recognize the importance of being a positive influence on others, especially the youth.

Leadership is about leading by example, and Jephthah's aspiration to ascend to the throne with the intention of being a role model demonstrates his commitment to embodying the values and principles he wished to instill in others. Today, leaders are expected to demonstrate integrity, humility, and empathy, and their actions serve as a guide for others to follow.

His rejection of a domineering approach to leadership further aligns with modern leadership philosophies. Effective leaders understand that leadership is not about exerting power and control over others, but about serving and empowering them. They strive to create an environment of collaboration, trust, and respect, where individuals are motivated to reach their full potential.

By aspiring to be a leader who inspires and motivates the downtrodden, Jephthah recognized the transformative power of leadership in uplifting communities and individuals. Modern leaders, too, have the opportunity to make a positive impact on those around them, whether it be in their professional or personal spheres.

They can serve as catalysts for change, encouraging others to overcome challenges, pursue their dreams, and contribute to the betterment of society.

Jephthah's aspiration to be a role model and inspire the young people of his land reflects the contemporary understanding of leadership as a source of guidance, inspiration, and empowerment.

Today's leaders strive to lead by example, create positive environments, and uplift those they serve. By embodying values such as integrity, humility, and empathy, leaders can inspire others to become their best selves and contribute to the greater good.

Munara was a well-respected, highly educated, professor of English with a Master's in Linguistics. Recognized by her peers for her keen intellect and strong work ethic, she was promoted to English Department Head at a leading University—a rare and prestigious accomplishment for a woman in her country. Yet, despite her significant accomplishments and obvious intelligence, like many women under Kyrgyzstan's authoritarian patriarchal rule, Munara faced serious gender discrimination and oppression.

When the chance to pursue a temporary project at Indiana University presented itself, the confident and determined linguist and mother seized the opportunity. Certain that her skills and experience would be valued elsewhere, and wanting to raise her young daughter in a place where she could pursue her dreams, once in the U.S. Munara sought asylum, and set out on a quest to claim a piece of the American dream for her little family.

But the dream soon became a nightmare. For four years Munara, while continuing to search for professional employment in her field, struggled to make ends meet by spending long hours driving a taxi. She sent out countless resumes, trying to find a position as an ESL instructor, but was told as a non-native speaker it was not likely she would find one.

Munara refused to give up. She joined the Upwardly Global Job Seeker Program in 2010, approaching her job search with the same level of dedication and perseverance that helped her make her way to the U.S.

By keeping in close touch with her Job Search Advisor, and applying the specialized advice and support she received, within seven months Munara landed a part-time medical interpreter job. With her unique multilingual skills and intercultural knowledge, it wasn't long before her new employer recognized the tremendous value someone with Munara's skills, education, and experience brought to the company.

Now in a new full-time role as Operations Manager, Munara has traded in low wages and endless hours driving a taxi for a challenging and meaningful position complete with a healthy salary and full benefits, and that allows her family time with her daughter who sees her mum as the greatest role model.

Whenever you are negotiating for a good deal, look out for such opportunities and take advantage where necessary. These are the things that remain after you have exited the scene. People will remember you for the impact you made on their lives more than the amount of money in your bank accounts.

 If you have the option to choose any of the above-mentioned privileges, don't hesitate to do so if you know you have what it takes to deliver the results at the end of the day. However, if your expertise is not up to scratch, then, work on them before demanding anything that you will be required to justify in the long run.

He has achieved success who has lived well, laughed often, and loved much; who has gained the respect of intelligent men and the love of little children; who has filled his niche and accomplished his task; who has left the world better than he found it, whether by an improved poppy, a perfect poem, or a rescued soul; who has never lacked appreciation of earth's beauty or failed to express it; who has always looked for the best in others and given them the best he had; whose life was an inspiration; whose memory a benediction.

To laugh often and much

To win the respect of intelligent people and the affection of children

To earn the appreciation of honest critics and endure the betrayal of false friends

To appreciate beauty, to find the best in others

To leave the world a bit better, whether by a healthy child, a garden patch, or a redeemed social condition

To know even one life has breathed easier because you have lived

This is to have succeeded.

(Often attributed to Ralph Waldo Emerson)

I thank you, Lord God,

for the ability to bargain to gain and remain.

I know with you I will make more impact on other lives.

May you restore to me any identity trait that is missing in my life

And help me rise above every physical or emotional challenge.

I refuse to settle for less in life

I shall scale over every huddle and defeat the enemy in Jesus' name.

I take charge of my destiny from today.

I know without you I am nothing,

so I depend on you for the grace to inspire and lead others

who look up to me in the mighty name

of Jesus Christ of Nazareth I pray.

Amen

Summary of points

i. Bargain to gain but it's better to remain in the hearts of people

ii. Your identity is what makes your totality

iii. You can make it with or without your biological parents

iv. "People will forget what you said, people will forget what you did, but people will never forget how you made them feel." Maya Angelou

v. You block your dream when you allow your fear to be bigger than your faith

vi. Never neglect your family for business; balance the two

vii. People will pay more for your talents if you are an expert

viii. Your resolution to succeed is more important than any other one thing

ix. Set new standards, take new challenges in life

x. ''Leadership is influence, it is nothing more, nothing less'' J. Oswald Sanders

xi.   Become a good role model to those you engage with by
       setting high standards

CHAPTER SEVEN

SEIZING OPPORTUNITY IN A CHANGING WORLD

"There are some men who, in a 50-50 proposition,

insist on getting the hyphen, too"

Lawrence J. Peter

From my little adventure in this journey called life, I have had my fair share of encounters with opportunities. Some were as tempting as a plate of freshly baked chocolate chip cookies, and let's just say I devoured those with great success. But there were also moments where I stumbled and ended up with crumbs on my face.

Opportunities are like hidden treasures, scattered all around us. They can sneak up on you when you least expect it, whether you're shaking hands in a business meeting or simply strolling down the street in search of a good cup of coffee.

They can be found in the most unexpected places—a chance encounter at a party, a conversation with a stranger on a long train ride, or even a quirky job interview question that catches you off guard.

Now, not all opportunities come with dollar signs attached to them. Some may not seem like much at first glance, but they have the potential to shape your life in unimaginable ways. Just ask Les Brown, the man who went from being an errand boy to a world-renowned DJ and motivational speaker.

He didn't have a fancy degree or professional training, but he had something more powerful—unyielding hunger.

One fateful day, when the main DJ had a meltdown on air, Les Brown saw his chance to step up and shine. While others would have panicked and called for backup, Les grabbed the opportunity by the mic and refused to let go.

He was hungry for success, and he was willing to give it his all, even if it meant leaping without a safety net. And guess what? He nailed it. His raw talent and determination caught the attention of the world, propelling him to greatness.

In this chapter, we're going to dive into the story of a young lad who found himself face-to-face with an opportunity that seemed out of place and inconvenient. But he didn't let that deter him. He recognized the hidden gem in chaos and took hold of it with both hands.

We'll explore the art of surviving amidst opportunities, even when they come with their fair share of thorns. Because let's be honest, not every opportunity is a bed of roses. Sometimes, you have to navigate through prickly situations to come out on top.

So buckle up and get ready for a wild ride as we unravel the mysteries of seizing opportunities. And remember, when life hands you a chance to shine, don't be afraid to grab the mic and show the world what you're made of.

Who knows? You might just end up becoming the DJ of your destiny, spinning tunes of success and inspiring others along the way. Now, let's get this party started!

Treat the following story as a joke!

Seizing the Opportunity: Daring To Take Risks!

There was this robbery in Guangzhou, China, the robber shouted to everyone: "All don't move, money belongs to the state, life belongs to you".

Everyone in the bank lay down quietly.

This is called the "Mind Changing Concept --> Changing the conventional way of thinking".

One lady lay on the table provocatively, the robber shouted at her "Please be civilized! This is a robbery and not a rape!"

This is called "Being Professional --> Focus only on what you are trained to do!"

When the robbers got back, the younger robber (MBA trained) told the older robber (who is only primary school educated), "Big bro, let's count how much we got", the older robber rebutted and said, "You're very stupid, so much money, how to count, tonight TV will tell us how much we robbed from the bank!"

This is called "Experience --> nowadays experience is more important than paper qualifications!"

After the robbers left, the bank manager told the bank supervisor to call the police quickly. The supervisor says "Wait, wait wait, let's put the 5 million RMB we embezzled into the amount the robbers robbed".

This is called "Swim with the tide --> converting an unfavorable situation to your advantage!"

The supervisor says "It will be good if there is a robbery every month".

This is called "Killing Boredom --> Happiness is most important."

The next day, the TV news reported that 100 million RMB was taken from the bank. The robbers counted and counted and counted, but they could only count 20 million RMB. The robbers were very angry and complained "We risked our lives and only took 20 million RMB, the bank manager took 80 million RMB with a snap of his fingers. It looks like it is better to be educated than to be a thief!"

This is called "Knowledge is worth as much as gold!"

The bank manager was smiling and happy because his loss in the CINOPEC shares are now covered by this robbery.

So who are the real robbers here?

This is called "Seizing the opportunity --> daring to take risks!"

A higher purpose

Jesse, a proud father of eight sons, had his peculiar way of assigning responsibilities. It seemed like a well-orchestrated plan: the first three sons were deemed fit to join King Saul on the battlefield.

Logical, right? If there was a need for reinforcements or someone to gather Intel, it would naturally be the fourth son, followed by the fifth, and so on. But no, life had a different sense of humor in store.

In a surprising twist, it was the last but not the least of them all, David, who was sent to check on the first three sons on the battlefield. Now, this wasn't just any ordinary visit. It was a national combat situation, where experienced individuals were expected.

I couldn't help but wonder if Jesse saw David as a sacrificial lamb, sending him off to the battlefield while preserving the "more precious" sons at home. Perhaps Jesse didn't have much confidence in David becoming the future King, even though he had been anointed just a few days or weeks prior.

Picture this: an August gathering, a quest for a new King, and Jesse conveniently forgetting to mention David's name or invite him to the grand occasion. The poor lad was relegated to herding sheep in the wilderness, deemed unqualified for the position. But little did they know, God had a different agenda. There was a higher purpose for David's journey to the battlefield.

And amid chaos, an incredible opportunity presented itself to David. Here was a chance for him to rise to greatness in the land, despite his lack of military training or membership in the prestigious National Boys' Brigade. It was an opportunity he recognized, and without hesitation, he seized it.

Beloved, when you find yourself in a challenging situation with no help in sight, remember that God has a better plan for you. There's a higher agenda from heaven, intricately woven into the fabric of your earthly experiences. God knows exactly whom to send and how to answer your prayers in unexpected ways.

You might be expecting help from influential individuals or well-to-do friends, but God, in His infinite wisdom, loves to take all the glory. So, don't be surprised if He uses the most unexpected people or events to pull you out of your predicament. It's all part of His grand design—a divine opportunity in disguise.

So, my friend, it's time to grab your opportunity now. Keep your eyes open and be ready to seize those hidden moments of greatness. And remember, while it may seem like hard work or disguised as ordinary circumstances, an opportunity is often dressed in overalls. As the brilliant Thomas A. Edison once said, "Opportunity is missed by most people because it is dressed in overalls and looks like work."

In the upcoming pages, we'll explore deeper into the mindset and actions required to recognize and seize opportunities. So, fasten your seatbelt and get ready for a thrilling journey of discovery and growth. Together, let's unlock the doors to a world of endless possibilities, armed with courage, determination, and a sprinkle of humor along the way.

*"Opportunity is missed by most people because
it is dressed in overalls and looks like work."*

Thomas A. Edison

Instead of the *fourth* son, the *eighth* son was sent. It was thus not surprising that Eliab the first son was angry to see David, the least of them who was sent to check up on them, bring them provisions, and take back word to their father. It was an opportunity to change his destiny and that of the entire land of Israel.

The youngster seized the opportunity to make a big impact in his life. He looked beyond the food, his brothers, their captain, and their father back at home. He took his chances. While soldiers were hiding in caves, dens, and holes he stood up to give his best shot at the opportunity.

Remember, some may be repeated, while other opportunities come but once. You must be sensitive to those that come your way in life. Most appear unexpectedly but carry what it takes to take you to the next level.

Many sisters have mixed the opportunity of meeting and marrying their future husbands and helpers because they *only* looked at the outward appearance of the gentleman that stood before or passed by them and was not what they expected or wished.

She missed her golden chance!

Once upon a time in a small town, there lived a sister whose sharp wit and quick tongue were matched only by her confident stride. With a vibrant spirit and a keen eye for opportunity, she navigated the bustling streets, always in search of something extraordinary.

One sunny day, as she made her way through the lively marketplace, her attention was drawn to a peculiar sight. A man, his face streaked with sweat and dirt, labored tirelessly, unloading crates of soft drinks into a humble store. His clothes clung to him, drenched in the essence of hard work. A powerful aura of determination surrounded him, despite his weary appearance.

Curiosity sparked within the sister's heart, and she couldn't resist the urge to approach this man of labor. But as she drew nearer, her impatience got the best of her, and her words spilled forth with a hint of condescension. "And who are you…and what might your name be?" she asked, her tone laced with an air of superiority.

Undeterred by her dismissive demeanor, the man turned to face her, his eyes twinkling with resilience. A gentle smile played upon his lips as he uttered words that would forever alter her perception. "My dear, I am Ben, the new country director of the esteemed soft drink brand," he revealed, his voice carrying the weight of his accomplishments.

The sister's world seemed to momentarily halt as his words sank in. Here stood a man who, beneath his outward appearance, possessed the power to command empires.

Mansions and valuable properties adorned his name in his home country, and he had chosen this unassuming town as his new abode, seeking not only a life partner but also a kindred spirit to share in his triumphs.

Regret washed over the sister as she realized the opportunity she had unwittingly let slip through her fingers. Her initial judgment, based solely on outward appearances, had obscured the true essence of this extraordinary man. In her haste to uphold her expectations, she had failed to see the golden opportunity that had stood before her, waiting to be embraced. By her initial demeanor, she missed out!

This tale serves as a touching reminder that the paths to greatness are often paved with surprises and unexpected encounters. It teaches us the value of looking beyond the surface, for within the unassuming exterior of a person lies a world of depth and hidden treasures.

Oh, dear reader, let this story stir your soul and ignite the fires of curiosity within you. Open your heart and mind to the enchanting possibilities that lie within unconventional situations and people. Embrace the thrill of uncovering hidden gems and be receptive to the extraordinary opportunities that may grace your path.

For in the smudged face of toil and the tattered clothes of labor, true character, and unbounded potential often reside. Do not let judgments cloud your vision, but instead, allow the beauty of humanity to captivate you and reveal the wonders that lie beneath the surface.

May this tale be a reminder to us all, to cherish the richness that exists within each person's story, and to approach life's encounters with empathy, understanding, and an unwavering belief in the boundless possibilities that await us.

So, seize your opportunities with an open mind and a willingness to look beyond the surface. Don't let your expectations blind you to the potential that lies within unexpected encounters. You never know when a chance encounter or a seemingly ordinary moment could be the turning point in your life.

More Missed Opportunities

I read a story about a man who missed a great opportunity! It seems that his friend took him for a ride one day, way out in the country.

They drove off the main road and drove through groves of trees to a large uninhabited expanse of land.   A few horses were grazing and a couple of old shacks remained.

The friend, Walter stopped the car, got out, and started to describe with great vividness the wonderful things he was going to build. Walter wanted his friend Arthur to buy some of the land surrounding his project to get in on the ground floor!   But Arthur thought to himself: - "Who in the world is going to drive 25 miles for this crazy project?"   The logistics of the venture were staggering!

Walter explained to his friend Arthur: "I can handle the main project myself but it will take all my money. However, the land bordering it where we are now standing will in just a couple of years be jammed with hotels and restaurants & convention halls to accommodate the people who will come to spend their entire vacations here at my park."   He continued: "I want you to have the first chance at this surrounding acreage because, in the next five years, it will increase in value 700 times."

As Arthur tells the story today: "What could I say? I knew he was wrong! I knew that he had let this dream get the best of his common sense so I mumbled something about a tight money situation and promised that I would look into the whole thing a little later."   "Later on will be too late" Walter cautioned Arthur as they walked back to the car. "You'd better move on it right now!"

And so Art Linkletter turned down the opportunity to buy up all the land that surrounded what was to become Disneyland. His friend Walt Disney tried to talk him into it but Art thought he was crazy! Art Linkletter missed a golden opportunity!

Have you ever kicked yourself in the Seat of the Pants because you missed a golden opportunity? Friend, this is how God works at times. He brings you so close to your breakthrough and expects you to be sensitive enough to spot and take advantage of. If you miss this, you may never have the same opportunity again!

Sometimes you may put your hope and trust in relatives, friends, and certain loved ones to support you in times of difficulties, but these may disappoint you. Those you think should understand your plight and support you will let you down. God will use unexpected people to provide for you. Help and deliverance will come from a different place altogether as you trust Him. But you must be sensitive when they come your way.

Queen Esther was admonished by her uncle Mordecai when the Jews had been slated for destruction by Haman their arch-enemy. She should not trust in her personality or her royal powers thinking nothing could be done to save the situation if she remained nonchalant or silent.

Mordecai's message to the queen was a reminder that their deliverance did not solely depend on her actions or abilities. It was a call to recognize that their ultimate help came from God, the true source of their deliverance. While they may not have known the exact details or timing of how it would unfold, they could trust that God would intervene in His way.

For the queen, this presented a unique opportunity to not only fulfill her role as queen but also to elevate her status before the King. It was a chance for her to demonstrate her queenly powers and make a significant impact.

The planned annihilation of the Jews served as a platform for her to showcase her influence and gain favor in the eyes of the King and the entire kingdom. It was an opportunity she almost missed, but thankfully, Mordecai reminded her of the significance of the moment.

In our own lives, we often encounter opportunities that may not always appear as such at first glance. We may overlook them because they don't align with our expectations or because we are preoccupied with other things. But the truth is, we don't need to pray for more miracles or wait for perfect circumstances. We need to be more sensitive to the openings that God brings our way.

Sometimes, seizing an opportunity requires us to be prepared, to step out of our comfort zones, or to be attentive to the needs of others. It could be a job opportunity, a chance to minister to someone in need, a moment to make a positive difference, or an opportunity to share our faith. These opportunities are gifts from God, and how we respond to them can make a lasting impact.

So, how do you perceive opportunities in your own life? Do you see them as obstacles or as stepping stones to something greater? It's essential to cultivate a mindset that recognizes the potential in every situation.

Like the two salesmen in the story, we can choose to see challenges as opportunities for growth and innovation. Even in the darkest moments, there can be a glimmer of hope if we are willing to change the narrative and seize our chances.

Don't let opportunities pass you by. Be sensitive, be bold, and be willing to embrace the possibilities that come your way. Trust that

God is orchestrating events for your benefit, and when you seize the opportunities He presents, you can make a meaningful and lasting impact in your own life and the lives of others.

"Opportunities multiply as they are seized."
Sun Tzu

How To Identify Opportunities And Maximize Them

Opportunity presents itself in various forms and sizes. It may manifest as a brilliant entrepreneurial concept, a valuable connection, or a shift in the market landscape. The question is, do you seize these golden chances or let them slip away unfulfilled? Regardless of whether you hold the title of CEO, possess marketing expertise, or harbor aspirations of becoming a future leader, the following insights will equip you to identify and pursue every opportunity with unwavering determination.

1. Have Filters

Not every opportunity is worth the effort. Taking on too many opportunities will spread your resources too thin and likely lead to multiple failures. Take stock of the resources you have and establish a clear direction for where you want to go. Then you can assess each opportunity for its true value and capability within the context of your aspirations.

In the digital age, where information overload is prevalent, it's crucial to filter through the myriad of opportunities that come your way. For example, as a CEO, you may assess potential partnerships based on their alignment with your company's values and long-term goals. By carefully selecting the opportunities that truly resonate with your vision, you can maximize your chances of success.

2. Put Optimism Aside

Do a diligent assessment of risk versus reward for each new opportunity that comes your way. Look for reasons why it won't work rather than getting excited about the reasons you think it will. Examine the opportunity through a lens that helps you see the worst possible case. If, after you beat it apart, it still looks shiny and bright then you'll be much more confident in pursuing its worthiness and potential.

3. Cultivate Networks

Building a robust network is pivotal for unlocking opportunities. Surround yourself with diverse individuals who can offer fresh perspectives and insights. Engage in industry events, join professional groups, and foster meaningful connections. The relationships you forge may lead to invaluable opportunities, collaborations, and mentorship.

In the era of professional networking platforms like LinkedIn, building connections is both accessible and vital. As an up-and-coming leader, you can leverage online communities and attend virtual conferences to expand your network.

Engaging with diverse professionals from different industries and backgrounds can open doors to collaboration, mentorship, and potential opportunities.

4. Embrace Calculated Risks:

Opportunities often demand that we step beyond our comfort zones and take calculated risks. Assess the potential rewards and weigh them against the associated risks. Undertake thorough research, analyze the pros and cons, and seek advice from trusted mentors or advisors. Do not allow fear to hinder you from embracing opportunities that could propel your progress.

Today's business landscape is ripe with examples of calculated risks paying off. Take the rise of Fintech startups as an example. By harnessing emerging technologies and challenging traditional banking models, these companies have disrupted the financial industry and seized opportunities in underserved markets. Embracing calculated risks involves thorough research, market analysis, and a strategic approach to innovation.

5. Continual Learning and Skill Development:

To seize opportunities, commit to perpetual learning and skill enhancement. Stay current with industry advancements, enroll in courses, attend workshops, and seek novel experiences. By consistently expanding your knowledge and honing your skills, you will be better equipped to identify and seize opportunities as they materialize.

In the age of online learning platforms and digital courses, acquiring new skills has become more accessible than ever. For instance, as a marketer, you can stay updated on the latest trends in social media advertising or data analytics through specialized online courses. By continually expanding your skill set, you position yourself to capitalize on emerging opportunities within your field.

6. Adopt an Agile Approach:

In our fast-paced world, agility is paramount. Be receptive to adapting and pivoting your strategies as needed. Opportunities may emerge unexpectedly, and an agile mindset allows for swift and effective responses. Maintain an open-minded and flexible outlook, prepared to adjust your plans as circumstances evolve.

Startups like Airbnb exemplify the power of agility in today's dynamic market. By adapting their business model from air mattress rentals to a global hospitality platform, they capitalized on a changing market landscape.

Embracing an agile approach involves being open to pivoting your strategies, responding to customer feedback, and embracing new opportunities as they arise.

7. Assess Realistic Requirements

So many opportunities end up requiring more time, money, or energy than originally anticipated. So many times people get halfway into a process only to discover they are stuck.

They don't want to abandon the serious investment they made, but they don't have the resources to go forward. Spend some time estimating the necessary hours, dollars, and skills required to fully pursue an opportunity to completion.

8. Be Clear on Objectives

To make the most of an opportunity, it helps to have a clear picture of why you want to pursue it and how it will benefit your path to success. Otherwise, you'll struggle with measuring performance and won't know whether to put in more time, energy, and resources, or cut your losses and bail.

Once you have decided to pursue an opportunity, establish a list of clear milestones with dates to make sure the opportunity warrants continued engagement.

9. Commit with Limits

A half-hearted effort on any opportunity will likely end up with a half-hearted result. Once you have set aside the resources and put objectives in place, you need to push full speed ahead to give the opportunity its best chance of success at least until it starts to fall apart. Even then, make sure you tweak and adjust to give it every possible chance to reach its potential within the limits of the resources you agreed to use.

10. Instead of chasing new opportunities all the time, focus on taking what's already working and making it better

80% of your sales come from 20% of your efforts, so isolate the 20% and do MORE of what is WORKING. That's why you must be tracking and reviewing analytics.

11. In today's market you don't need a USP, but a UCP – Unique Connection Point

How do you connect with clients in a way that is different from competitors? You need to be more patient, understanding, and empathetic to build connections and affinity with your market.

12. A BIG mistake people make is thinking the untapped market is the best place to go

But the fast track to success is picking busy markets where the action already is. You see, niche products that tap into bigger markets are where the money is. Find out what your user search behaviors are and exploit this opportunity.

13. Mindset

A lot of what drives us to take action is when our backs are against the wall. If you want to accelerate your money and business to growth, you need to envision something that you don't currently have in your life that you want, and then reverse engineer the numbers of what it would take to buy the item (or pay off the debt, if that is the case).

14. Have explicit goals and visualize intensely

Always have lofty explicit goals and visualize them intensely. Assume the attitude that if you don't reach your goals, you will die! This type of gun-to-your-head forces survival pressure mindset, no matter how briefly used, stimulates your mind, forces you to use your time effectively; and illuminates new ways of getting things done.

15. Take Decisive Action

The success of companies like Uber can be attributed to their ability to take decisive action in seizing opportunities. By recognizing the need for disruption in the transportation industry and swiftly launching their innovative ride-sharing service, they transformed the way people commute. Taking decisive action involves being bold, making informed decisions, and executing plans with determination.

Ultimately, seizing opportunities requires decisive action. Develop a bias for action and avoid excessive analysis or procrastination. When you spot a promising opportunity, create a well-defined action plan and pursue it with unwavering determination. Be proactive, focused, and persistent in your pursuit.

Remember, opportunities are not passive entities; they require active engagement and effort. By having filters, embracing a growth mindset, fostering networks, embracing calculated risks, pursuing continual learning, adopting an agile approach, and taking resolute action, you can position yourself to capitalize on exceptional opportunities that cross your path.

Embrace the realm of possibilities and embark on a transformative journey of growth and accomplishment.

Qualified to do the unqualified

Like this shepherd lad, you and I may be unqualified to send help or supplies to people in various forms of challenges or battles in their lives and yet, He calls us from the wilderness- just as we are and sends us out there into the world(battlefield) to be a blessing to our brethren in need.

You may look inadequate in yourself but God knows you can make it because; you have the anointing of the Anointed inside you, as an anointed of the Lord. Be bold and move to the battlegrounds where your gifting and talents are required.

Bargain to gain no matter the challenges you find yourself in. You have something unique to offer here on earth no matter who you are or your educational background.

A tourist asked a boatman: 'Do you know biology, psychology, geology, and criminology?' The boatman said no to all questions. The tourist then said, what the hell do you know on the face of this earth then? You will die of illiteracy.

After a while, the boat started sinking.

The boatman asked the tourist; Do you know 'swimology' and 'escapology' from 'crocodilogy'? The tourist replied no.

Boatman says: 'Well you will 'drownology'. And 'crocodilogy' will eat your 'assology' and you will 'dieology' because of your 'mouthology'

Hahahahaha!!!

So you see, precious one, you know something that someone does not know. You have something unique and peculiar to you. Don't allow anyone to intimidate you or despise your abilities or capabilities. You can make it with or without *biology, psychology, geology, and criminology.*

Just master your field and become an expert in whatever you do. You never know how far you can get with it. You may end up in the Whitehouse or Buckingham Palace one day. Become an expert in whatever field you find yourself.

Here are twenty-one reasons why this is a critical pursuit:

1. Search engines are making a clear shift in favor of quality — The changes are (and will continue to be) big, but they're going in a consistent direction — that of better quality content. Search engines will continue to improve the quality of games, and only high-quality content will win.
2. No one cares what you think if you aren't an expert — I know that sounds harsh, but I'm not talking about your friends or social conversations here.
3. You will understand your business better — Knowing the subject matter of your business cold is the first step in creating a business that runs efficiently.
4. Creating great content is much easier (you will know something new!) — The key to great content is sharing information or perspectives that are new to the reader. If you know far more than your competitors, this becomes relatively easier.
5. Building a lean content marketing team is easier — An expert perspective on the subject matter will help you understand what help you need.
6. Determining the scope of your content marketing opportunity is easier too, because you know the market so well.
7. You can predict upcoming changes to your market better — With expertise comes more knowledge of the major players in your industry, and the things they're likely to do. No, you can't predict everything, but expertise can help you get ready for change.
8. Communities will form around you — This one is simple. Genuine experts attract attention.
9. People trust experts — People are more likely to believe your opinion when you know more.

10. People will want to work for you — Being known as an expert tends to attract smart, motivated employees who can make a tremendous difference in your business.

11. People will want to buy from you — A deep understanding of your topic makes you more trustworthy, and that makes you the more inviting choice when it comes time to purchase a product or service. This is particularly true if you combine being an expert with a strong -sense of ethics.

12. The media will want to interview you — Both traditional and new media depend on experts to flesh out stories. Being a visible expert in your field makes you an attractive person for the media to interview.

13. Other media will want you to write for them — Looking for guest posting opportunities on major sites? This is so much easier when you're recognized for being exceptionally well-informed in your field.

14. Other experts will want to meet you — Experts are drawn to other experts. And that can open out to an introduction to *their* audience or business partners.

15. Other experts will want to collaborate with you — No expert is looking for collaboration with a person of thin, weakly researched content.

16. Growing a social media following is easier — This eventually happens, even if you don't work at it. People will figure out where your social profiles are and want to connect with you. Of course, this goes much faster if you *do* work at it well enough.

17. Your posts or exhibits will get more comments — People will want to share their thoughts with you and develop a connection with you.

18. Your articles will draw more links — No matter what anyone may tell you, incoming links are still the key driver in corporate

rankings. Attracting high-quality natural links more easily is pure gold.

19. The distribution of your content on social networks will grow exponentially. More tweets, plus ones, and likes will spread your expertise further every day.

20. Your conference presentations will draw more people — Doing presentations is one of the most underestimated parts of a content marketing strategy.

21. Experts make more money — For a business owner, this is the bottom line. People will pay more for your products or services if you are a recognized authority or an expert in your field.

In the grand tapestry of life, opportunities are the colorful threads that weave together our successes and dreams. They come in various shapes and sizes, sometimes disguised as challenges or unexpected encounters. It takes a keen eye and a determined spirit to spot them and seize them with gusto.

Imagine yourself as the captain of your ship, sailing through uncharted waters of possibilities. As you navigate this vast ocean of opportunities, remember to anchor yourself with a solid foundation of knowledge and expertise. Be the master of your craft, the maestro of your field. Know it inside out, upside down, and even sideways. Become the go-to person whom others turn to for guidance and support.

But don't stop there, my ambitious friend. Take it a step further. Be the one who not only knows but also teaches. Share your wisdom and insights with others, guiding them on their paths to success. In the realm of opportunities, being a beacon of knowledge and a helping hand is a surefire way to stand out from the crowd.

Picture yourself in a room full of experts, each trying to impress with their vast array of skills. But amidst serious faces and intense discussions, let your unique charm shine through. Be the person who adds a sprinkle of laughter to the mix, lightening the atmosphere and making connections with a witty remark or a well-timed joke.

As you embark on this journey of seizing opportunities, remember that sometimes the greatest opportunities lie in what is already working. Instead of constantly chasing the next big thing, focus on polishing and improving what you already have. Take that 20% of your efforts that yield 80% of your results and give it the royal treatment. Nurture it, refine it, and watch it blossom into something truly remarkable.

And finally, my fellow opportunist, always hold onto your dreams with unwavering determination. Visualize your goals with such intensity that they become an inseparable part of your being. Let them fuel your drive and light a fire within you. Embrace the mindset that failure is not an option and that every opportunity seized brings you one step closer to your ultimate success.

So, go forth with character, determination, and a touch of commitment. Embrace the dance of opportunities that life presents, and with each step, leave your mark on the world. Remember, it's not just about seizing opportunities; it's about creating your own destiny. Now, my friend, go out there and make your mark on the canvas of life with every opportunity that comes your way.

Bon voyage!

Heavenly Father I thank you for the many privileges

you have given me in life.

I believe in your ability to make great opportunities

available to me today.

Please help me to be more sensitive to the opportunities

you bring on my path and to dare to make a difference in it all.

I ask that you assist me become more productive

with my talents and being an expert in my field.

Grant me more grace so I can be who

and whatever you have purposed for me to be in life

I trust you to do all these for me and many other

blessings in the name of Jesus Christ my Lord.

Amen

Summary of points

1. Your ability to seize opportunities determines what comes to you

2. Opportunities are missed by most people because they look like work

3. Don't despise people anywhere; they may be carrying your blessings

4. Luck has little to do with it, be more sensitive to opportunities

5. Dare to be daring

6. You don't need all the degrees or certificates to make it in life

7. Become an expert in your field of operation

8. Don't pretend to be what you are not

9. Experts make more money

10. Go expert or go home…

CHAPTER EIGHT

UNVEILING THE 12 PILLARS OF LIFE'S ACHIEVEMENT

"Always bear in mind that your resolution

to succeed is more important than any other."

Abraham Lincoln

I trust that you have been inspired to step out and challenge the status quo as you fearlessly navigate the treacherous path of bargaining and fighting for what rightfully belongs to you in life.

Our journey, my dear reader, has been nothing short of a roller coaster ride, with twists, turns, and a few unexpected loop-de-loops along the way. But hey, who said negotiations were a walk in the park? Strap on your seatbelt, because we're about to take it up a notch!

Let's rewind to where it all began—the tale of a young, scrappy lad who emerged from the wilderness to become the leader of a nation. Talk about a rags-to-riches story that would make Hollywood weep with envy!

We witnessed his transformation from an underdog to a force to be reckoned with, thanks to some clever strategic moves that would make Sun Tzu himself raise an eyebrow.

But hold on tight, folks, because we're about to hit the climax of our narrative. Picture our fearless hero, facing off against a seasoned warrior in a battle that could make or break his destiny.

What does he reach for? Five ordinary-looking stones. Oh, but my friends, these stones were no ordinary pebbles you'd find skipping across a pond. No, no, no! These little gems symbolized bargaining nuggets—powerful nuggets that could make the Giant himself tremble in his oversized sandals.

Imagine the surprise on the faces of those gathered around as our hero steps forward, armed not just with courage but with a strategic wit that could outsmart even the trickiest of car salesmen. Those seemingly insignificant stones held within them the power to shift the balance of the entire kingdom.

Who would have thought that bargaining nuggets could be found in something as innocent as a handful of rocks? Life has a funny way of surprising us, doesn't it?

Now, let's get down to business. Through my meticulous research and a touch of divine inspiration (don't worry, I won't claim divine intervention on my tax forms), I've uncovered the *Twelve Bargaining Nuggets of Success.*

These precious gems, my dear, are the keys to unlocking your full potential in the art of negotiation. They're like a secret weapon hidden in plain sight, ready to propel you towards victory, be it in the boardroom or the battleground.

But wait, there's more! Just possessing these nuggets isn't enough. You need to wield them with finesse like a skilled magician pulling a rabbit out of a hat. That's where our bargaining strategies come into play.

We'll explore an arsenal of techniques and approaches that will make your opponents quiver in their boots. From the "Smooth Talker" to the "Charm Offensive," we've got the playbook to make negotiation a game you'll win every time.

So buckle up, my ambitious friend. Prepare to be empowered, entertained, and maybe even a little bit amazed. With the Twelve Bargaining Nuggets of Success and our arsenal of strategic maneuvers, you'll be unstoppable.

Get ready to negotiate anything like a boss, laugh in the face of adversity, and walk away from the bargaining table with a swagger that says, "I came, I saw, I conquered... and I got a killer deal!"

Now, let's dive headfirst into this final chapter, where legends are made and fortunes are won. Are you ready to seize the day and make your mark in the world of negotiation? Then let's do this thing!

Before we proceed, I want to extend my heartfelt recommendation for my book, "THE THREE 'S' OF SUCCESS (The Staff, the Sling, and Stone - Vol. 1)," which serves as the foundational part of this series.

I have made adjustments to ensure its relevance within this chapter. Additionally, I invite you to explore my book, "OVERCOMING THE BATTLES OF LIFE," a timeless classic that will ignite your inner fire and propel you to greater heights of personal renewal and empowerment.

So, let us embark on this journey together, as we unravel the significance of the lad's actions and his remarkable bargaining powers in the face of the entire army on the battlefield.

Your willingness to apply these nuggets will determine your success as you navigate life's negotiating table. Come, join me, and let us unlock the gateway to triumph in this troubled world of ours.

NUGGET #

1. **FAITH-** Foundation and Pillar of life

"Faith sees the invisible,

believes the unbelievable,

and receives the impossible."

Corrie Ten Boom

The young lad's choice of stones symbolized his unwavering faith in God as the cornerstone of his life. The Lord served as a mighty fortress, supporting and guiding him through the wilderness and the land of Bethlehem. It was God who propelled him towards his breakthroughs, providing unwavering support and strength in the face of any challenge.

His decision to gather those stones also reflected his refusal to become complacent or settle for mediocrity. Despite being anointed as the future King of Israel, he remained determined to establish a stronger foundation and build towering pillars for both personal and national growth. He recognized the importance of preparing himself for a higher calling in life.

Just as a solid foundation is vital for the construction of any significant structure, the lad understood the significance of laying a strong foundation upon which greatness could be built. Without such a foundation, even the most magnificent edifice would crumble in an instant. He realized that true success required a solid footing in faith, determination, and unwavering resolve.

"It is not the beauty of a building you should look at;

it's the construction of the foundation that

will stand the test of time".

David Allan Coe

Just as pillars are essential for supporting and reinforcing a structure, so too are they necessary in our journey toward success. These pillars serve as the strongholds that hold everything together, providing stability and resilience. Without solid pillars, the entire structure is prone to collapse.

At each stage of our journey, we must erect new pillars to support the next level of growth and development. These pillars represent our beliefs, values, and principles that anchor us in the face of challenges. Just like the iron rods that reinforce the pillars, we need strong foundations of faith, determination, and unwavering conviction to hold everything firmly in place.

In the story of David, his unwavering faith served as the foundation and pillar that supported his negotiation with the opponent. The people around him, paralyzed by their unbelief, lacked the necessary foundations and pillars of trust in God's power.

David, however, erected new foundations and pillars of absolute confidence and trust in the Lord. It was this unwavering faith that enabled him to bring down the giant and emerged victorious.

Similarly, in our own lives, we must tear down the pillars of doubt and demolish the old foundations of fear and anxiety. To succeed at the negotiating table of life, we must establish new foundations built on absolute trust in God's ability to guide and empower us. We must have faith that transcends our current achievements and propels us to aspire to greater heights.

God has extraordinary plans for each one of us, and these plans require solid foundations of faith and unwavering trust in His divine providence. No matter how far we've come, there will always be the next level to strive for. But achieving that next level requires unwavering faith and unshakable trust.

So, my friend, it is time to dismantle the pillars of doubt and fear. It is time to lay new foundations of faith and trust in God's guidance and provision. With these solid foundations in place, you will be well-equipped to navigate the negotiating table of life and achieve remarkable success.

Remember the words of Psalm 11:3, "If the foundations be destroyed, what can the righteous do?" As a righteous individual, you have the power to establish strong foundations and build pillars of unwavering faith. Embrace this truth, pull down the pillars of doubt, and rise to new heights of success and fulfillment.

Get ready to lay your solid foundations and build your pillars of unwavering faith. The negotiating table of life awaits you, and with God as your guide, there is no limit to what you can achieve. Prepare to negotiate your way to greatness and let your faith be the cornerstone of your success!

"Faith is like a radar that sees through the fog-

the reality of things at a distance

that the human eye cannot see."

Corrie Ten Boom

NUGGET #

2. **INTEGRITY-** As a Witness

"A life lived with integrity –

even if it lacks the trappings of fame and fortune

is a shining star in whose light others

may follow in the years to come."

Denis Waitley

The use of stones as witnesses holds great significance in establishing trust and accountability between parties. When there is a risk of forgetting or denying promises or contract details in spiritual, business, or social matters, a large stone is set as a witness and reminder for the future.

By using a stone as a witness, individuals are bound by their words and pledges, ensuring their commitment to fulfill what was declared or agreed upon in the proposed deal. The presence of the stone serves as a constant reminder of the obligations undertaken, leaving no room for denial or contradiction.

In my tribe, the Akan people, we have a saying, "gyi wo buo" or "take back your stone," which signifies the fulfillment of one's promises and the recognition of their actions matching their words.

In the realm of negotiations and bargaining, this principle carries great weight. It emphasizes the importance of upholding commitments and honoring the terms discussed. The use of a stone as a witness symbolizes the integrity and accountability needed in the negotiation process.

Incorporating this concept into your negotiations fosters trust and transparency. It underscores the significance of keeping one's word and promotes a sense of reliability and honesty. Just as a stone stands as a witness, ensuring that commitments are not forgotten or denied, so should individuals uphold their promises in the bargaining arena.

Remember, the power of a stone lies not only in its physical presence but also in its representation of honesty, reliability, and trustworthiness. As you navigate the negotiating table of life, let the stones of your commitments stand as a testament to your integrity and determination to honor your word.

Embrace the significance of stones as witnesses in your bargaining journey, allowing them to serve as a reminder of the importance of staying true to your promises. With this understanding, approach negotiations with confidence, knowing that you are bound by your words and committed to fulfilling your agreements.

And Joshua said unto all the people,

Behold, this STONE shall be a WITNESS unto us;

for it hath heard all the words of the LORD

Joshua 24:27

Indeed, the son of Jesse displayed a remarkable level of integrity through his actions. By choosing the stones and boldly declaring his intentions to defeat Goliath, he demonstrated his unwavering commitment to his words and promises. He didn't just talk the talk; he walked the walk.

In a world where many people struggle with keeping their word and following through on their commitments, the son of Jesse serves as an example of integrity in action. He understood the power of consistency and reliability in building trust and credibility. His actions aligned with his words, creating a strong foundation of trust among those who witnessed his determination.

Integrity is a rare and precious trait, often tested in times of challenges and difficulties. It is easy to make grand promises when things are going well, but it is during the moments of adversity when true character shines. The son of Jesse remained resolute in his convictions, even in the face of a formidable opponent like Goliath.

Unfortunately, many of us today struggle with maintaining such unwavering integrity. We may say one thing and do another, causing instability and distrust in our relationships and dealings. We must reflect on the son of Jesse's example and strive to be people of integrity in all aspects of our lives.

Let us learn from his steadfastness and commitment to his word. May we strive to be men and women of our word, fulfilling our promises and staying true to our convictions. By doing so, we can inspire trust, build strong relationships, and navigate the troubled world with honor and integrity.

"A single lie destroys

a whole reputation of integrity."

Baltasar Gracian

The transformation of the Apostle Peter is indeed a powerful testament to the impact of integrity in one's life. Before the infilling of the Holy Spirit, Peter's character revealed vulnerability and a propensity to compromise in challenging situations. However, the outpouring of the Holy Spirit on the day of Pentecost marked a significant turning point in his life.

As Samuel Richardson wisely said, "Calamity is the test of your integrity." It is in the face of challenging moments that our true character is laid bare. However, the transformative power of the Holy Spirit can bring about a profound change within us, just as the tongues of fire ignited a new sense of boldness and fearlessness in Peter.

The tongues of fire symbolize the presence and work of the Holy Spirit, which can consume any traces of fear, timidity, and compromise within us. When we allow the fire of the Holy Spirit to burn within us, it empowers us to stand firm in our faith, speak the truth boldly, and maintain unwavering integrity.

May you also experience a fresh infilling of the Holy Spirit, allowing His fire to burn away any fear and anxiety that may cause you to waver in your faith and compromise your integrity. Embrace the transformative power of the Holy Spirit, and let it fuel your courage and conviction to live a life of integrity, speaking the truth and remaining steadfast in your commitment to Christ and His promises.

Integrity is a precious virtue, but it can be fragile, particularly in times of success and prosperity. It is during these moments, often referred to as the "summer months of success," that the temptation to compromise our integrity can be greatest. Stay vigilant and steadfast, relying on the power of the Holy Spirit to guide and strengthen you in upholding the truth and maintaining your integrity.

Let the story of Peter's transformation be a reminder of the transformative power of integrity. Embrace the fire of the Holy Spirit within you, allowing it to fuel your unwavering commitment to truth and righteousness, even in the face of adversity. Through integrity, you will not only honor God but also inspire those around you with your unwavering character and steadfastness.

In a troubled world where integrity is often challenged, may you be a shining example of unwavering faith and unyielding integrity, making a positive impact on those around you. May your life be a testament to the power of integrity, shining brightly in both the summer and winter seasons of your journey.

Let your yes, be YES!

And your no, be NO!

---

3. **EQUITY-** Free and Fair Fight

Stones, in addition to their symbolic significance, also held a practical role as scales of measurement in ancient times. They were used in balances to weigh and measure various items, including money and foodstuffs. The balance or scale itself represented the ideals of fairness and justice, ensuring that transactions and exchanges were conducted on an even playing field.

In the context of the battle between David and Goliath, the selection of stones also carried a deeper symbolism of fairness and objectivity. Despite the vast difference in size and strength between David, a young lad, and Goliath, the Philistine giant, the battlefield was a level ground where both contenders willingly engaged in combat. There was no manipulation or coercion involved; it was a confrontation based on the principles of fairness and free will.

The battle between David and Goliath encompassed both physical and spiritual dimensions, and these aspects were perfectly balanced and unbiased. Just as Goliath called upon his gods to grant him victory and spoke derogatorily about David, the young shepherd, David, in turn, called upon the God of his fathers, Jehovah, to deliver the giant into his hands.

The Philistine indirectly insulted David by referring to him as a dog and threatened to leave his body to be devoured by birds of the air.

In response, David cleverly compared Goliath to the lions and bears he had previously conquered in the wilderness. Both warriors, despite their differing backgrounds, were experienced in their respective fields, be it warfare or shepherding, and neither voiced any complaints of unfairness or injustice in their confrontation.

Furthermore:

- The warrior had a *spear* as support while the shepherd had a *staff*

- The giant had a sword but the lad had a sling

- He had a bronze helmet but the youngster had a shepherd's turban

- A warrior's coat of mail, and the youth had a shepherd's smock

- He a bronze armor on his legs, and the boy had shepherd's socks on his legs

- The giant had a shield while the lad also had a shepherd's bag

- The giant could throw a *spike* (javelin) while the lad could sling a stone

- The warrior had an aerial advantage while the lad had a terrestrial advantage

- They both had moral support from their respective armies

- Both had the backing of their supreme deities before the fight

- They both enjoyed the blessings of their Kings

- They both had their countrymen to cheer and back them

The use of stones as a symbolic tool and the emphasis on fairness and balance in the battle between David and Goliath serves as a reminder that success is not solely determined by physical strength or societal expectations. Rather, it is the combination of courage, strategy, and a reliance on a higher power that can lead to triumph.

The story of David and Goliath highlights the importance of maintaining integrity and facing challenges with a spirit of fairness and impartiality, regardless of the odds stacked against us. Thus, the fight was free, fair, and balanced in all parameters.

In our own lives, we should strive to emulate these principles, approaching our lives with a sense of balance and fairness. Whether we face physical or metaphorical giants, let us remember that true victory lies not only in our abilities but also in our unwavering trust in the guiding principles of fairness and justice.

Beloved, your Heavenly Father is not partial. He knows exactly what you can handle and will not bring any fight that's above your strength. As David stepped in front, he knew the battle was unbiased, open, and fair. He could not complain or blame anyone in the crowd; not his family nor the King if he failed to finish the foe.

They all had a leveled ground to play the gamble for their lives. At the end of it all, one was more successful and carried the day. It took the anointing of the LORD upon David's life and his skill to win the fierce fight.

There are so many people today who complain and murmur about their situations and circumstances in life and claim the world is not fair; their parents and family have never been fair to them, even the Almighty and all-knowing God has not been fair and reasonable towards them.

These sometimes blame their misfortunes on their environment. They believe if they had been born into a better family or in a different environment, they would have made it to greater heights in life.

Well, I came to announce to you precious one, the world and its systems may not be fair and just to you and me, but God knows very well why he placed you in that locality, family, or institution. It is to fulfill a specific assignment and a divine purpose on earth. He holds the whole world in the hollow of his hand. Whatever He created, He saw to be good and perfect including you and I. So why complain and murmur?

No one in this world is better than you. You may not have certain material things in life today, but it doesn't mean you can't have them one day. All that you need in this life has been deposited within you.

Just recognize them, and harness them (your talents, treasures, and time) and you can be sure to chalk great success for generations unborn. Put to good use all that nature has deposited in you. You are perfect and there is none like you neither will there be any on this planet.

All you need is the anointing and presence of God with you in any endeavor you take. This was the secret of the chap which made him triumph in the clash with the giant. The anointing and presence will place you ahead of others in life and bring you before Kings, Princes, and great people.

4. EXTRA ABILITY- Strengthen yourself

When the Israelites were suffering from thirst in the wilderness during their journey to the Promised Land, it was the presence of a rock (stone) that brought them deliverance and relief. While they could endure hunger for extended periods, thirst was unbearable. In their time of need, the LORD intervened miraculously on two occasions by providing water through a rock in the desert.

Moses, their leader, had the authority to bring forth water from the rock by either striking it or speaking to it. Following his actions, water would abundantly flow, allowing the congregation and their animals to drink and quench their thirst (Numbers 20:11). The rock (stone) became their savior, providing them with life-sustaining water.

May the rock (stone) in your life bring liberation and salvation to those connected to your destiny. Unfortunately, for Moses, this same symbol contributed to his downfall. He disobeyed divine instruction by striking the rock instead of speaking to it. This act provoked God, leading to Moses being denied entry into the Promised Land.

His mishandling of the stone (representing Jesus) hindered him. Let us be mindful of the value of what we have in our lives, ensuring that we do not abuse or misuse them, as the consequences can be severe.

As we learned in the previous pages, the symbolism of the five stones was connected to Jesus. The young shepherd had confidence and assurance that he was safe and secure in the mighty hands of his Savior.

He firmly believed that God was capable of saving and delivering him from the ferocious giant he faced. He embraced the spiritual principle that "for me to live is Christ, and to die is gain" (Philippians 1:21). The young lad had such strong faith in his Savior that even if he were to die in the battle, he believed he would live again one day.

Jesus proclaimed, "I am the resurrection and the life. The one who believes in me will live, even though they die, and whoever lives by believing in me will never die. Do you believe this?" (John 11:25-26).

As he held the lifeless stones in the palms of his hands, he felt the supernatural power and strength of Christ flowing through his mortal body. This infused him with courage and gave him the determination to risk his own life for the deliverance of the land. He willingly sacrificed himself for the sake of the entire nation, disregarding his future ambitions.

The story of the young lad and the rock emphasizes the significance of faith in Jesus Christ and the willingness to lay down our lives for a greater cause. It reminds us of the transformative power and salvation found in Him.

May we hold firm to our faith, allowing the resurrection power of Christ to flow through us, empowering us to face challenges with courage and selflessness.

The Incredible Power of Sacrifice

As a prisoner of the Imperial Japanese Army in the jungles of Thailand during WWII, Ernest Gordon, a commander in a Scottish infantry battalion, saw firsthand the depths of depravity that can happen when a man sinks to his lowest.

At age 24, Gordon was captured while escaping from Sumatra after the fall of Singapore. With other prisoners, he was marched into the jungle to build the notorious bridge on the River Kwai.

Starvation, beatings, disease, and dawn-to-dusk slave labor were hallmarks of the death camp. The Scottish and British soldiers, normally bastions of composure, good cheer, and self-discipline, were slowly influenced by death's destructive grip. Morale broke down, along with concern for one's fellow man.

Over time, "nothing mattered except to survive," wrote Gordon. "We lived by the law of the jungle, survival of the fittest. It was a case of 'I look out for myself and to hell with everyone else.' The weak were trampled underfoot, the sick ignored or resented, and the dead forgotten. All restraints of morality were gone."

Then, slowly, something remarkable began to emerge in the camp.

- o *Selflessness*. A few officers began to pool their meager resources. They sent food to the sick prisoners holed up in the makeshift dispensary.
- o *Compassion*. Gordon himself became gravely ill, and two fellow soldiers, Dusty and Dinty, volunteered to come by every day and wash his wounds.

"Several men," Gordon wrote, "in the midst of widespread degradation and despair, kept their integrity inviolate and their faith whole." The supreme example of a different way of living came to a climax one horrific evening after a long day of hard labor.

That night, when the tools were counted, a Japanese guard announced that one shovel was missing. One of the prisoners had stolen the shovel to sell on the black market, it was assumed. The crime was heinous, and the guard railed. The perpetrator had maligned the Emperor himself, an act punishable by death.

The guard lined up the men in the work party and demanded that whoever took the shovel confess. No one did. The guard ranted and screamed, denouncing the men for their wickedness. His rage reached a new level.

"All die! All die!" the guard shrieked. He pointed his rifle at the crowd and set his finger on the trigger. The prisoners knew he was serious.

Calmly, quietly, from the back of the work party, one solitary man stepped forward.

"I did it," the man said.

The guard unleashed his fury on the man. In front of the rest of the prisoners, a contingent of armed guards standing by, he beat the man bloody with the butt of his rifle, crushing the man's skull.

When the tools were counted again, it was found that all the shovels were there.

The guard had miscounted. One man died in the dust and dirt of the death camp by the River Kwai. One man died so that others might live.

"It was dawning on us all," Gordon wrote, "that the law of the jungle is not the law for man. We were seeing for ourselves the sharp contrast between the forces that made for life, and those that made for death.

"Selfishness, hatred, envy, jealousy, greed, self-indulgence, laziness, and pride were all anti-life. "Love, heroism, self-sacrifice, sympathy, mercy, integrity, and creative faith, on the other hand, were the essence of life, turning mere existence into living in its truest sense.

"These were the gifts of God to men."

It is indeed a challenging question to consider how many of us today would be willing to lay down our lives in the face of death, even with the knowledge that God can raise us immediately afterward. The story of Isaac and Abraham illustrates a profound display of faith and trust in God. Isaac, being the son of Abraham, the father of faith, had such an unwavering belief that even if he were to die on the altar of sacrifice, God would raise him back to life. His faith was rooted in the assurance of a better place in paradise after death.

Similarly, the three Hebrew boys—Shadrach, Meshach, and Abednego—exhibited remarkable faith in the face of severe threats from King Nebuchadnezzar. They refused to bow down and worship the golden image set up by the king, knowing that their God was able to deliver them from the burning fiery furnace.

Nonetheless, even if God chose not to intervene in the way they expected, they made it clear to the king that they would not compromise their devotion to the one true God.

These stories highlight the unwavering faith and trust in God displayed by individuals who were willing to lay down their lives for their beliefs. They recognized that the Lord was their salvation and strength, which empowered them to face seemingly insurmountable challenges without fear or hesitation.

In today's world, such steadfastness and willingness to sacrifice one's life for the sake of faith may be rare. Nevertheless, the underlying message in these accounts is not necessarily about seeking death, but rather about living a life of unwavering devotion to God and standing firm in our beliefs, even in the face of adversity. It calls us to have a deep trust in God's faithfulness and sovereignty, knowing that He can deliver and provide for us in all circumstances.

While the specific circumstances may differ, the principle of unwavering faith and trust in God remains relevant today. We are called to stand firm in our convictions, even when faced with opposition or challenges. The story of the young lad facing the giant Goliath serves as a reminder that when we place our faith in the Lord and rely on His strength, we can face any obstacle or adversary with confidence and courage.

5. ACCOUNTABILITY- Root out the rot

In discussing the concept of accountability, we delve into the symbolic significance of stoning as a form of punishment in ancient times. Throughout various cultures, including among the Jews and other tribes, stoning was employed as a means of dealing with serious offenses such as blasphemy against God's name, gross violations of the Law, or rebellion against high authorities (Leviticus 20:2, 24:14, Deuteronomy 13:10).

These acts were considered abominations and required complete eradication from the community. They invoked divine judgment, with the Lord commanding that those who defiled His name or spoke irreverently about Him or His people should be subjected to the punishment of stoning.

In the context of David and Goliath, Goliath's defiance and insults toward the armies of Israel were not only acts of defiance but also a defilement of the name of the Lord, who is the Supreme Commander and ruler of His people. Through his actions, Goliath incurred God's anger and judgment, necessitating his execution and the eradication of sin from the land. It was an unpardonable act of blasphemy that demanded swift action.

David, filled with righteous indignation and passion to execute judgment on behalf of God, acted following the Law and spiritual principles. The choice of a stone as his weapon of choice surpassed the conventional spears or swords.

His alignment with the Holy Scriptures allowed him to carry the divine authority and mandate of God to execute justice. When the first stone from his sling struck Goliath, the giant fell dead to the ground, bringing about divine retribution.

It is important to note that this account serves as a powerful reminder that, regardless of the time it takes for individuals to change their ways, a day of judgment will always come. God, the ultimate judge, will bring every deed to judgment, and any evil harbored within individuals will be met with punishment unless it is rooted out.

Applying this concept to our lives as students or individuals, we are reminded that we, too, face a day of accountability. We will be tested, and if we fail, we will bear the consequences. While we may enjoy freedom and autonomy in our present circumstances, we must remember, a day will come when the stone of life will be thrown at us. Should we survive, we should offer gratitude to God, but if we fail, we will be found lacking.

Our works will undergo the test of fire, and if they withstand the scrutiny, we will have saved ourselves. However, if they are consumed by the flames, we will suffer loss. It is therefore crucial that we purify our hearts, lead lives characterized by holiness, and engage in good works, ensuring that we are not disappointed in the end. Repentance becomes the sole pathway to escape destruction and find redemption.

By aligning our lives with the principles of accountability and righteousness, we can navigate the challenges we encounter, knowing that our actions carry weight and consequences.

Accountability holds immense significance across various contexts, including the historical practice of stoning as a form of punishment. Throughout different cultures, including among the Jews and other tribes, stoning was implemented for severe offenses such as blasphemy against God's name, gross violations of the Law, or rebellion against higher authorities.

These acts were deemed abominable and required complete eradication from the community. As a divine judgment for such sins, the Lord commanded that those who defiled His name or spoke irreverently about Him or His people should face stoning as the prescribed punishment.

Goliath, through his defiance and insults towards the armies of Israel, not only defied but also defiled the name of the Lord, who is the Supreme Commander and ruler of His people. His actions invoked God's anger and judgment upon himself, necessitating his execution and the eradication of sin from the land. It was an act of unpardonable blasphemy that demanded decisive action.

In David, the Lord instilled a deep sense of indignation and passion to execute judgment on His behalf. Aligned with the Law and spiritual principles, David recognized that a stone would be the most fitting tool or weapon for this task, surpassing the conventional spears or swords. David's adherence to the Holy Scriptures enabled him to carry the divine authority and mandate of God to dispense justice.

Thus, when the first stone from his sling struck Goliath, the giant fell lifeless to the ground.

Had David's act been driven by personal motives or carnal desires, overcoming the Philistines would have required an array of larger stones. However, because it was the Lord Himself executing justice, no human resistance could withstand His wrath manifested through David's sling and stone.

This account serves as a solemn reminder that regardless of the time it takes for individuals to change their ways, a day of judgment will inevitably arrive. God, as the ultimate judge, will scrutinize every deed, and any evil harbored within individuals will face punishment if not addressed.

As students, we too are subject to a day of accountability. We will undergo testing, and if we falter, we must bear the consequences. While we enjoy freedom in the present, a day will come when the stone of life will be cast upon us. Should we emerge triumphant, our gratitude should be directed toward God. Yet, if we fail, we will be deemed lacking.

In the pursuit of success, our actions will be subjected to the trial of fire. If our works endure the test, we will safeguard ourselves and reap the rewards. However, if they are consumed, we will suffer loss and face disappointment. To ensure a favorable outcome, it is crucial that we purify our hearts, lead lives of holiness, and actively engage in righteous deeds. Through repentance, we can evade destruction and attain redemption.

Accountability is a fundamental principle that permeates every aspect of our lives. Just as the stone symbolized divine justice in David's encounter with Goliath, we must recognize that we will all be held accountable for our actions.

Therefore, it is incumbent on us to embrace repentance, cleanse our hearts, and strive for righteousness. By doing so, we can navigate the trials of life, avoid disappointment, and ultimately find success and salvation.

6. **ROYALTY-** Embracing Your Royal Identity

The significance of stones extends beyond their physical properties, as they also symbolize spiritual royalty and priesthood. In the instructions given to Moses, the Lord commanded that precious stones be lined in the breastplate of the High Priest's garment, which represented true righteousness and was essential for ministering before the Lord (Exodus 28:17-21). The breastplate, adorned with precious stones, served as a requirement for the High Priest to enter the Holy of Holies.

These stones also bore the names of the twelve sons of Israel, representing the original royals and pioneers of the land. In the New Jerusalem, their names are written on the twelve gates of the royal city (Revelation 21:12).

Moreover, in ancient times, the crowns of kings were adorned with expensive and precious stones, symbolizing their glory and honor (2 Samuel 12:30; 1 Chronicles 20:2). This implies that certain precious stones carry both priestly and royal symbolism, representing a spiritual mandate.

As David carried the stones in his bag, he was symbolically preserving his future honor and royalty as an upcoming king. He had the awareness that he would become one of the greatest rulers of the nation and therefore needed to guard this destiny diligently.

Nonetheless, for the sake of the entire land, he willingly traded his precious honor and future nobility by going into battle. He laid down his glory and potential kingship for the greater good, which ultimately led to even greater glory and grace.

In the pursuit of success, it is essential to recognize the deep significance of your spiritual heritage. Just as Jesus, our High Priest and the King of Kings, traced His lineage back to David, a shepherd boy who carried the spirit of royalty within him, your journey holds a divine purpose.

Jesus, starting with a simple stone, worked great miracles and wonders that ultimately propelled Him into royalty and dignity when He married Michal, the daughter of Saul, the first king of Israel. This was not a coincidence but a divine embeddedness in His spirit from birth, unveiling His royal identity to the world.

Dear friend, in your hand and your spirit, you may possess something extraordinary, even a form of royalty. Through Christ, we are described as a royal priesthood, a peculiar people, a chosen generation, and a holy nation (1 Peter 2:9). You are not a commoner but a joint heir with Christ in the Kingdom of our Heavenly Father.

Know that the Spirit bears witness with your spirit, affirming that you are a child of God and an heir of His divine promises. If you share in Christ's sufferings, you will also share in His glory (Romans 8:16-17). Therefore, do not belittle yourself or consider yourself insignificant in this world. You are special and precious to God. You are the apple of His eye, His beloved bride, and the queen of His Estate. You are God's royal child, destined for greatness.

As you navigate the path to success, let the awareness of your royal identity guide you. Walk with pride and confidence, embracing your calling and purpose.

Remember you carry the heritage of God, and with it comes divine authority and potential for extraordinary accomplishments. May you find strength and inspiration in knowing that you are a chosen and cherished child of God.

7. **UNITY** in diversity

"I take as my guide the hope of a saint:

in crucial things, unity; in important things, diversity;

in all things, generosity."

George Bush (1989-93)

The five stones also symbolize unity within the Body of Christ. Just as the human body has many parts with specific functions, believers represent the various parts of the Church of God and have unique roles to play.

We are interdependent, relying on one another for survival and security. If one part is lacking or weak, it affects the entire body, and if one member is strong, the whole body is strengthened.

In the Body of Christ, we have the fivefold ministry consisting of apostles, prophets, evangelists, pastors, and teachers, which is given for the equipping of the saints, the work of the ministry, and the edification of the church (Ephesians 4:11-12). We all work together in harmony, pursuing the same goals and running towards the same target.

When the sons of men decided to build a city and a tower that reached the heavens, their unity of mind and language allowed them to accomplish their mission without hindrance. However, it took the intervention of the Godhead—the Father, Son, and Holy Spirit, who was in perfect unity—to scatter them and disrupt their plans.

Unity is crucial in the Body of Christ. When believers come together, united in purpose and spirit, there is power and effectiveness in fulfilling the mission of the Church. Just as the five stones worked together to bring victory to David, so too does the unity of believers enable them to overcome obstacles and accomplish great things for God's kingdom.

And the LORD said, Behold, the people is ONE,

and they have all ONE language;

and this they begin to do:

and now nothing will be restrained from them,

which they have imagined to do. Go to, let us go down,

and there confound their language,

that they may not understand ONE another's speech.

So the LORD scattered them abroad from thence upon the

face of all the earth: and they left off to build the city.

Genesis 11:6-8

United we stand, divided we fall!

As David picked the stones one after the other, he was putting together the spiritual structures and pillars of the Body of Christ. It was no coincidence that the lad gathered only five stones.

He perceived in his spirit that, before he could bring down this mountain of a monster, he had no choice but to call upon Jesus because, at the mention of his name, every knee bows. This he did by selecting the five stones and declaring that, he comes against the opponent in the name of the LORD of Hosts.

Indeed, as believers, we are being built into a spiritual house under the leadership and guidance of the fivefold ministries. We need to be submissive to the authority established within the church, as this helps maintain the spiritual structures and pillars of the Body of Christ.

Unity and togetherness are vital in any organization, whether it be the church, a nation, or any other group. When there is unity among the main structures and pillars, it fosters cooperation and collaboration, leading to the achievement of common goals. On the other hand, confusion and rivalry only result in divisions and factions, which hinder progress and growth.

Ministers of the Gospel, politicians, and executives in both the private and public sectors should recognize the significance of their respective roles and work in unison. Each individual has a specific and special contribution to make in equipping the saints and fostering the development of the people they lead. By embracing unity and appreciating the diversity of gifts and callings, we can create a harmonious environment that promotes growth and serves the greater good.

In summary, unity, submission to authority, and recognizing the unique roles within the Body of Christ and other organizations are essential for their effective functioning and the accomplishment of their missions.

"I dream of the realization of the unity of Africa,

whereby its leaders combine their efforts

to solve the problems of this continent.

I dream of our vast deserts, our forests,

of all our great wildernesses."

Nelson Mandela

8. **IMPERISHABILITY-** Beauty in the heart

The great and magnificent temple built by Solomon the *wisest* man who ever lived was adorned with lots of precious ornaments, minerals, and stones of great value and worth.

The symbolism of the precious ornaments and stones used in Solomon's temple is indeed profound and carries spiritual significance. These materials were carefully chosen to represent various aspects of worship, spirituality, and divine attributes.

In the New Testament, the perspective shifts from physical temples to the understanding that our bodies are now considered temples of the Holy Spirit. We are called to decorate our inner selves with the precious stones and ornaments found in the Word of God, rather than relying on external, man-made things.

Just as David held the precious pebbles and swung one in his sling, we are called to exhibit the beauty of Christ and the Holy Spirit embedded in our spirits. Our lives should reflect the imperishable and valuable qualities found in the Word of God, such as love, joy, peace, kindness, patience, and more.

It is time to let the light of Christ shine through us, showcasing the glory and power of the Lord to the world. The perishable and fading nature of man-made things should not be our focus. Instead, within our hearts, we should lay abundant and imperishable precious jewels and stones of the Spirit.

By embracing and manifesting these qualities, we become living testimonies of God's grace and power. Our actions and character should radiate the light of Christ, so that others may see our good works and give glory to our heavenly Father.

Therefore, let us strive to decorate our inner selves with the virtues and qualities of the Spirit, letting our light shine before others. May our lives reflect the beauty of Christ and the power of the Holy Spirit, leading others to glorify our Father in Heaven.

9. **IMPECABILITY-** Impenitent and Harden Heart

"A NEW HEART also will I give you,

and a new spirit will I put within you:

and I will take away the STONY HEART out of your flesh,

and I will give you a HEART OF FLESH".

Ezekiel 36:26

The account above speaks of God's promise to give His people a new heart and a new spirit, removing the stony heart from them and replacing it with a heart of flesh. This symbolizes a transformation from a hardened and rebellious heart to a heart that is responsive, obedient, and sensitive to the leading of God.

In the context of David selecting stones and the story of Goliath, the symbolism extends to the need for a change in the hearts of the people of Israel. Their stony hearts represented their rebellion and disobedience, and David's actions were a call for repentance and a return to the Lord.

The idea of speaking with integrity and using words in the direction of truth and love, as mentioned by Miguel Angel Ruiz, aligns with the need for genuine confession and alignment between one's words and heart. It emphasizes the importance of honesty, self-reflection, and avoiding gossip or self-deprecating speech.

The broken and contrite heart, as mentioned in Psalm 51:17, is pleasing to God. It signifies humility, repentance, and a willingness to submit to His will. Isaac's submission to his father Abraham, even in the face of great uncertainty and danger, exemplifies this brokenness and humility.

The international evangelist and preacher Benny Hinn rightly asserts that God anoints dead people and this highlights the concept of dying to self and surrendering our desires and passions to God. It is through brokenness and humility that we become vessels that God can use for His purposes.

Ultimately, the call is for believers to be transformed inwardly, with their hearts and affections set on Christ and the eternal things. It is a challenge to not just hear the Word of God, but to become doers of the Word, allowing our lives to be shaped by His truth.

Indeed, the quote by Dietrich Bonhoeffer, "When Jesus bids us come to Him, He bids us to come and die," emphasizes the importance of dying to self and surrendering our desires and ambitions to follow Christ wholeheartedly. It speaks to the need for complete surrender and submission to God's will, even if it means letting go of our plans and preferences.

To be "impeccably" dead to self means to be unwavering in our commitment to deny ourselves, take up our cross, and follow Christ. It requires us to put to death our selfishness, pride, and worldly attachments, and instead live by God's purposes and desires for our lives.

By dying to self and embracing humility, we open ourselves up to the transformative power of God. It is in this state of surrender and brokenness that we become vessels for His glory, allowing Him to work in and through us to accomplish His plans.

In summary, the call to be "impeccably" dead to self underscores the need for total surrender, self-denial, and submission to God. It is through this process of dying to self that we find true life and become effective instruments in God's hands.

10. **RESTORABILITY-** Restoration from Rejection

"Throughout history,

no one has suffered more than God.

He has suffered because his children fell away from him.

Ever since the fall, God has been working tirelessly

for the restoration of mankind.

People do not know this brokenhearted

aspect of God."

Sun Myung Moon

The stone was also used in the New Testament as a symbol of the rejection and neglect of Christ who became the Chief Cornerstone. Christ as the stone is revealed in threefold ways:

- To Israel, Christ, not coming in the Messianic glory but in the form of a servant, is a stumbling stone and Rock of offense
- To the Church, Christ is the foundation and Chief cornerstone
- To the Gentile world powers, Christ is to be the Striking Stone of destruction.
- Israel stumbled over Christ; the church is built upon Christ; Gentile world dominion will be crushed by Christ.

The symbolism of the stone in the New Testament represents the different responses to Christ. To Israel, Christ was a stumbling stone and a Rock of offense because He did not come in the expected Messianic glory but as a humble servant.

To the Church, Christ is the foundation and Chief cornerstone upon which the faith is built. And to the Gentile world powers, Christ is the Striking Stone of destruction that will ultimately crush their dominion.

Despite the rejection and neglect Christ faced, He remained sinless and steadfast in fulfilling His purpose. In the same way, David, as a shepherd boy, faced opposition and challenges but held onto his faith in God's promises. Both Christ and David teach us the importance of enduring contradictions and opposition, and remaining faithful to God's calling even in the face of adversity.

The verse from Psalms 118:22-23, "The stone which the builders refused has become the headstone of the corner. This is the LORD's doing; it is marvelous in our eyes," emphasizes that God can turn our rejections and neglect into something marvelous and significant. He can restore what the enemy and society have taken away and bring forth abundance and restoration in our lives.

As believers, we can find hope in Joel 2:25-26, where God promises to restore the years that were lost and bring blessings and satisfaction to His people. Our faith in God's ability to restore and redeem is essential as we face challenges and setbacks in life.

In summary, the stone symbolism in the New Testament highlights the different responses to Christ, the need to endure contradictions and opposition, and the assurance that God can restore and bring forth blessings in our lives. Through faith and trust in Him, we can experience His marvelous work even in the face of rejection and challenges.

There is restoration for your tribulation!

11. PROFITABILITY- Investment and Income

Among the major sources of foreign exchange and income for a nation are the exports and imports of precious natural resources and minerals, such as gold, oil, bauxite, coal, and various precious stones, including diamond, emerald, beryl, chalcedony, and topaz.

After the Queen of Sheba had benefited from the profound wisdom and deep insights of King Solomon, she expressed her gratitude by presenting him with precious stones (2 Chronicles 9:10; 1 Kings 10:2, 10). These stones served as currency and represented her nation's wealth, income, and personal investment. They symbolized her appreciation and the value she placed on their trade relationship.

Similarly, the stones chosen by the shepherd boy David represented his investments and income in life. These stones symbolized the fruits of his labor and the potential for financial transformation. By using them in battle, David made a significant deposit and investment in the outcome of the warfare. He had the confidence that his sacrifice would yield abundant returns in the future.

In life, it is essential to have your eyes open to the numerous investment opportunities available to you. Though it may require parting with some of your resources, such sacrifices can lead to greater benefits and returns. As stated in Ecclesiastes 11:1, "Cast your bread upon the waters, for you will find it after many days."

Remember the principle of sowing and reaping. Giving generously, whether it is your time, talents, resources, or tithes and offerings in the house of the Lord, is rewarded abundantly. As mentioned in 2 Corinthians 9:6, "Whoever sows sparingly will also reap sparingly, and whoever sows bountifully will also reap bountifully."

Indeed, the scripture from Malachi 3:8-10 emphasizes the importance of fulfilling our financial obligations to God, specifically in terms of tithes and offerings. It addresses the act of robbing God when we neglect to give what is rightfully His.

The passage highlights that by withholding tithes and offerings, we are depriving God of His portion. This not only impacts our relationship with Him but also affects the overall spiritual well-being of the nation as a whole. However, when we obediently bring all the tithes into the storehouse, we open ourselves to the blessings and provisions that God promises.

God challenges us to test Him in this matter of giving. He invites us to trust Him and see if He will not open the windows of heaven and pour out blessings upon us in abundance. The blessings He provides may extend beyond material wealth and encompass various aspects of our lives, including our finances, relationships, and overall well-being.

Therefore, it is essential to continue investing wisely and giving generously, knowing that our acts of giving are not in vain. When we fulfill our financial obligations to God, we position ourselves to receive His blessings and experience His provision in ways that surpass our expectations.

Let us remain faithful in honoring God with our tithes and offerings, understanding that our obedience in this area can lead to blessings and financial abundance that we may not anticipate.

12. **LOYALTY-** Remain loyal to the Law

"The game is my life.

It demands loyalty and responsibility,

and it gives me back fulfillment and peace."

Michael Jordan

The use of stone tablets to inscribe the commandments of God served multiple purposes. First, it demonstrated the power and authority of God, as He chose this unique and durable material to convey His laws. By writing with His finger, God emphasized the divine origin and significance of the commandments.

Second, the use of stone tablets ensured the preservation and longevity of the Law. Unlike other writing materials that could easily perish or be damaged, stone tablets were durable and could withstand the test of time. This was important because the Law was not meant to be a temporary set of guidelines but a lasting covenant between God and His people.

Furthermore, the stone tablets symbolized the seriousness and immutability of the commandments. The permanence and solidity of stone conveyed the unchanging nature of God's laws and the importance of adhering to them faithfully.

However, despite having the Law written on stone tablets, many of the Israelites failed to internalize its true meaning and significance. They treated it as an external symbol rather than allowing it to transform their hearts and guide their actions. The ultimate purpose of the Law was not just to be engraved on physical stones but to be written on the tablets of their hearts, influencing their thoughts, attitudes, and behaviors.

In the New Testament, we see a shift from external stone tablets to the internal transformation of the heart through the work of the Holy Spirit. The apostle Paul speaks of believers being transformed by the Spirit and having the law of God written on their hearts (2 Corinthians 3:3). This inner transformation allows us to live out the principles of God's law in a genuine and heartfelt manner.

Therefore, while the stone tablets served their purpose in the Old Testament as a tangible representation of God's commandments, the ultimate goal is for the Law to be internalized and lived out in the lives of God's people through a heart transformed by His Spirit.

"The foundation stones for balanced success are:

honesty, character, integrity,

faith, love, and loyalty."

Zig Ziglar

Indeed, David understood the importance of internalizing the Law and keeping it in his heart. While the Israelites in the wilderness had the Law written on stone tablets and displayed on their doorposts as a reminder, David took it a step further by writing it on the tablet of his own heart. This demonstrates a deeper level of commitment and personal connection to God's commandments.

By comparing his heart to the stone tablets on which the Law was inscribed, David acknowledges the significance of having a transformed and obedient heart. It is not enough to merely externalize the Law through physical symbols or rituals; true devotion and loyalty to God require a genuine internalization of His commandments.

David's statement reflects his desire to align his thoughts, desires, and actions with God's Word. He recognized that by keeping God's commandments in his heart, he would be less likely to fall into sin and would live a life that honored and pleased God.

In essence, David's declaration highlights the importance of personal transformation and a deep, heartfelt commitment to God's laws. It is a reminder that true obedience stems from the innermost being rather than external displays or rituals alone. Just as the stone tablets were precious and carefully preserved, David treasured God's Word in his heart, valuing its transformative power and guidance in his life.

This teaches us the timeless lesson that genuine obedience to God goes beyond outward observance and rituals; it requires a heart that is softened, receptive, and obedient to His commands.

Whenever the word of God is not hidden in our hearts, we are highly susceptible to sin. The people of Israel could provoke the anger of the LORD on themselves through idol worship and other forms of disobedience and detestable deeds because, the Law was only read to them from stone tablets or inscribed on their walls and doorposts, but were not inscribed or imprinted on their hearts.

Their hearts and minds were not so attached to the commandments of God: as such, were not loyal in keeping them rather, they were more interested in displaying them on stone tablets and walls.

"Achievement of your happiness

is the only moral purpose of your life,

and that happiness, not pain or mindless self-indulgence,

is the proof of your moral integrity,

since it is the proof and the result of your loyalty

to the achievement of your values."

Ayn Rand

May we learn to hide the word of God in our hearts by consistent studying, memorization, and meditation on the Law of God day and night that we shall be careful to do everything written in it, then will our ways be prospered (Joshua 1:8).

Be a loyal Law "lover"

Not a sensational stone "scriber"

In this troubled world, let us infuse our journey with an unwavering spirit of power and determination to overcome. These bargaining nuggets of success will ignite a fire within us, fueling our resolve to rise above challenges and make a profound impact.

Let us be fueled by the power of these nuggets, empowering us to break through barriers, defy limitations, and conquer the impossible. Embrace the storms that come our way, knowing that within us lies the strength to weather any tempest and emerge stronger.

In the face of uncertainty, let our determination be unyielding. Press on with unwavering faith, confident in the promises these nuggets hold. We are not merely survivors in this troubled world, but conquerors, destined to achieve extraordinary feats and leave an indelible mark.

In every endeavor, let us be driven by an unrelenting passion to make a difference. Channel the power within, drawing from the depths of our souls, to bring forth transformative change. In a world longing for hope, let us become beacons of light, catalysts of progress, and instruments of love.

No matter how arduous the journey, persist with unwavering resolve to succeed. Harness the power of these nuggets to overcome obstacles, defy mediocrity, and shatter confining boundaries. With each step, let determination resonate as a testament to the extraordinary potential within us.

In the face of adversity, let our spirits soar with unwavering confidence. Stand firm, unshaken by raging storms, for we carry within us the power to change the world. With these nuggets as our armor, we are equipped to withstand any trial and emerge victorious.

So, in this troubled world, let power and determination to succeed be a force that cannot be contained. Be relentless in the pursuit of excellence, unwavering in the commitment to make a lasting impact. Together, forge a path of triumph, inspiring others to embrace their power to succeed.

With hearts ablaze and minds set on victory, march forward armed with these bargaining nuggets of success. Be a generation that refuses to be defeated, a generation that dares to dream big and leave an indelible legacy of transformation.

In this troubled world, let power and determination be the catalyst for change, propelling towards a brighter future. With these nuggets as our compass, navigate storms, overcome obstacles, and emerge as champions of hope.

So, go forth with unwavering power and determination, destined for greatness in this troubled world. Embrace these nuggets, unleashing a tidal wave of courage and resilience. Together, ignite a revolution of transformation, making this troubled world a place of triumph and prosperity.

With the power of these bargaining nuggets coursing through veins, prevail. Succeed. And leave an indelible mark on the troubled world, shaping its destiny.

Embrace the power within, ignite the flame of determination, and navigate this troubled world with unwavering strength. Let power and determination be the anthem resounding through the ages, echoing in hearts, inspiring all who dare to dream and persevere. Together, rise above challenges, illuminate darkness, and create a legacy of triumph that inspires generations.

Let power and determination be the force that cannot be contained. Let it be relentless, unwavering, and unwavering. Let us be champions of hope, catalysts of change, and architects of a brighter future in this troubled world.

I am deep in Christ,

I always bring out deep and precious pearls within me.

The LORD is my foundation and pillar.

He has become my salvation and investment.

I am a royal priesthood and a peculiar person.

I am a loyal "lover" of the Law and not just a "subscriber"

My deficiency with God's efficiency is a great sufficiency.

There is certainly restoration for all my tribulations

In me dwell the precious jewels of love, peace, and joy

in the Holy Spirit. My light is shining everywhere I go

In Jesus' name, I pray.

Amen.

Summary of points

i.   Pull down the pillars of fear and erect that of faith

ii.   A single lie destroys a whole reputation of integrity.

iii. Your deficiency with God's efficiency is a great sufficiency

iv.   You are His royal baby so walk with pride and confidence like a Prince or Princess

v.   Say only what you mean. Avoid using the word to speak against yourself or to gossip about others.

vi.   "When Jesus bids us come to Him, He bids us to come and die".

vii. Refuse to abuse Christ, else you will end up with a crisis

viii. Whenever the word of God is not hidden in your heart, you are highly susceptible to sin.

ix.   There is restoration for all your tribulations

x.   Have more investment in God by faithfully helping the needy, tithing and giving offerings

FINAL WORD

The question of identifying and *Unleashing Your Bargaining Power* is a personal and introspective one. It requires self-reflection and an understanding of the strengths, skills, and unique qualities that you bring to the table. It's important to recognize and appreciate your value.

Confidence plays a crucial role in navigating life's challenges, including those encountered in the metaphorical "boardroom" of life. We have explored the essential principles and strategies that can empower you to navigate the challenges and uncertainties of life with confidence and determination.

Throughout these pages, we have delved into the concepts of self-awareness, recognizing your worth, harnessing your strengths, and embracing the power of negotiation.

We have learned that true bargaining power begins with a deep understanding of oneself. By acknowledging our strengths, skills, and unique qualities, we gain the confidence to face life's negotiations head-on. We have discovered that confidence is not a static trait but a dynamic quality that can be cultivated through self-reflection, continuous learning, and a willingness to step outside of our comfort zones.

We have learned that in a troubled world, possessing advanced intelligence in negotiation is a significant advantage. It encompasses the ability to analyze complex situations, understand diverse perspectives, and make informed decisions that lead to favorable outcomes.

By cultivating our intellectual acumen, emotional intelligence, and adaptability, we can navigate the intricacies of negotiation with precision and purpose.

In our exploration, we have discovered that applying the concept of advanced intelligence is not limited to individual brilliance but also relies on collaborative intelligence. Building relevant relationships, fostering trust, and seeking mutually beneficial solutions and strategies are critical components of successful negotiation in a troubled world.

By working together and leveraging the collective intelligence of diverse stratagems, we can address complex challenges and forge innovative solutions.

As we journeyed through the metaphorical boardroom of life, we explored the importance of strategic thinking, effective communication, and adaptability. We have recognized the value of setting clear goals, preparing diligently, and embracing opportunities for growth and success in any endeavor.

In a troubled world filled with challenges, we have revealed that our bargaining power lies not only in our abilities but also in our ability to build strong relationships and collaborate with others.

We must seek those qualities which leave indelible marks in the hearts of the people we engage with and not only the material gains as an outcome. Unity, empathy, and understanding are crucial elements in achieving mutually beneficial outcomes in negotiations.

Remember, in a troubled world, negotiating with advanced intelligence is not just about personal success but also about fostering a greater sense of harmony and progress. It is about finding innovative solutions that address societal challenges and uplift humanity as a whole.

Throughout this book, we have emphasized the significance of integrity, ethical conduct, and fairness in all our negotiations. By upholding these principles, we not only protect our interests but also contribute to a harmonious and prosperous society.

As we conclude this book, I encourage you to carry the wisdom and insights you have gained into every aspect of your life. Remember that your worth is immeasurable, and your bargaining power is limitless. Approach negotiations with confidence, preparedness, and a commitment to finding win-win solutions.

In this troubled world, filled with uncertainties and obstacles, you can overcome challenges, achieve your goals, and create a life of fulfillment and success. Harness your inner strength, embrace the power of strategic negotiation using the advanced intelligence suggested in this book, and strive to make a positive impact on the world around you.

May the knowledge and principles shared serve as a guiding light on your journey to success. May you navigate the complexities of life with grace, resilience, and unwavering determination. Always recall you possess the bargaining intelligence of success that can transform your life and the lives of those around you.

Thank you for embarking on this journey with me. I wish you the very best in all your future negotiations and endeavors. May you continue to thrive and achieve greatness in this troubled world. Remember, your bargaining power is the key to unlocking a world of endless possibilities.

Go forth with confidence and resolve, armed with the power of these advanced intelligence, and negotiate your way to a brighter future in this troubled world. Don't forget, always and forever, you possess the ultimate Bargaining Power!!